Naval Brigades in the South African War 1899-1900

MOUNTING A 4.7 GUN WITH PLATFORM MOUNTING ON GUN HILL, CHIEVELEY
(Note the cross beams which are being sunk in the ground. This was one of the two platform 4.7's which afterwards took part in the fighting at terrace and Pieter's Hills)

Naval Brigades in the South African War 1899-1900

The Campaigns of the Royal Navy During the Anglo-Boer War

Thomas T. Jeans

LEONAUR

Naval Brigades in the South African War 1899-1900
The Campaigns of the Royal Navy During the Anglo-Boer War
by Thomas T. Jeans

First published under the title
Naval Brigades in the South African War 1899-1900

Leonaur is an imprint of Oakpast Ltd

Copyright in this form © 2012 Oakpast Ltd

ISBN: 978-0-85706-958-0 (hardcover)
ISBN: 978-0-85706-959-7 (softcover)

http://www.leonaur.com

Publisher's Notes

Contents

Every officer or man who has had the good fortune to serve with either of the Naval Brigades landed during the war, and has come safely through it, will remember for the remainder of his life, with the most lively recollections of pleasure and gratitude, the time when he was the guest of the British Army, and had the honour of sharing its work and its glory.

Introduction

Despite the fact that so much has already been written on the subject, I feel assured that this little contribution to the history of the struggle in South Africa needs neither explanation nor excuse. It is the story of how, at a time when their comrades of the land service were in dire need of help, the seamen hastened to place their ships' guns on improvised carriages, took them ashore, and in the nick of time enabled our military forces to cope on equal terms with the Boer artillery.

Many years will elapse before we can forget the surprise and dismay occasioned at home when, after the apparent successes of Talana Hill and Elandslaagte, it became known that the enemy had put into the field heavy guns of high velocity, large calibre, and long range, brought on travelling carriages from the forts at Pretoria and Johannesburg. These guns inevitably outranged and overmatched the British field artillery, rendering position after position untenable, until, within three weeks of the outbreak of the war, Ladysmith itself was in danger from the heavy pieces of ordnance mounted on the encircling hills. Then came the delight and the immediate sense of relief when the news was received of the dramatic and unexpected appearance of the naval guns in the beleaguered town.

To the remarkable prescience and ingenuity of Capt. Percy Scott, the admirable energy and promptitude of Capt. the Hon. Hedworth Lambton, and the zeal and resourcefulness of all the officers and men associated with them, it was due that the Naval Brigade, with guns of equal power to those possessed by the Boers, was able to reach the front before the investment was complete, or, as Sir George White said, 'when it became evident that I was not strong enough to meet the enemy in the open field.'

Outside Ladysmith, both during and after the siege, in the Cape

Colony and in the hostile States, the entry of naval detachments upon the field of action was not attended by circumstances such as had made the appearance of the *Powerful's* brigade so significant and dramatically effective. But the part played was quite as important, the work performed was fully as arduous, and the difficulties surmounted demanded an equal amount of smartness, endurance and courage.

The description of the share taken by the naval guns in the relief of Ladysmith demonstrates most clearly the tremendously heavy calls made upon the little force, and the excellent manner in which all responded. The energy which the bluejackets infused into their performance of duty, their high spirits and the magnificent marksmanship, earned the commendation of all the military officers they served under. As one general said of the seamen who were helping him, 'They were worth their weight in gold.'

The Naval Brigade on the Western line of operations, first under Lord Methuen, and then accompanying the field force to Bloemfontein, Pretoria, and eventually to Komati Poort, was perhaps not called upon so frequently to meet artillery of equal power, but it conclusively proved that heavy guns, even on roughly constructed mountings, could keep up with infantry marching at unusual speed. At Graspan it had the opportunity of doing a splendid bit of work worthy of the highest traditions of the service. In the march from Poplar grove across the *veldt*, after the terrible bombardment of Cronje's *laager*, often for considerable distances without water and always on reduced rations, the zeal, the cheerfulness and the discipline of all was beyond praise.

And then that wonderful movement of Grant's guns over a thousand miles, including a seventeen days' chase of de Wet, during which, as we are told, it was never necessary to bring a man before the commanding officer for any crime, neglect of duty, slackness, or other offence whatever! This constitutes a record that must ever be remembered to the credit of those immediately concerned, as well as of the navy itself.

The words of Lord Roberts might well find an echo through the Empire:

I wished Capt. Bearcroft and the Naval Brigade goodbye today. They leave for Cape Town tonight, carrying with them the thanks and good wishes of the army in South Africa for the able assistance they have afforded throughout the war.

The two services had worked together harmoniously from the

beginning—a circumstance abundantly gratifying, but bringing with it no surprise. They were inspired by the same ideals and the same patriotic spirit, and were fighting for the same national end.

The narrative of the experiences of the bluejackets and marines, as it appeared in the despatches, is most thrilling. But still more interesting is the tale as here told by those who participated in the dangers and difficulties of the campaign, who were eyewitnesses of the events they describe, and who have interspersed their descriptions with anecdotes and sketches which could find no place in official documents. As was the case in the brigades themselves, so with the writers in this volume, nearly every branch of the service is represented, and members of the gallant sea regiment which lost so heavily at Graspan conjoin forces in its pages with executive, engineer, and medical officers, as they did in their work in the field.

Even so we are only shown a portion of the share which the navy has taken in the war. The work of the brigades was the outward and visible sign of the influence exerted by our naval strength in every sea, and of that silent pressure exerted upon foreign opinion which assured for us the neutrality of the world.

Our maritime security throughout the struggle has been a great source of confidence at home, while the circumstances in connection with the transmission of our soldiers thousands of miles across the sea, with as much safety as if they were but crossing our own territory, has been a wonderful object lesson of the vital importance of the navy to the empire. That is the indirect but nevertheless most important share of the navy in the war. A direct share was that provided by the blockading squadrons and the ships patrolling the South African waters. Theirs was perhaps the most arduous and least recognised work, demanding on some occasions diplomatic discretion and tact, any lack of which might easily have precipitated international complications, and it was fraught also with peril, for the ships were short-handed, while often it was utterly unexciting and monotonous. A description of the proceedings at sea and upon the coasts might have enhanced the value of the book as an historic record of events, but limitation of size has precluded this, and I must be content with merely the bare mention of that most useful work,

There never has been a time in the history of the navy when we could not point to the use of seamen landed for the purpose of assisting their soldier comrades, but this feature of naval life has naturally become more common and more prominent owing to the increase of our responsibilities in many distant and isolated parts of the world. If the time should come when the navy again has to fulfil its primary function in the clash and clang of action, our seamen may find, not only in the prowess of their ancestors under Blake and Hawke and Nelson, but in the gallant deeds of those who recently served in the brigades in Africa and China, example and incentive to emulate them, and to add still more brilliant pages to our naval history.

I have had very great pleasure in writing the introduction to this volume, it was my good fortune to be able to bring the writers together, and I would commend their work as descriptive of a little known aspect of the South African war,

Chas. N. Robinson,

Castelnau: November 1901,

CHAPTER 1

Formation and Departure of the First Naval Brigade

Directly the Suzerainty Question was raised by the South African Republic it was felt that war was inevitable, and after the Bloemfontein Conference war clouds began quickly to gather.

Throughout South Africa there was intense excitement, more perhaps in Cape Colony than in loyal Natal, for here the outspoken and braggart opinions of the large section of disloyalists added to it.

At Simonstown, the headquarters of the Cape Squadron, little else was talked of; war, and the chance of a Naval Brigade being required, being the sole topics of conversation wherever naval men were gathered together. And, down in our hearts, we fervently hoped that the Republics would not 'back down' and that we should be given a chance to help wipe out 'A Certain Stain.' Nobody who has not lived in South Africa knows what that stain meant to every Englishman.

In England on October 7, 1899, 25,000 men of the First Class Army Reserve were called out, and from Pretoria two days later President Kruger issued his cheeky ultimatum to H.M. Government, containing the following demands and giving until 6 p.m. on October 11 for reply:

1. That all questions in dispute shall be settled by arbitration, or such amicable way as may be agreed;

2. That troops on the Transvaal borders shall be instantly withdrawn;

3. That all reinforcements which have arrived in South Africa since June 1 shall be removed from the country;

4. That H.M. troops now on the high seas shall not be landed in South Africa.

This meant war in bitter earnest, and H.M. Government replied, regretting these peremptory demands, which were impossible to discuss; and as the Transvaal Government stated, in their note, that a refusal to comply with these demands would be regarded as a formal Declaration of War, the British Agent at Pretoria was instructed to withdraw.

On October 12 commandoes poured across the Natal frontier, and, on the other side, Boers derailed and destroyed an armoured train patrolling the line south of Mafeking.

Troops were but few in number; some were hurried up to Kimberley just in time, and with the enemy arrogantly proclaiming their determination to drive every Britisher into the sea by Christmas time, the navy was asking to be allowed to famish a brigade to stem the tide of invasion. On the 18th, orders came down to Simonstown for two 12-pounders with full field guns' crews of bluejackets to be held in readiness to proceed to Cape Town. The Royal Marines began to think that they were to be left out, but happily this was not to be, for on the following day the orders were amended, and as many marines as could be spared were to form the gun escort of the first Naval Brigade.

Then commenced a general bustle all round. Time was short and many things had yet to be done.

The two senior officers detailed to land—one in command of the whole brigade and the other of the marines—were ordered by the G.O.C. to attend at Cape Town, to arrange details and receive confidential instructions.

Khaki clothing, not then supplied to the Navy, was obtained from the Ordnance Stores at Cape Town, piled into and on top of cabs, hurried to the station and sent down by rail to Simonstown.

The officers met to discuss final matters and arrange personal business, khaki was issued, also military great coats, to the bluejackets, all equipment was got ready, and marines' belts, pouches, and rifle slings were scrubbed and dyed a colour meant to be khaki, but not quite, with permanganate of potash.

Some stout men, for whom no khaki could be found large enough, tried the experiment of dyeing their white clothing a coffee colour. The result may best be left to imagination. However, everything eventually was arranged and on October 20 the Naval Brigade landed from H.M.S. *Doris* (flag), *Monarch* (guardship), *Powerful* (from China, homeward bound), and *Terrible* (to China, outward bound). There was tremendous enthusiasm in the fleet. All hands on board manned and cheered ship, and a hearty reply was given from every boat as it pulled ashore laden with its khaki-clad bluejackets, stokers, and marines. Inside the dockyard the brigade was formed up for inspection by the rear-admiral commanding the station, who made a short address, and specially confided the care of the guns to the marines, saying, 'The corps must prevent them at all hazards from being captured. With such an escort, I rest assured that if the guns don't come back, no bluejackets or marines will come back either.'

There were many dismal faces among those left behind, nothing but cheerful smiles on the faces of those chosen as they formed 'fours' and wheeled through the dockyard gates on their way to the station.

The brigade was composed as follows:

Commander Ethelston of H.M.S. *Powerful* in command.

Major Plumbe, R.M.L.I., of H.M.S. *Doris* 2nd in command.

9 Naval officers.

68 bluejackets.

7 Marine officers.

290 N.C.O.'s and men of the Royal Marines.

The guns were two 12-pounder 8-cwt. guns on ordinary field mountings.

The road to the railway station was packed with an enthusiastic, cheering crowd of friends and well-wishers. At the station the brigade entrained for Cape Town, and so well had the secret been kept, no one knew what was to be the destination of this force. There were many conjectures; not a few men said, in sorrowful tones, that they were only going to Cape Town, to be stationed in the castle for garrison duties, and so release some soldiers for duty up country. The scene all along the line was splendid. Thousands of people turned out and waved and cheered vociferously. At Cape Town (Salt River Junction) a staff officer boarded the train, gave orders, printed and otherwise, the engine whistled and started for——where?

All necessary precautions were taken against surprise, and orders issued in case of being attacked, blown off the line, or otherwise rudely interfered with. After proceeding for many miles it gradually became

15

known that the destination *might* be De Aar. The trip went along splendidly and smoothly with little or no excitement. Arrangements had been made for the issue of rations, &c., and, to the joy of every one, *rum* was to be issued daily. It required some tact and patience on the part of all concerned to shake the men together, comfortably and well, and it speaks well for their discipline that no man had to be pitched into for any fault. Keen to do their duty to the utmost and thoroughly and sincerely loyal to their officers, it was very difficult to find fault with them, though naturally the unusual conditions under which they found themselves tended to get them a little 'out of hand' at first. On the route we got occasional items of war news. The telegram announcing the victory at Glencoe met us at one station and was received with round after round of cheering and much enthusiasm.

The country until the Great Karroo is reached was very picturesque, but there are no words to describe the desert. A never-ending tract of waterless and treeless country, with an occasional house, apparently put there by mistake. Beaufort West, a town of importance, with many sympathisers of the Republics, was passed, and eventually De Aar was reached. A large depot was being formed here, and one could not help being struck with the fact that it was a place very exposed, and open to attack and capture. One amusing incident occurred on the train. It was reported that a man speaking with a foreign accent was seated on the engine, and would give no satisfactory account of himself or of his movements, nor would he produce his pass or permit to travel on the line. It soon became known amongst the men that he was a spy. There couldn't be a doubt of it, &c., &c.

An officer interviewed him, could get no explanation from him, and promptly had him placed in a luggage van, handcuffs on, and a sentry mounted with orders to shoot him if he attempted to escape. Eventually it was discovered that the foreign spy was a German boasting of an English name, who was travelling up and down a certain section of the line as railway and traffic superintendent.

Staff officers on the line could not give us any information as to our destination, and all conversation with civilians was forbidden and men kept in the train.

From De Aar the train was sent eastwards with a pilot engine to look out for pitfalls. The commander attached himself for duty as amateur engine-driver and lookout man to this pilot engine, and at the end of the journey when we reached camp it was hard to distinguish

16

him. He was as black as a chimney-sweep. The experience had been a trying one.

It was reported that we might be attacked or blown up, and there was great keenness amongst the men to be ready and under fire and get in their first shot at '*they* Bo-ers.'

On the way to Stormberg Junction, which was now known to be the Naval Brigade's destination, we passed through Naauwpoort Junction, an important place held by half a battalion of the Berkshire Regiment, and which the Boers ought to have occupied at once.

We saw a number of refugees at Naauwpoort, who had been sent out of the Orange Free State, and they looked very miserable and depressed, and asked many awkward questions as to our doings, movements, and destination. Secrecy was the order of the day, and even then it was hard for the men not to talk.

Stormberg, an important railway junction, about fifty miles south of the Free State border, was eventually reached on Sunday evening, October 28, and it was a great surprise and pleasure for the Naval Brigade and marines to have so especially cheery a welcome from the Berkshire Regiment—old friends and comrades of McNeill's *zareba* days in the Soudan. The manner in which the officers and men of this regiment treated us was beyond description. Nothing could possibly be kinder, and it was a sad parting when goodbyes had to be said later on.

Everyone was very glad to get into camp at last and put in a satisfactory sleep, for we had been working at tension during this train journey, and what with the crowding and jolting had got very little.

Now that camp was formed the hard work of daily routine camp life began.

The weather was bitterly cold at night and very hot by day. Every morning we stood to arms at four o'clock, shivering with cold and excitement, waiting for an attack by the Boers at dawn, but it never came. But we could not slack up a little bit. It was always present in one's mind how necessary it was to keep the men aware of the fact that they were on active service—conditions very different from those of peace. After the outposts were relieved, and mounted infantry sent out, a good deal of necessary shaking-together drill had to be done, working parties went away to dig and work on defences, washing parades were held as often as possible, if water and time permitted, and before dusk the night outposts marched away. These outpost duties fell very heavily on the officers and men, but were always performed cheerfully, willingly, and intelligently. The men were generally away from camp for twelve hours, and on arriving in camp were immediately detailed for other duties, and there was no taking off of boots and clothes except for washing, and even all parties sent away for washing took their arms with them and had a covering party on the look-oat for the slim Boer, who is an expert in the art of sniping from safe cover.

The Naval Brigade camp at Stormberg was pitched on a plain surrounded by high *kopjes* (or rocky hills), fairly well put into defence by Berkshires and the Naval Brigade. It is difficult for those who know the place to realise how the disaster to General Gatacre's force on December 11 occurred. The Berkshire Mounted Infantry and infantry, from their experience of the country for some months, must have known every inch of the ground.

The country south of the Orange River is of very peculiar formation, and admirably suited to Boer tactics—Boers possessing, as they do, that most important qualification, mobility. Boers were known to be moving south near Norval's Pont and Bethulie, armoured trains were busily occupied, and the men of the Naval Brigade had many exciting times careering about with their mule guns. Probably this is the first time in the history of the navy that muleteers have been borne on ships' books.

The excitement at Stormberg began to increase as soon as General Buller arrived at the Cape, and the Naval Brigade expected to be moved forward and take a part—a very prominent part too we fully intended it should be—in the general advance. Stores and provisions were piled into the place as quickly as possible, ready for expected troops. We now heard that the first Boer prisoners were to be put on board the *Penelope*, and others on the cricket ground at Simonstown. One day in camp we had a general alarm, turned out hurriedly, and then found out that it was only for practice—very necessary, of course, but disappointing, as we thought we were in for a fight.

After being in camp for nearly a fortnight, the Naval Brigade got sudden and hurried orders to strike camp and prepare to move. Now was our time, we thought, and every one worked his hardest to get things together quickly, and take them to the station as ordered. We felt certain that we were to move forward to fight some Boers who were known to have crossed the Orange River, and were supposed to be marching on Naauwpoort and Stormberg. Preparations had previously been made to provision the various fortified places round about,

Operations on
the South of the
Orange River

as we expected to be attacked at any moment.

On arriving at the station, we were grievously disappointed to hear that our movement was to be by train to the rear, probably to Queenstown, and when it was whispered that General Sir Redvers Buller had, for strategic reasons, decided to withdraw the troops from Stormberg, there was much regret expressed, and men were actually seen to be weeping from disappointment. Never was disappointment more plainly written on men's faces. It was some considerable time before the news leaked out that our destination *was* Queenstown, and we heard eventually that probably the disaster at Nicholson's Nek was the primary cause of this hurried evacuation of Stormberg.

A. E. Marchant.

CHAPTER 2

Recalled to Our Ships

Queenstown was reached at 7 p.m. on November 2, and a large and enthusiastic crowd of inhabitants welcomed us. They seemed to look upon the arrival of the Naval Brigade as their salvation. Camp was pitched that night, and next day the remainder of the Stormberg garrison arrived and all necessary precautions for defence immediately taken in hand. Before leaving Stormberg all stores were loaded up and those burnt for which no room was available, and the defences destroyed. The Naval Brigade had their first experience of the real discomfort of camp life on active service soon after their arrival here, for suddenly a gale (or dust storm) sprang up and blew most things away.

News of the progress of the campaign was very hard to get, especially from Natal; the wildest rumours flew round, and very sinister were some of these. We were much amused at getting letters from Simonstown saying that the Naval Brigade at Stormberg was surrounded on all sides, and likely to be cut up. We also heard of the Naval Brigade's doings in Ladysmith and the death of poor Egerton.

A remount depot had been formed at Queenstown, and the officers of the brigade were promptly fitted out with all necessary horse equipment, and occasional riding parties did much to pass the time. Cutlass drill on horseback as tried by two of the officers one day led to a most amusing, and quite unintended, cavalry charge into the middle of the tents, their frightened steeds not being used to such treatment. Though we begged them to go through their interesting performance again, they were much too modest to do so.

Queenstown itself is a charming little town lying on a plain with a range of hills to the north. The inhabitants treated us well, and we were eventually very sorry to leave. The Berkshires' band used to play inspiriting tunes, and the fair inhabitants, many of them Boer sympathisers, no doubt, enjoyed the unusual treat, and often were to be seen in our camp, as guests. But we were very suspicious of everybody, and the men were instructed never to give any information whatever to strangers, and taxed their imaginations to give ingenious and misleading replies. To one visitor, who, on being shown the guns, asked: 'What do they fire?' the private of marines, remembering his orders, had a brilliant inspiration, and replied: 'Oh, them there guns? Well, you see, when our fellers 'ave to go away from camp on dooty we fires biscuits after 'em. It saves a deal of trouble.'

The duties at Queenstown were very heavy for our men, and there was plenty of digging and building for them to do; the weather being bitterly cold at night, and exceedingly hot during the day. Sometimes there was as much as forty-five to fifty degrees variation in temperature, varied by occasional gales of wind, and dust storms, quite enough to spoil one's 'stretch off the land' and temper. It was very amusing on one night, when the top-gallant halyards of the mess tent carried away, to see officers in varicoloured night garments running about trying to keep the marquee from travelling heavenwards. However, by dint of hard work, hard language, and a number of strong men the situation was saved.

Some reinforcements were sent up to this garrison, but when the railway west of Queenstown was cut it was decided to withdraw the garrison altogether, and with bitter expressions on all sides, and much sympathy from the Berkshires, the Naval Brigade was entrained for East London. This disappointment was awful to us, as we quite thought that all our chances of being in action had gone. We returned horses, saddlery, water-cart, and all army stores, and actually handed over the guns to a second lieutenant of Royal Artillery. To return without their guns was an exceedingly great blow to our men, and the night before we left it is vouched for that two of the gun's crew approached an officer, and, after a good deal of scratching of heads and shuffling of feet, asked permission to disable their guns.

When asked 'what the devil they meant?' they answered, 'Well, sir, seeing as how we can't take 'em back ourselves, we don't want 'em to fall into the hands of nobody else.' There were heavy hearts when the goodbyes were said to our friends in the garrison. The Berkshire band played ns away, and a big crowd assembled at the station to see the last of the Naval Brigade, who during their short stay in garrison had become exceedingly popular. Every one hoped to meet us again, and still hoped to meet us fighting.

At East London we were met by the senior naval officer, who said it was quite true that we were to rejoin our ships. We had fondly hoped that Natal might be our goal. Here the *Terrible's* men of the Naval Brigade embarked on board a transport for passage to rejoin their ship, and to see some fighting in Natal, and the remainder embarked on board the *Roslin Castle*, and left immediately for Simonstown. Champagne to drown one's sorrows and quench one's thirst was the order of the night, and after a good dinner, a smoke and sing-song, we, to a certain extent, forgot our sorrow and took a more cheerful view of the situation; but the disappointment and disgust at being sent back, bloodless, to our ships may be better imagined than described. At East London we heard how well the Natal Naval Brigades had been doing, and wished and hoped for our chance to come.

On the way round to Simonstown there was deep-seated anger at the thought of being on the point of rejoining the fleet without having a chance of fighting, and we wondered if we should be badly chaffed. Imagine our joy on arriving on Sunday, November 19, to see men in khaki parading on board the ships, and to receive a signal that a new Naval Brigade was being organised, that we were to form part of it, that we were to be entrained at four o'clock that same afternoon, all under the command of Flag Captain Prothero, and that we were going to join Lord Methuen's column for the relief of Kimberley. Round after round of cheering rent the air, and there was a good deal of handshaking and congratulations. Those of us whose wives were living at Simonstown were lucky enough to be able to get ashore for a few hours, and then off to the front again.

A. E. Marchant.

CHAPTER 3

Battle of Belmont

The force was reconstituted, more guns and more bluejackets were taken, the whole of the force being made up to something like 400 of all ranks—half of these being marines; four 12-pounder 12-cwt. guns on improvised mountings (Scott's), with guns' crews, stokers for stretcher-bearers, and a medical staff.

The same tremendous enthusiasm was shown on this day as on October 20. The rear-admiral inspected us on the lawn of Admiralty House and wished us Godspeed; a south-easter blowing with unaccustomed vigour gave us a final send-off, and we left to join Methuen's Kimberley relief force in the highest spirits.

The whole town and dockyard turned out, and with drums beating and colours (if we had them) flying we marched gaily to the station, entrained for Cape Town, being cheered all along the route, and left at 9 p.m. that night for De Aar. Shortly after leaving Beaufort two trains collided and blocked the line, and as our commanding officer had orders to get on to Lord Methuen as quickly as possible, he decided to transfer all our train load into another train about half a mile ahead. It was a tough job, but the men, splendidly helped by a squadron of South African Light Horse, worked with a will from 10 p.m. till 2 a.m. and did it, and we proceeded. The collision looked a suspicious affair, but it was quite impossible to apportion the blame. Probably Boer sympathisers were about. All necessary precautions were again taken to guard against surprise, or to resist an attack, and we arrived at De Aar without further incident. Rum was again regularly issued, and was a very cheering addition to our midday meal.

Lord Methuen waited for the arrival of the Naval Brigade at Witteputs before making his advance on Belmont, where a hard fight took place on November 23, in which the Guards and Northumber-

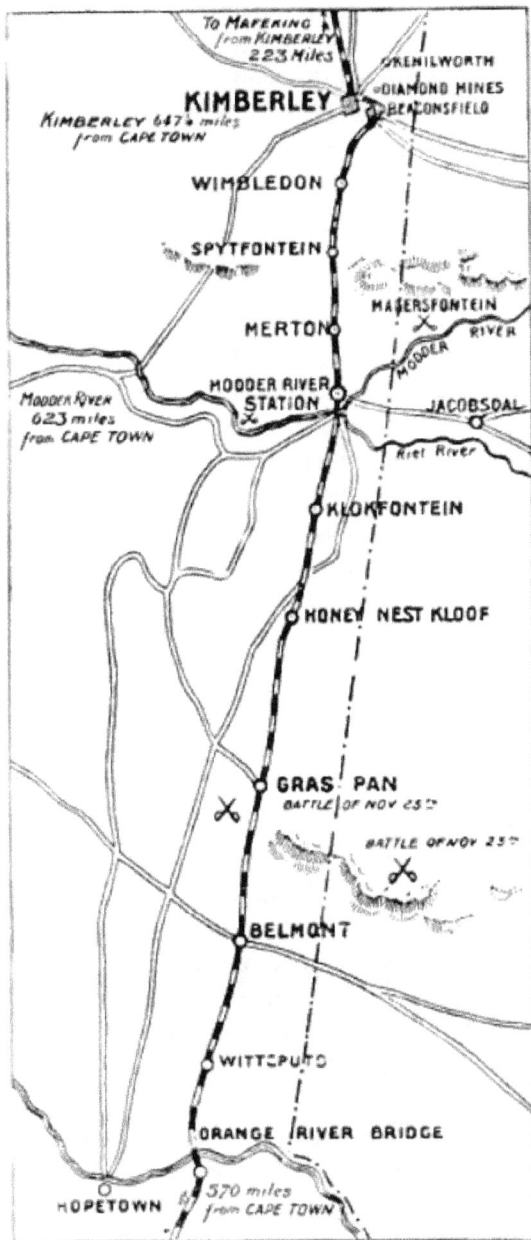

LORD METHUEN'S ADVANCE

land fusiliers behaved splendidly and suffered heavily, and the Naval Brigade came under fire for the first time daring the war. The Naval Brigade was delayed marching with the force on account of the late arrival of its transport, and the night march that followed was a particularly trying one. All baggage of officers was cut down to 35 lbs., swords were left behind, and much of the men's gear packed in a railway truck as base luggage. One officer's horse, with brand-new saddlery, &c., bolted and was never seen again. The horse was loot, so probably it was a judgment.

At 8.30 p.m. the Naval Brigade column, somewhat resembling a long gipsy caravan, was finally mustered and got under way, the mules being very troublesome, wagon loads heavy, and drivers not quite experienced yet in their work. After some time two wagons got hopelessly stuck in the heavy going, and the rear guard of one company of marines was left to bring them along as well as possible. It seemed a hopeless and endless task, but by dint of hard work and perseverance the column did eventually reach the camp at Belmont, where water was very welcome. A night march with obstinate mules is a very trying experience. The Naval Brigade was fortunate enough to come into action and under fire, but did not have very much to do in the fight. The going was very heavy and in places very rocky for the 12-pounder guns on improvised, dockyard-built wooden mountings. The weather was very hot; and mules and men were much distressed and dead beat after this trying night march and fight.

A short description of this action taken from Captain Prothero's despatches is interesting.

. . . . .I marched out of Belmont by road in company with Colonel Hall's battery of field artillery. After clearing Belmont *kopjes*, we turned off the road on the open veldt; day was just dawning, and we could see the top of the line of *kopjes* held by the enemy. We were then advancing towards the centre of his position, over very rough ground intersected with dykes. This tried our gun- mountings very severely. Unfortunately, one gun capsized, but was soon righted, and I was relieved to find that there was no damage done, and that the dockyard work stood the test so well.

On proceeding to higher ground, a view of the Boers' position was then obtained—a long line of *kopjes*, which looked very much higher at dawn of day than they really were, the light be-

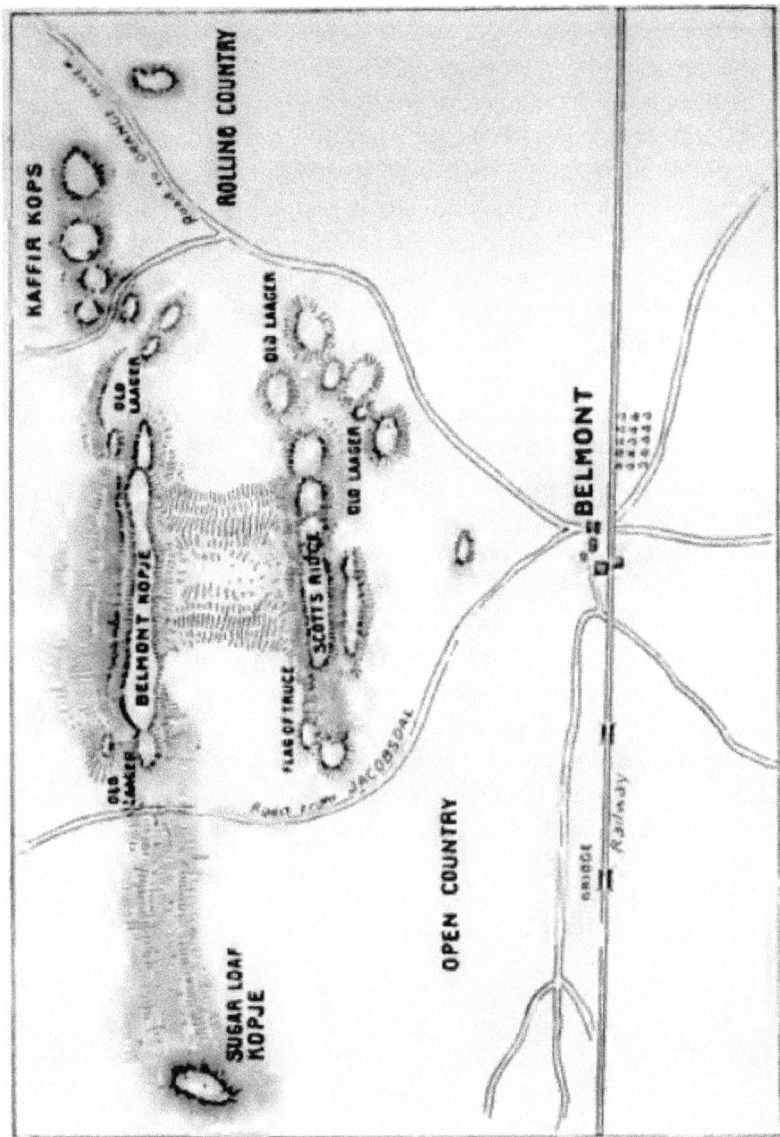

BATTLE
OF
BELMONT

ing very bad indeed, and the sun coming up behind the *kopjes* cast dark shadows, which made it very hard to distinguish any object. In addition to this there was a mist round the lower part of the *kopjes*. Firing was now going on in our front, the Boers evidently having been repulsed. Colonel Hall here turned away to his left, and to the left of the Boer position, on the understanding that I should take up a position across the railway line on higher ground, and he would soon communicate with me. This I did, but had great difficulty in taking my heavy ammunition wagons and guns across the railway line, finally succeeding. I here brought the battery into action to try the range of the extreme depth of the Boer position, but after firing a range-finding shot, and not seeing it pitch, I limbered up. . . .

I then turned to the left between two *kopjes*, and found the Boers on the rear *kopje*, firing upon advancing infantry. I immediately got the battery into action, and at 1,700 yards shelled the Boers, who were firing on our troops, the practice being excellent.

The Boers were very soon silenced and retreated.

I received orders from the general to take my guns, if possible, on to a low *kopje*, about eight hundred yards from my front, so as to shell the retreating Boers from their position.

I limbered up, and advanced as quickly as possible over very rough ground, and advancing well ahead myself to survey the *kopje*. I found, when I arrived on top, that it was impossible to take wheels over it, so reluctantly had to give it up. Here my officers, men, and mules were almost dead beat, and the battle over.

Having watered my mules, I returned to the camp with the remainder of the troops.

A. E. Marchant.

CHAPTER 4

The Action at Graspan

The general advance along the railway was recommenced at 1.30 p.m., the armoured train moving abreast of the division, and being followed by another train with the naval 12-pounders on tracks. Lieutenant Dean was in command of these, and their mule teams had been lent to the field batteries, in order that the exhausted horses might reserve their strength till actually in contact with the enemy.

Our destination was two shallow dams, about seven miles north of Belmont, and as it was expected that their possession would be contested, the advance was exceedingly slow to allow of very careful scouting ahead. However, the Boers were good enough not to give any trouble, and at sunset a final halt was called, and the division bivouacked for the night, between two small *kopjes* on either flank, the Naval Brigade occupying the post of honour on the extreme right, and throwing out a company of marines to hold a narrow *nek* of rising ground in the right rear.

The local topography of this narrow *nek* became tolerably well known that night, for on the opposite side lay the two dams from which water had to be obtained.

The men, carrying water bottles and mess tins, were taken across a company at a time, and will not readily forget these excursions. The night was extremely dark, except for the occasional treacherous light of a quarter moon; great boulders brought them up with a 'round turn' and barked shins; loose stones tripped them and spilt the water they carried; and deep holes, concealed by long grass, laid pitfalls for those who had managed to steer clear of other dangers.

These dams were only three-quarters of a mile away, yet the double journey occupied two hours, and as they were very shallow, with about twelve inches of mud and three of water, more mud than water

Officers landed with the Naval Brigade to defend Stormberg, and who afterwards took part in the Action at Graspan

1. Commander A. P. ETHELSTON [killed]. 2. Major J. H. PLUMBE, R.M.L.I. [killed]. 3. Lieutenant W. T. C. JONES, R.M.L.I. [wounded].
4. Captain GUY SENTON, R.M.A. [killed]. 5. Midshipman C. A. E. HUDDART [killed].

was brought back. However, we tried to imagine it was rum.

By the time water was obtained and fires burning brightly it was reported that our commissariat wagons had dragged themselves up, so the gunner went off in the dark to hunt for them, and after a long search returned with sufficient tinned meat and ship's biscuit to issue a small ration to all. As a great luxury, the officers opened a tin of preserved kidneys, and these, biscuits and muddy water, eaten round the fires, formed our supper.

The fact, however, that this was 'real soldiering' made the fare seem luxurious, and, in the circumstances, the 'sardine, beer, and onion' suppers after a long 'coal-ship' day could not stand comparison.

Supper being finished we smoked round our fires and discussed the situation generally, the chances of getting some sleep and the probable events of tomorrow.

'We must get the chance of a "show" before reaching Kimberley,' was the general opinion, and the 'show' we meant was a little infantry work in addition to our long-range artillery business.

Almost as this opinion was expressed, out of the darkness into the light of our fire stepped the good fairy we had invoked, a somewhat dust-grimed A.D.C., inquiring 'Is this the Naval Brigade?'

'Yes, old chap. Sorry we can't give you a drink.'

'I want the officer commanding.'

We directed him to Captain Prothero, and heard him say as he handed the captain some orders, 'You will have a nice job tomorrow, sir, something more to your liking.'

Immediately the officers were summoned, and the captain read the laconic order, 'The enemy, about four hundred strong, hold a hill on our line of advance two miles to the north. The Naval Brigade will lead the attack, supported by the K.O.Y.L.I. and a field battery. . . .' Then followed precise instructions as to movements and dispositions.

'Goodnight, sir,' said the A.D.C., and disappeared.

At last the navy was to have a 'show' all to herself; the news seemed almost too good to be true, and it was some short time before we could believe it and realise our luck.

The officers went to their companies, and told them there would be work for them next day, though the actual arrangements were kept secret. A thrill of excitement ran through the brigade.

'By Jove, what sport!' said a midshipman.

'What luck!' said an officer of marines.

'Is it really true, sir?' asked a company sergeant, radiant with the anticipation of an infantry job; everyone felt a sense of subdued joy and satisfaction that *something* was going to happen tomorrow. The only people that night who did not share equally in the good news were the fifty bluejackets manning the guns on the railway, who would have to stay with them, and would not be able to take part in the infantry attack.

The men lay down by their arms and the officers in groups of two and three, but sleep was long in coming, fitful and but little refreshing when it came.

The night was very cold; the wagon with our blankets, great coats, and waterproof sheets had lost its way in the darkness and could not be found; it was impossible to find a spot where we could lie down without resting on the sharp corner of some rock, and in our thin cotton khaki we shivered through the night. It was our first experience of a very cold night after a hot day, and without our blankets we did not enjoy it.

The picket in the right rear was relieved at 11 p.m.

Saturday, November 25.—The picket was withdrawn at 2.30 a.m. and the brigade stood to arms at 3 a.m. Magazines were charged and rifles carefully examined. This being done we marched silently down to the place of assembly and were joined by the cavalry, mounted infantry, and the K.O.Y.L.I., the remainder of the 9th Brigade forming up in rear and the Guards in charge of the baggage. At 3.45 a.m. an advance was made in mass of quarter-column, the spaces between companies being slightly opened out. The mounted troops bore away to the flanks, and in the growing daylight we could just make out a hill ahead of us which we imagined was our objective and on which we could see a few figures moving against the sky-line. As we drew nearer a murmur of disappointment ran through the ranks, for these moving figures turned out to be our own scouts and we were afraid our chance had gone.

However, the Boer position was not nearly reached yet.

The whole division advanced parallel to and about a mile on the right of the railway, the cavalry well away on the flanks, the two field batteries well to the front, and the Naval Brigade proudly leading the infantry. Slowly puffing along the line on our left was the armoured train, with the naval 12-pounders on trucks behind it, and away on our right the sun was just appearing over the horizon.

The air was delightfully cool and bracing, and we marched over

PLAN OF GRASPAN.

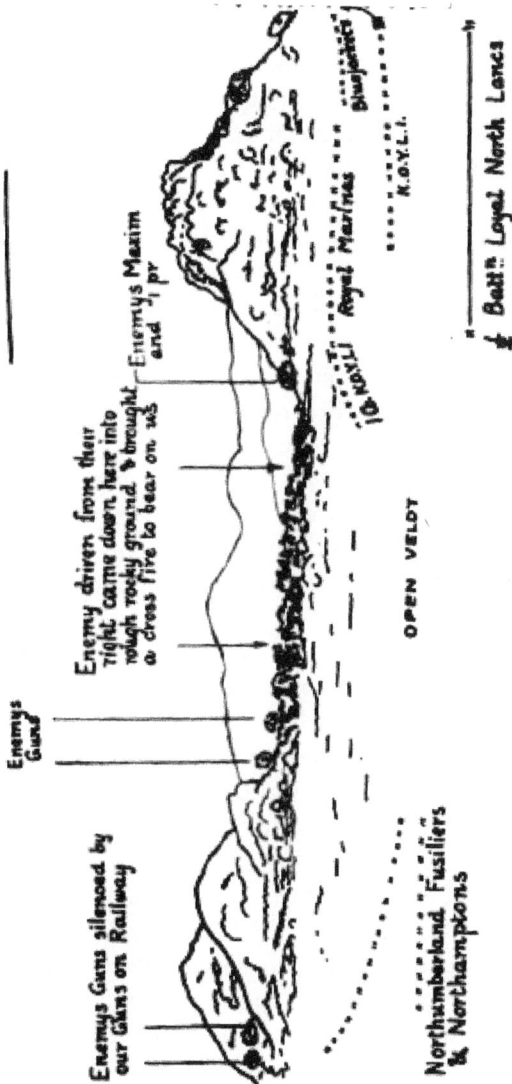

Enemy's Guns silenced by
our Guns on Railway

Enemy's
Guns

Enemy driven from their
right came down here into
rough rocky ground & brought
a cross fire to bear on us

Enemy's Maxim
and 9 pr

OPEN VELDT

Northumberland Fusiliers
& Northamptons

.... K.O.Y.L.I.

.... Royal Marines

.... Bluejackets

.... K.O.Y.L.I.

——— Battⁿ Loyal North Lancs

the *veldt* at a steady pace, the 'going' being very good. Occasionally we halted for a few minutes.

After marching for a couple of hours the scouts came in touch with the enemy and found their main body strongly posted in a position very similar to that at Belmont, except that the line of *kopjes* they held was broken in their left centre and the *kopjes* themselves did not run so high. The extent of the position was about three miles from flank to flank, running eastwards at right angles to the railway. The right flank was beautifully drawn back, and the field of fire commanded was, if possible, more nearly approaching the ideal than even that at Belmont, with splendid opportunities for posting and concealing guns amongst the rocks, whilst attacking artillery had no commanding positions to seize and would have to unlimber in the open. There was not the slightest cover for an attacking force except for an occasional ant-hill dotted here and there over the *veldt*, which extended for thousands of yards round the front and flank and was covered with rank brown grass about eighteen inches high.

Away on the enemy's extreme left stood a boulder-strewn *kopje*, higher than the rest, a fortress in itself. It appeared to be almost isolated, but we found later that a low-lying spur, covered with great rocks, ran out towards and a little in front of it from the central *kopje*, and gave splendid cover for a deadly cross-fire as we advanced to the attack.

Its strength and size were such that it evidently formed the key of the position, and it was against it that the attack was ultimately pushed home.

A field battery now galloped out and commenced shelling it at a range of about 2,500 yards. On our left the naval guns and the other battery were also in action and were being vigorously replied to by two Boer guns.

Thus about seven o'clock—we had already marched for three hours it must be remembered—the general position was as follows. The Naval Brigade, extended to single rank, leading, and the 9th Brigade, similarly extended in support, were opposite the right centre of the Boer position and distant about 3,500 yards. The Guards' Brigade was guarding the baggage on the railway, the cavalry were hovering round the enemy's right to intercept their retreat, one battery and the naval guns were busy on our left, and the second battery far away on our right flank was pouring shrapnel over that isolated *kopje* on the Boer left.

At this point the intended attack on the Boer left flank commenced to develop. The Naval Brigade, now extended to four paces, the K.O.Y.L.I. and the half-battalion of Royal North Lancasters were ordered to move away to the right, and the remainder of the 9th Brigade, consisting of the Northumberlands and Northamptons, pushed on, straight ahead, for the centre of the enemy's position, to demonstrate against this point and to act as a containing force.

Slowly we laboured across the front of the *kopjes* whilst the guns merrily pounded away, and extended as we were in a line about eight hundred yards long, perhaps longer, this diagonal march of nearly two miles was very tedious.

Not quite certain why this movement was taking place, for only the commanding officers knew exactly what we were intended to do, we trudged along through the coarse grass, keeping our left shoulders well up to avoid the ugly rocky *kopjes* in our immediate front. The sun was beginning to be very hot and we were becoming somewhat 'droopy,' as no one had had any breakfast, except a few who had been wise enough to save a little biscuit or bread from their supper over night, and we had been marching already for three hours and a half. The men were taking frequent 'pulls' at their water bottles, and the advice to 'Save your water, men, you'll want it presently,' had not much effect. Lucky were those who still had a little two hours later.

Now and then a *greis*-buck would get up and scamper down the line; and sometimes a covey of frightened partridges would remind us that we had rifles in our hands, not shot-guns.

We glanced at the *kopjes* and almost wondered why the guns poured such a tempest of shrapnel over them; rarely did we catch sight of a figure moving among the rocks, and with the exception of the enemy's guns on their right, vigorously replying to our own, the whole position looked harmless and untenanted.

At 7.45 we were some seven hundred yards from the base of the isolated *kopje* on the Boer left, and the field battery ceased firing. Almost immediately from the rocks, which a moment before seemed lifeless, there opened the wild crackle of Mausers.

Bang! Bang! the battery commenced again, firing over our heads. Even now our firing line was continuing its diagonal march, but at the moment we heard the crackle of musketry and the whistling of bullets each man instinctively turned to his front and the line paused.

Captain R. C. Prothero, R.N., led the advance, and Major J. H. Plumbe, R.M.L.I., Captain A. E. Marchant, R.M.L.I., and Colour-

Sergeant Dyson were in advance of the various marine companies.

Midshipman T. F. J. L. Wardle acted as A.D.C. to Major Plumbe and accompanied that officer. In some places the line was somewhat crowded and 'bunched,' but the average extension was about four paces.

As supports, there were seven companies of the K.O.Y.L.I., which later on reinforced the right of the firing line, and in reserve, the half-battalion of the Royal North Lancasters.

The composition of the firing line from right to left was as follows:

1 company of bluejackets:
        Comm. A. P. Ethelston
        Lieut. Hon. E. S. H. Boyle
        Gunner E. E. Lowe
        Midship. C. A. E. Huddart
            „   W. W. Sillem
                                                    55

'A' Company R.M.A. Captain Guy Senior
'B'   „   R.M.L.I Lieut. W. T. C. Jones
'C'   „   „   Lieut. F. J. Saunders
                                                    190
1 Company of K.O.Y.L.I.   85
                                                   ─────
        Total strength of firing line   330

The brigade paused and half wondered what all this crackling going on in front meant; there was a sound of whistling in the air, and instinctively we raised our left arms as if to protect our faces from a hail storm.

Advance! Advance! And on we went at the 'quick'; the crackling grew fiercer and we looked anxiously to see if anyone was hit.

Down dropped three men, falling forward; 'Get up!' shouted an officer, but only one rose and he was dazed and bleeding from the back of the neck—a shrapnel had burst overhead.

A few paces forward and the line sank down; officers shouted the distance—600 yards; non-commissioned officers gave, 'Volleys! Ready! Present! Fire!' and those of the men who heard obeyed. Fire control was, however, almost impossible; the men were too far apart and the noise of the enemy's fire drowned all orders.

Officers and men quickly grasped the situation and used their rifles independently. This was our first halt after coming under fire, and from here onwards the attack took the form of a succession of short rushes.

The line worked automatically, firing, rushing on and dropping down to fire again. Men advanced, crouching low, some holding their water bottles in their left hands, ready to moisten their lips at the next halt; the scorching heat and overwhelming excitement had parched our throats, and each drop of water gave us strength for another spring.

As the line halted each man threw himself at full length on the ground, drew himself to a tuft of grass, loaded his rifle, adjusted his sight and fired at the top of the *kopje*. Only an occasional head was visible there, and it is an extraordinary fact that, though under fire for the first time, many men, in order to make their aim more accurate, actually lowered their sights frequently as they advanced, disregarding the rule laid down of fixed sights below 500 yards, and thus displaying a most unexpected coolness during a period of intense excitement.

The Boer fire was hottest between 500 and 200 yards—a short-range fire in front from the crest of the hill sending down a continual stream of bullets—ploughing up the ground all round us, splashing against stones and rocks, and flying by with a shriek, or whistling past us with a noise like the crack of a whip. But a far more deadly cross-fire swept the line from our left. This came from the before-mentioned rocky spur jutting out from the central *kopjes*, and down to which the Boers had poured, to reinforce their left, and to get away from the fire of the guns near the railway.

Here they were unmolested, except for an occasional shell, and could use their rifles with deliberation.

Most of our casualties took place whilst dashing on; some were shot as they lay firing, all remained helpless where they were struck down on the open veldt and frequently were hit again and again as they lay. Those who could do so dragged themselves to an ant-heap or tuft of grass and waited for the next bullet to hit them. Others, regardless of wounds, struggled on till brought down by another.

The officers lost heavily. Commander Ethelston, Major Plumbe and Captain Senior were shot dead. Captain Prothero, R.N., and Lieut. Jones were both severely wounded, and Midshipman Huddart was mortally wounded whilst struggling to advance after being twice hit.

Nearly all the petty officers and non-commissioned officers were killed or wounded, but the line still advanced without the slightest wavering. One may well ask how the men were led?

Drill books have taught that men should not lie down during the last 500 yards of the attack, because of the supposed impossibility, once they had laid down, of making them rise and face a short-range magazine fire.

It is certain, however, that the whole attack would have been swept away if they had remained on their feet continually, and there was no difficulty whatever in making them 'rise up' again. They wanted no leading; they were only too anxious to close with the enemy and get it over; many, in fact, had to be restrained to prevent the line losing its cohesion. If an officer sprang up, all his men followed like clockwork; there was no hesitation, and so it continued till the foot of the *kopje* was reached.

Here we were to a great extent sheltered by the very steepness of the *kopje*, and paused to take breath in this 'dead space,' the bal-lets flying past well overhead. Whilst we waited, our supports of the K.O.Y.L.I. rushed across the fire-swept belt we had just crossed and reinforced our right, bayonets were fixed, and on we went again.

Climbing was difficult and we had in places to haul ourselves up on hands and knees, painfully and slowly. The frontal fire never ceased till we were within twenty-five yards of the top, and then we knew the Boers thought it was time to quit. With a last scramble and rush we gained the crest only to find the enemy flying down the other side.

We still had to keep under cover, for they gained the shelter of some rocks a few hundred yards in rear of the *kopje* they had just va-cated, and opened fire. We were also again enfiladed from the left, but two companies of supports, swinging round their right and manning the left of the *kopje*, completely commanded the rocky spur to which the Boers were still clinging, and quickly drove them out.

The only thing now to be done by infantry was to dislodge the few Boers who remained to cover the main retreat. This was done by men of various corps, but luckily for the enemy they were partially screened in this retreat by the smaller *kopjes*, and, as they had already jumped on their horses and obtained a good start, they got away al-most unscathed until they were at long range, when a few probably useless volleys were sent after them. They had purposely galloped through the *dam* (pond)—the only water supply—to stir up the mud and spoil it for drinking.

Officers and men were terribly disappointed at not closing with them, and still more so when their wagons and baggage could be seen trekking northwards across the open *veldt* as fast as they could go, and we were powerless to stop them. The batteries galloped round and fired a few shrapnel, but did little damage, and the cavalry horses were in such poor condition that they had to give up the pursuit.

Meanwhile the remnant of the Naval Brigade assembled under Captain Marchant, R.M.L.I., the senior unwounded officer present, and the work of collecting the wounded and burying the dead commenced.

Many were the anxious inquiries for those who no longer answered to their names. They lay in little brown patches, dotted over the *veldt* at the foot of the dearly-won *kopje*, some dead, others with life fast ebbing, most of them helpless with wounds. Looking down from the top of the *kopje* we could see the surgeons and their orderlies already moving amongst them, stopping at each prostrate khaki figure to give first aid, or turning it over to make certain that life was extinct and passing on to the next. Many that day owed their lives to Fleet Surgeon Porter and his stoker stretcher-bearers, who had followed close in rear of the firing line, and had done their work under the hottest fire.

Already the collecting-place for the wounded had been formed, and backwards and forwards toiled the stretcher men, in the terrible heat, with their human burdens.

Now, down from the *kopje*, came the survivors to look after their messmates and lend a hand in getting them to the ambulance. 'For God's sake, a drop of water!' was each man's cry; one, mortally wounded and with one arm smashed, unable to pull out the stopper, had bitten off the metal neck of his water-bottle in the agony of thirst and pain.

As they found a messmate they would ask, 'What's up, Towney?'

'They've got me' would be the reply, and the injured part proudly pointed out.

The number of marvellous escapes had been very great. There was scarcely an officer or man who had not had his clothes or accoutrements shot through; one officer, over six feet high and very broad, had four bullets through his uniform without being even scratched.

The marines of the brigade added that day yet another leaf to the laurel wreath, the badge of their corps. They had lost two officers and nine men killed, and one officer and seventy-two men wounded (including eleven non-com.'s) out of a strength of five officers and 190 men: or a percentage loss of 44.[1]

The bluejackets had not suffered so severely, losing two officers and two men killed, and one officer and five men wounded: a percentage of 18.1. This was to be accounted for by the fact that they were further from the very accurate cross-fire which swept the line.

The cause of this excessive loss was explained by Lord Methuen in his despatch: 'the Naval Brigade attacked in too close formation.'

Perhaps as the *kopje* was peak-shaped every man individually took the summit as his point of direction, and so closed in on the centre.

It must be remembered that neither the bluejackets nor marines, who took part in the assault on this position, were specially selected men, but were chosen haphazard from several ships on the Cape station, and were simply a fair sample of the men composing the crews of our ships all the world over. Those remaining would willingly have changed places with them and would have done every whit as well as they did.

While the greater part of the brigade were doing infantry work on the right, the remainder, consisting of fifty bluejackets under Lieutenant Dean, with Lieutenant Campbell and Midshipman Armstrong, were working the 12-pounders on the extreme left.

Extracts from the report of Lieutenant Dean give a concise and vivid account of his share in the day's work. The report was published in the *London Gazette*, March 30, 1900. Short notes, in some explanation, are inserted in brackets. In it he says:

Arrived at Graspan [the station] at 5.45 a.m., and observing the enemy, in an apparently strong position 5,000 yards in advance, I detrained two guns—not having enough men to handle more—and at 5.55 a.m. fired one round to test the range.
[*The mule teams of these guns had been lent to the Field Artillery, and consequently fifty men were only just sufficient to both haul and fight the two guns.*]
I then waited till the Royal Artillery with six guns took up a position on my right front and opened fire on the enemy. I did the same, and subsequently advanced to ranges of 4,000, and ultimately 2,800 yards, acting from time to time on requests I re-

---

1. The company of K.O.Y.L.I. forming the extreme left of the line suffered very severely and lost all their officers. It is said that, being found by their major, uncertain what to do, or where to go, he sang out, 'Come along, my Orphans,' and the name stuck to them. Private Doran, R.M.L.I., Major Plumbe's servant, died of his wounds on the way down to Simonstown.

ceived from the officer commanding Royal Artillery who was attacking the same position, *viz.* two strongly fortified *kopjes* on either side of the railway, with a well-protected gun in each. About 8 a.m. I received verbal orders to retire from my position, as the Royal Artillery were about to move away to the right, and it would be untenable for my two guns. The Royal Artillery were already moving off when I got the order, and the Boer guns, having got our range accurately, were pouring on us such an effective shrapnel fire, that I judged it impossible to carry out the order without either leaving the guns or suffering very heavy losses, both amongst our own men and the company of Royal Engineers who were helping us, if we attempted to retreat with them.

[*The field battery was still able, though it had already lost several horses, to 'limber up' and retire in a few moments, but the two naval guns could only be very slowly dragged to the rear by their own gun's crews aided by the engineers.*]

I therefore continued to fire as briskly as possible at the Boer guns, with such effect that we continuously put them out of action, first one and then the other for as much as fifteen or twenty minutes at a time. Their shells burst with the utmost accuracy, and both our guns and ammunition trolley were spattered all over with shrapnel balls; but owing to my system of making all hands lie down when we saw their guns flash, and remain till the shell burst and the balls flew by, we had only six men wounded, when, at 9.30 a.m. the Boers finally ceased firing and abandoned their position.

[*The Boers had left standing certain telegraph posts along the line and knew their exact ranges; this fact accounts for their accurate fire and for the quickness with which they found the different ranges as the guns advanced along the railway, alongside which they were obliged to remain on account of the ammunition trolley.*]

[*The fire was so accurate, that an officer with the company of Royal Engineers supporting them, stated that very frequently both guns and crews were hidden from view by the dust raised as the shrapnel balls struck the ground, and that he was surprised to see a single man unhurt each time it blew away.*]

To the above extracts it must be added that every man with the guns did his duty exceedingly well, and special praise, if any individual selection must be made, should be awarded to the two No. 1's, who laid their guns with the greatest coolness and accuracy, showing no more excitement than they would at an annual prize-firing or quarterly target practice on board ship, though so heavily handicapped by engaging an entrenched and cunningly concealed enemy whilst they themselves were entirely exposed on the open *veldt*."

Thus was fought the action of Graspan (or Enslin), in which the Naval Brigade took so considerable a share.

The approach of the relieving army towards Kimberley was now opened up as far as Modder River.

W. T. C. Jones.

CHAPTER 5

After Graspan

From the bravely won hill the remnant of the Naval Brigade marched to Enslin Station and bivouacked. Here Lord Methuen visited us, saw the men and congratulated them on their splendid gallantry, making very touching allusions to the killed and wounded.

Colonel Money of the 1st Northumberland Fusiliers, who commanded the whole firing line and led the attack, also came to congratulate and condole. The men killed were buried near the foot of the *kopje*, but the three officers were buried next morning at Enslin, a little east of the siding there, on a bare, red plain; a pity almost that they should not have remained with the men who had fallen with them and beneath the shadow of the hill they had laid down their lives to gain.

Our men put up a rough, wooden cross, and the Australian Light Horse fenced the grave in, a deed for which the navy will be forever grateful.

A very sad evening was spent by the remnant of the brigade, for our casualties had been great. Only three officers who took part in the attack had escaped injury. Some incidents which occurred to the writer at the top of the *kopje* after its capture are worth relating. One wounded man was heard to say that he would not mind being wounded so much if he had only been able to see his enemy and get a shot at him. Another good old soldier, his thigh fractured by a bullet, was seen sitting down, quietly licking each bullet before putting it into his rifle, just as old soldiers were accustomed to do in the Martini-Henry days, and shooting away steadily.

The Boers were still keeping up a heavy fire from the rear of their position, and the writer was ordering a man to take shelter and reply to this fire, when he heard a bullet strike very close. The man seemed not to realise the order and appeared dazed. In a few seconds he came up and said, 'Beg pardon, sir, I didn't understand and I feel all over numb.'

He was asked if he had been hit but did not think so, though, on examining him, it was found he had been shot clean through the body—evidently hit whilst the order was being given.

Shortly afterwards, whilst the writer was collecting men to drive these Boers out of it—a very ticklish piece of work— somebody sang out 'All right, sir, we're coming along,' and, turning round, he saw with relief the 'bad hat' of the company, following him closely and 'seeing red' as they say in books. His bad record was wiped out that day and no one prouder of the fact than he, or more ready to 'go a bust' again directly this little job was over.

The rear-admiral telegraphed promoting Captain Marchant to major, pending the decision of the Admiralty, and appointing him to command the Naval Brigade until the arrival of a senior officer. This was a great honour, for seldom has an officer of the Royal Marines had the good fortune to command a Naval Brigade in action. He was the senior unwounded officer after the fight.

A telegram from Her Majesty the Queen, through the rear-admiral, was also much appreciated by the Naval Brigade, and was read to them at a special parade:

> The queen desires that you will convey to the Naval Brigade, who were present at the action at Graspan, Her Majesty's congratulations on their gallant conduct. At the same time express the queen's regret at the losses sustained by the brigade.'

Meanwhile the wounded had been despatched to Simonstown in the ambulance train; and Kimberley was still waiting to be relieved.

The Boers, driven back from Belmont and Graspan, had fallen back to the Modder River, entrenching themselves on both banks astride of the railway, the bridge over the river having already been destroyed.

We only halted for one day at Enslin, and on November 27 the force moved forwards, the Naval Brigade going by train to Clockfontein, where they bivouacked close to the railway.

We entrained at 4.30 next morning and proceeded under escort of the armoured train to a dip a mile and a half further on, detraining men, guns, and ammunition, and taking up a position west of the line on a low crest, the only good position for naval guns, 4,800 yards from the banks of the Modder.

Just after sunrise the infantry were all in position, and at 5.40 a.m. the battle began. The enemy got our range at once, sending three shells over us and among the wagons. Luckily the shells did not burst and no damage was done, but we thought we were going to have a very warm time of it. Our guns promptly engaged these guns, well hidden in small emplacements, and temporarily silenced two of them.

The marine escort was all the time well extended and hidden as much as possible, lying down on the hot ground.

The field artillery boldly advanced over the crest, and came into action under a long range rifle and pom-pom fire, whilst the infantry, also sweeping down from this crest in extended order, bravely advanced to within 800 yards of the river, but could go no further, for the rifle and pom-pom fire from the banks and trenches was terrific. They simply lay down and hugged the ground as closely as possible. The Highlanders suffered terribly from the sun—it became a terribly hot day, and the backs of many of their knees were burnt so badly, that afterwards, many of them could hardly walk.

It was difficult to see any Boers, or to see the result of our shooting, so presently the four naval guns moved forward to try and find a better position; as they came over the crest they too came under a hot Mauser and pom-pom fire, and the position not being more favourable and the risk to guns and crews much greater, they retired again, keeping up a brisk fire.

Late in the afternoon a field battery arrived, having made a tremendous forced march, and though evidently pretty well played out, most gallantly went into action on our left, and materially supported our left flanking movement. A few companies managed to get across the river in this part of the field, and the effect on the enemy was immediately seen in the redaction of fire. Just about this time Lord Methuen was wounded, and the infantry who had crossed were recalled.

Night fell and no one knew quite whether we were victors or not. The fact that our men had been able to cross the river, however, decided the enemy to wait no longer, and in the morning we woke to find them gone and their guns with them.

The day had been terribly hot and every man in the force was pretty well exhausted by the end of the day—practically no water being obtainable all through those scorching hot fourteen hours of fighting. The infantry were certainly too much distressed to make a

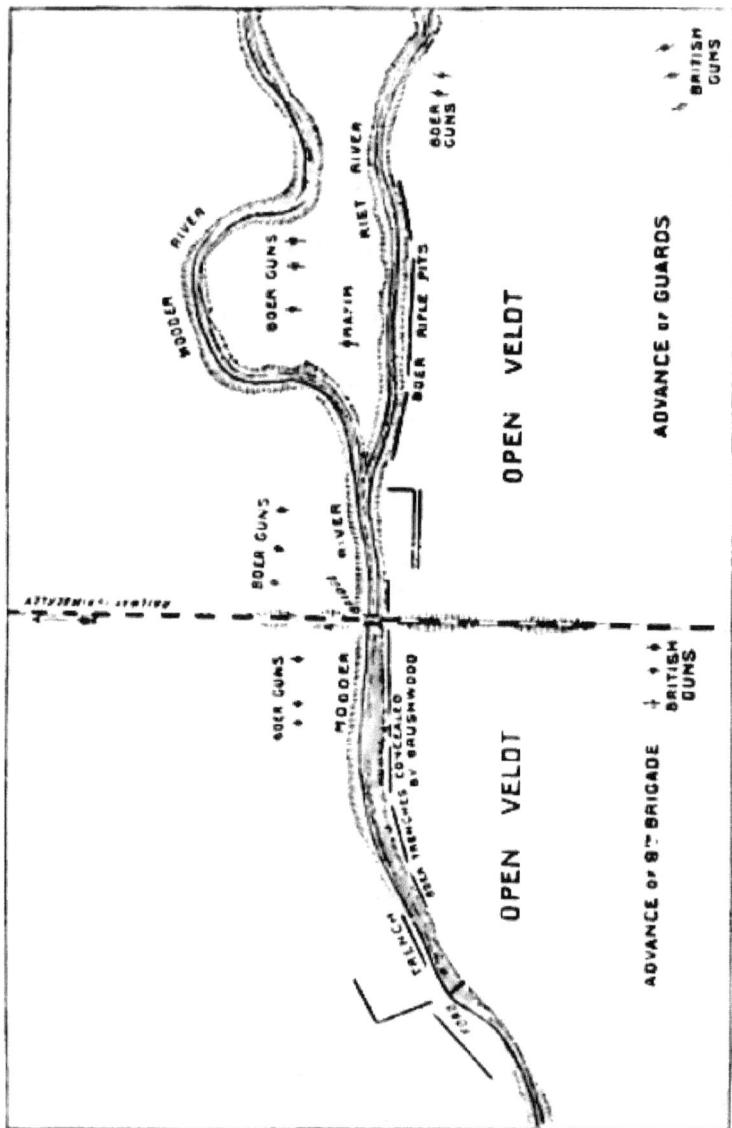

The Battle of Modder River

night attack with the bayonet, and the enemy slipped away comparatively unscathed.

At daybreak the army moved down to the river and occupied both banks, the Naval Brigade doing themselves rather well, by taking up a position close to the little hotel, the billiard room of which the officers used as their mess.

Our shrapnel fire must have been wonderfully effective, for hardly a tree but had its bark scored or branches torn off, and the few houses standing were simply riddled. Judging by the number of Boer horses killed the enemy must have suffered considerably, though only a few dead were found, and it was supposed, at the time, that more had been sunk in the river.

The position they had occupied was one of extraordinary natural strength, and in the hands of disciplined troops ought to have been almost impregnable.

Whilst here Com. de Horsey (H.M.S. *Monarch*) arrived to fill poor Com. Ethelston's place and took over the command of the brigade. He brought with him reinforcements to fill the vacancies caused at Graspan.

The general idea was to move on Jacobsdal, capture the town, and at the same time hold the railway and the river between, but on reconnoitring the position to which the enemy had retired, it was found to be too strong to leave in front of such a widely extended front, which we should not be strong enough to hold in much force, so the original plan was dropped, and the next thing to do was to turn him out.

Whilst we waited to bring up supplies, rest the troops and reconnoitre, the Boers were busily entrenching themselves on the Magersfontein Hills, and it became evident that much more heavy artillery was needed. Lord Methuen therefore telegraphed to the rear-admiral asking for a naval 4.7 gun—one was in readiness in the dockyard at Simonstown, mounted on a travelling carriage—and it arrived in due course and was taken north of the river. Daily it bombarded the Boer trenches with lyddite and common shell.

About this time Captain Bearcroft, R.N., H.M.S. *Philomel*, arrived to take command of the brigade, and Major Urmston, R.M.L.I., H.M.S. *Powerful*, took over the marines.

On December 9 a reconnaissance in force was made, the 4.7 advancing and vigorously shelling the trenches, though it was not successful in making the Boers unmask their guns.

Then came December 11, and the Battle of Magersfontein, when the projected assault at daybreak failed and the Highland Brigade lost so heavily. The 4.7 shelled the trenches at long range, but could not do the work of six guns, and failed to keep down the enemy's fire; and though maintaining their ground all night, the infantry had to fall back upon the river next day, their sufferings from thirst having again been very great.

The naval 12-pounders and a marine escort were left on the south of the river to protect the new deviation bridge and the accumulated stores.

The night after the fight was a time of the utmost anxiety for these four guns and their feeble escort, for but few other men were available, they were cut off from an exhausted army by the river, and had an enormous quantity of stores to protect, which it ought to have been the enemy's primary object to destroy. Luckily they wanted the pluck and dash to do so. If they had—and we all fully expected them to try—we should have had our work cut out to keep them off. Our relief when morning broke was intense. During the morning and before the army fell back, swarms of locusts were mistaken for the dust of an approaching commando, and caused much anxiety.

A. E. Marchant,

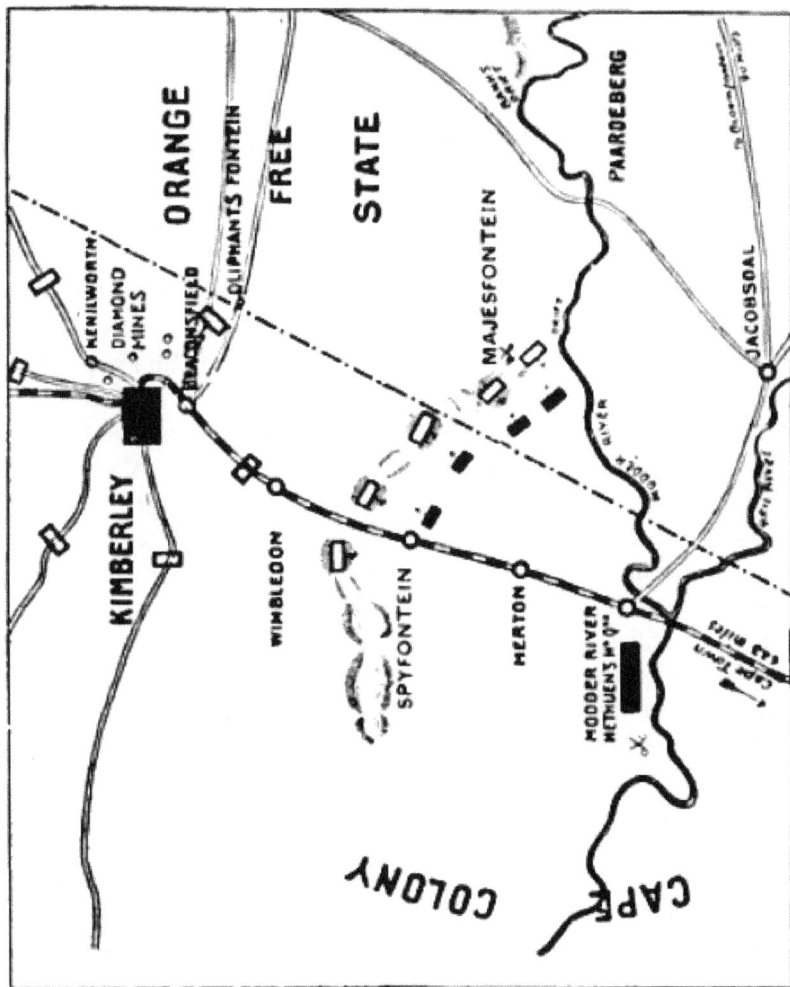

BATTLE

OF

MAGESFONTEIN

CHAPTER 6

Relief of Kimberley

The Kimberley Relief Force was checked, but this was probably a blessing in disguise, for had Lord Methuen been successful, he was hardly strong enough to hold the whole railway line, and might have had his communications cut, before sufficient supplies could have been hurried into the town. The army now settled down on the Modder and waited for reinforcements—a weary two months. All the naval guns were placed in position on December 14, north of the river, near a ganger's hut and close to the railway, and at dawn next day opened fire on the trenches for three hours. We could see the enemy very distinctly, and he quickly replied, landing a few shells near the infantry and field artillery who were demonstrating.

The daily bombardment and exchange of shells went on for a long time, and eventually the naval force was much split up, being sent to detached positions on the outpost line. Thus one 4.7, after the arrival of a second from Simonstown, was placed south of the river on the right rear, two 12-pounders on the extreme right on the north bank, all in emplacements and with small marine escorts.

One morning the ganger's hut, and the guns near it, came in for a heavy bombardment. Without previous warning three or four Boer guns opened a very heavy, well directed, and sustained fire on them for an hour. Thirty or more shells fell within a radius of a hundred yards round them and the hut, and extraordinary to relate, did no damage whatsoever, except to the two dogs which had attached themselves to the brigade, one of them being killed and the other injured. It reminded us of the mule at Matanzas in the Spanish-American war.

An amusing thing occurred that morning. When the bombardment commenced the officers were at breakfast in the hut, and one, slightly deaf and more hungry than the others would not take shelter—our guns were not replying—in the railway cutting close by. Presently he came to the door, filling his pipe with a self-satisfied expression of having made a thoroughly good breakfast, when a shell burst not ten yards from him. He then sauntered back to the 'cutting' merely remarking, 'I heard that,' and evidently congratulating himself on the fact that he was not so deaf as he thought.

Two officers tried to pass the uncomfortable hour in this cutting by trying to play picquet. It was a funny game to watch and listen to. One would perhaps be declaring his hand when the warning sound of a shell coming along would be heard. 'Tierce to a Queen, three; fourteen aces. I say old chap that one's coming pretty close.' *Crash* would come the shell, burst in the ground above us or go singing overhead. 'That's all right, now where had I got to,' and the hand would be counted again, but that game was sadly interfered with; no one could ever remember whose deal it was or what the previous score was, so eventually it was abandoned—a great pity, for it provided a good deal of amusement—for the others. A naval searchlight now arrived, worked by bluejackets, and each night kept up her constant beam-wagging to Kimberley, giving her the news of the outer world, whilst in return the Kimberley light spelt out on the clouds the names and condition of patients in hospital, wounded or ill. The midshipman in charge died of enteric and the one sent up to replace him died also.

Previous to the war the banks of this river had been favourite spots for picnics from Kimberley, on account of their beautiful shade. Now, after an army had been encamped there for a few weeks the whole camp was one arid waste. Not a living thing could move without raising a cloud of white sandy dust. Batteries, field and horse, trotting out for exercise; regiments marching in and out from the outpost line; staff officers and orderlies galloping in every direction, countless horses and mules, kicking and squealing on their way to and from water, innumerable A.S.C. wagons, all were hidden in the clouds of dust they raised.

In pure sport, whirlwinds—sand devils they were called—little and big, coiling and twisting, and ever growing larger and larger, whirled their way through the camp at all hours of the day, carrying up corkscrew columns of dust which could be traced a thousand feet or more into the sultry blue sky above. Three days out of five, to break the monotony of existence, regular sandstorms, walls of sand dust, rushed through the camp blowing down tents, stampeding animals and filling everything with sand. On the approach of one of these we would take

51

refuge in our tents, with door flaps closed and curtains fastened down, whilst the air inside filled with sand and the tent shook and swayed. It was a morning's work after one of these to clear the sand away.

Thirst here—for the first fortnight at any rate—was almost intolerable, for water was very scarce, and what we got had to be boiled first, and was a long time cooling. Indeed, the most valuable personal property was a man's canvas water cooler, and life would have been almost intolerable without one.

For two hours after sunrise and for two before sunset, the heat of the sun moderated, and a cool bracing breeze blew through the camp, bringing with it a keen sense of the enjoyment of living and a feeling of perfect health. It was during these hours of the day that the 4.7's dropped lyddite into the Magersfontein trenches, for then the grim shoulder of this hill stood out clearly from the plain, the trenches and watering parties could be plainly seen through the big naval telescopes, and there was no mirage to dazzle the captains of the guns.

On January 2 the general monotony was relieved by the news of Pilcher's capture of rebels at Sunnyside, and six days later a reconnaissance in the direction of Jacobsdal was made, the Orange Free State frontier being crossed for the first time. Meanwhile our strength had dwindled, enteric and other fevers 'of sorts' had accounted for many, and bluejackets were so scarce that one of the 4.7's was handed over to the Royal Marine Artillery—to their great pleasure and pride.

Early in February Grant's two 4.7's arrived and after a few days were sent down to Enslin.

On the 8th Lord Roberts himself arrived in camp and immediately things began to hum.

First went Grant's guns, then Dean's two 12-pounders, and by the 12th the Guards' Brigade and the 9th Brigade alone remained with Lord Methuen.

On the 12th the South African Field Force invaded the Free State, three days afterwards Jacobsdal, the Boer base for their Magersfontein position, was captured, on the 16th Kimberley was relieved and the day previously Cronje evacuated Magersfontein and trekked hurriedly eastwards.

As soon as the evacuation was known Lord Methuen advanced and occupied the position. It was a great disappointment to the Naval Brigade not to be allowed to go over these trenches, in front of which we had been sitting for so long, but orders were received to march to Jacobsdal to join in the general advance, so on the 17th the remaining

'Little Bobs,'
one of Grant's 4·7's

Was dragged 1,038 miles through the Orange River and Transvaal Colonies by spans of 32 oxen

two 12-pounders and the 4.7's started off, nearly all our personal gear having to be left behind.

On the 18th Jacobsdal was reached, and Grant's guns were found there, very proud of having made several brilliant marches and of having kept well up with the infantry.

Dean's guns were still ahead, chasing Cronje.

A. E. Marchant.

CHAPTER 1

Capture of Jacobsdal

Lord Roberts landed at Cape Town on January 10, 1900, and the dark cloud which had overshadowed South Africa since that disastrous week of Stormberg, Magersfontein and Colenso, seemed to sweep aside at his mere coming. A few days later, and the news that he had asked for two more 4.7's flew, like wild-fire, round every ward-room and lower deck of the little squadron anchored in Simon's Bay, and officers and men, fretting and fuming at their forced inactivity, eagerly sought to be included in the two guns' crews. Week after week they had landed, and loaded down with all the paraphernalia of modem warfare, toiled up Red Hill in the scorching heat, cursing and sweating, to practise the attack on the steep slopes of Simonsberg and get into training for the day when they should be wanted.

Now only six officers and fifty-nine men *were* wanted—and these were chosen from the *Doris,* and the trim little *Barrosa*, the fierce desire to avenge previous reverses, adding zest to the grim content of those selected, and keenness to the disappointment of those who saw yet another chance of landing slip by.

These two guns were quickly mounted on travelling carriages, built in the dockyard, and with their crews, stores and ammunition formed the last complete naval unit landed under Lord Roberts.

They were known as Grant's guns,[1] and the following account refers more particularly to them, but at Jacobsdal they joined the Naval Brigade which had fought under Lord Methuen and from that place to Bloemfontein their fortunes were merged in those of the whole brigade under Captain Bearcroft of the *Philomel.*

We landed at Port Elizabeth on January 31, entrained our guns,

---

1. Commander W. L. Grant of the *Doris* was in command.

stores and ammunition, left the same night for the north, and eventually ran into Modder River Camp just before dawn on March 3. As the train came to a standstill among the silent tents, day broke, and our naval guns, a mile away on the crest of a slope, opened their customary fire on the Boer watering parties at Magersfontein, the dull boom of the bursting shells coming back to us.

We stayed here for five days, encamped on the banks of the Riet River, and, at the end of this period, were taken fifteen miles down the line to Enslin, where we disembarked our guns, and again pitched our nine tents.

Whilst at Modder River, violent sandstorms swept through the camp every afternoon, and at first, when the red dust and sand came whirling through the tents, and the fierce gusts shook them, the bluejackets, 'standing by' for squalls, wanted to 'ease' or even 'let fly' weather sheets, and it was not till, on one or two occasions, the tents nearly collapsed, that they reluctantly, in future, hauled 'taut' the wind'ard tent ropes on the approach of a storm.

'We ain't —— sailors no longer, Bill; we're only —— soldiers,' was the explanation offered for this unseamanlike proceeding.

Whilst at Enslin we received our transport, consisting of thirteen wagons, two small carts for carrying water barrels, and 284 oxen. With these came a motley, laughter-loving crowd of forty-two native drivers, and to look after all four colonial conductors.

Fifteen wagons had been promised, and had actually been sent, but orders were received to return two. One had stuck badly in a *drift* miles away, another had broken down already. These two were 'returned' and everybody was satisfied and content.

On Monday afternoon, February 12, ammunition, three days' provision, and the little kit each man was allowed to take, being stowed on the wagons, we hauled down the white ensign hoisted on a telegraph pole between the guns, formed into 'line ahead,' and leaving the tents and most of the personal gear behind crossed the railway, and bivouacked for the night at the foot of Enslin *kopje*.

This was our first night without cover, and we were to invade the Free State next morning, so small wonder that the novelty of the experience, the roughness of the ground we lay on, and the excitement as to what the next few weeks had in store for us, hindered sleep.

Up and ready by 4 next morning, we waited whilst the Highland Brigade swung by. After them came the 82nd Battery, followed by a 6-inch howitzer battery with their short stumpy guns, rumbling past with a clatter of wheels and stamping of hoofs; we looking curiously at them, and they still more curiously at us, for this was our first meeting, and we were destined to march together a good many weary miles.

Now came the turn of the naval guns, and they quickly brought up the rear. First went 'Little Bobs,' the *Doris* gun, with horse shoes nailed on her carriage for luck, and the muzzle of her long chase pointing over the backs of the two 'wheeler' oxen. After her came 'Sloper' with a crew of *Barrosa's*, giving place to 'Little Bobs,' for she was a flagship gun, with a flagship crew, so must go first. Close behind were two ammunition wagons and a water-cart; then came the officers' conspicuous hooded ambulance and headquarter wagon, whilst the remaining ten ammunition wagons and the second water-cart formed the rest of this patriarchal procession.

An hour later, we entered the Orange Free State, and our spirits rose exceedingly, especially when, that long stretch of twisted and broken down wire fencing which marked the boundary having been crossed, word was passed that now we were getting eighteen-pence a day extra, for being in an enemy's country.

During this march there were several delays owing to the snapping of the gun trek-chains. Oxen are accustomed to work in a span of sixteen—eight pairs, and the chains are made sufficiently strong for this strain. The guns, however, had two spans to each, and the result was that the oxen, unused to this arrangement, started badly by jerking instead of steadily hauling. This jerking tried the chains very severely, and 'Sloper,' whose carriage was heavier than 'Little Bobs,' had frequently to be left astern with a broken chain. Each time it was mended with strong wire carried for the purpose, but meanwhile the wheels, broad though they were, would sink into the soft, loose soil, and try oxen and chains to the utmost to restart them.

It would only be by dint of much lashing and yelling of native drivers that the oxen could be persuaded to pull 'all together,' the guns' crews would haul on the drag ropes, and if the trek chain held, along would trundle the big wheels. They always seemed to say on these occasions as they started out of a hole, and rolled briskly on, 'There you see, just give a steady pull—all together—and we'll come out of anything.'

At 9.30 a.m. we debouched into the sandy plain surrounding Ram Dam and halted, whilst Kelly-Kenny's 6th Division marched eastwards under a seemingly endless dust cloud, twenty-four hours ahead of us,

57

twenty-four hours behind General Tucker and his division. With the 6th Division had gone a section of the Naval Brigade from Modder River, consisting of two 12-pounders; these did most excellent work during the pursuit of Cronje. As yet unused to the extreme heat we felt it very severely that day, crouching under the wagons to obtain shade, and when the sun sank, bathing in the cool liquid mud of the dam.

That night three horses arrived, one for the commander, another for the doctor, and the third for the commander's A.D.C. This last, a big, white, bony animal, with a prominent tumour on his belly, was an old 9th Lancer horse, with a highly extraordinary and eccentric action, and very difficult to control. The midshipman himself, fat and not too active, had no idea of riding, yet plucky youngster that he was, with hands up and knees away from saddle, always carried orders across a most treacherous undermined *veldt* or along a rock-strewn road, at a hand gallop. The plump, rosy-faced boy, bumping along on this queer looking beast, became well known to most people in the army during the next few weeks. Poor boy, he was too young and wanted the physique to stand the work and climate, and died of enteric at Bloemfontein.

During the day another brigade had arrived, and at daybreak next morning the now completed 9th Division pushed on again.

Waterval Drift on the Riet River was reached by noon, after a march of fifteen miles in six hours and a half, and very weary was every one, for the heat of those last three hours was excessive. Every ambulance was crowded with men overcome by it, and many of the bluejackets only just managed to crawl into camp, and the oxen, too, were much exhausted by the terrible heat, plodding wearily along with protruding tongues, heaving flanks, and deep, pitiful sobs.

All that afternoon a huge convoy had been slowly wending its way into the plain bordering the *drift*. This was the main supply column for the whole army, and every wagon was captured twenty-four hours later by a few Boers who managed to stampede the oxen.

Till 5 p.m. we halted, and then refreshed by a bathe in the river, were ordered to cross the *drift*, and as the banks were high and steep and the road down to the river-bed very bad, half a battalion of The Royal Canadian Regiment was told off to take the guns over.

Arrived at the top of the bank, the oxen were unshackled and taken across the river. Drags, ropes, and check-ropes were then hooked to the axles of the great iron wheels, and a company being told off to each, and hauling and checking alternately, the guns were, one by one, safely lowered down into the riverbed.

It was most amusing to hear naval words of command being 'sung out' to soldiers. At one moment, when great care was necessary, the gunner sang out, 'Handsomely, men, handsomely!' whereupon, instead of checking, they hauled all the heavier. 'Handsomely, I tell you!' shouted the gunner, getting red in the face, and harder than ever they hauled.

'Avast! Heaving,' he shrieked, and then, suddenly understanding, sang out, 'Stop, you idiots, stop!' at which they did, with broad grins on their perspiring faces.

Among all this shouting was the quiet 'Starboard, men, starboard,' or 'Port a bit,' 'Steady,' from the petty officer of the gun to the men on the limber-pole.

Once safely in the river-bed, all manned the drag-ropes and ran the guns, one after the other, up the opposite bank as if they were things of no weight; and were not they pleased with themselves, these Canadians, and long will they remember bringing 'Little Bobs' and 'Sloper' through a difficulty.

Our wagons took two hours to get across, and it was half-past nine before the last had reached the new bivouac.

Orders came to start at 1 a.m., so after a hurried supper we rolled ourselves in our blankets and took what sleep was possible.

Off again at one, we were soon marching silently along, under a brilliant full moon, the soft yielding ground smothering the noise of hoofs and rumbling of wheels.

The night air was cold and bracing, the moonlight glorious, only fading when the sun rose, and there was very little dust, so that the thirteen miles marched that night were performed under the best possible conditions, and everyone was most thankful to be spared the heat of the sun.

We were marching for Wegdrai Drift on the Modder River, and bivouacked there at half-past six in the morning—a red bare plain of great extent.

Twenty-seven miles had been accomplished in eleven marching hours during the preceding twenty-five hours; not a bad result when it is remembered that the first fifteen to Waterval Drift were across open *veldt*, the only track being that which the guns made for themselves. Add to the twenty-seven miles three hours' hard work, getting across Waterval Drift, and it will be allowed that we had done a good day's work.

We bathed in the Modder later on that morning, among a number of Highlanders carefully washing themselves and their clothes—most entertaining they were. 'An' what wa'd the bairns think of me noo?' said a huge, bearded reserve man, as he knelt on a rock, naked but for his helmet, whilst he washed his flannel shirt and smoked a pipe. His face and neck were burnt black, his jet black beard stood straight out, six inches long, all round his face; he had a red belt round his waist, where sand had got under his kilt and irritated the skin, and his thighs and knees were the colour of his face. What would his bairns have thought of him?

Five miles from this place was Jacobsdal, a little white-faced village, nestling in a cluster of dark green trees, and daring the afternoon a brigade and a battery went on to capture it, the mounted sections of the C.I.V.'s going with them and gaining their first experience of an enemy's fire. We watched the interesting little operation from a safe distance and gained our first sight of the enemy. They were quickly driven out of the town, took refuge behind some farm buildings till the artillery fire made it too hot for them, and then bolted for their lives, lying down on their horses' necks and disappearing over a ridge with our shrapnel bursting over them.

Sheep were plentiful and dinner in the officers' mess that night was a splendid meal. Our table a stretcher, our light two candles, and to eat, lambs' chops, liver and kidneys, and new potatoes. The presence of the potatoes was easily explained: our faithful stokers had been for a walk.

Friday, February 16.—At half-past eight we inspanned and marched into Jacobsdal, escorted by the same half-battalion of Canadians. These men, who had cheerfully waded through the river, and hauled our guns across two days ago, now helped us on our way with songs. Four hundred lusty voices roared out the chorus of 'They all love Jack,' then a pause as they washed the dust out of their throats and gathered breath for 'We'll rant and we'll roar like true British sailors,' and many more, till they were too husky and dry, and their water-bottles would stand no more squeezing.

Frenchmen there too, a whole company of them. Proud of being Frenchmen, proud of being Britishers, and prouder still of escorting and marching alongside British naval guns. And weren't our men pleased, grinning with pleasure, and only regretting that there were no convenient 'pubs 'where they could stand them a 'wet.'

There was practically no food in Jacobsdal, but some of us found a box of bicarbonate of soda, and another of tartaric acid, and bought the lot. These made splendid 'fizzy' drinks; 'an improvement even on seidlitz powders,' said connoisseurs, as they begged for a second.

CHAPTER 2

Unexpected Orders to March

Extracts from Diary. Saturday, February 17.—Still remaining at Jacobsdal, which is full of typhoid cases from the Magersfontein trenches. Late in the afternoon two 12-pounders from Modder Camp join company, reporting that the remainder of the Naval Brigade with two 4.7's is on its way, but the roads are very heavy, and the guns are coming along with difficulty, and may get stuck.

Everybody is asking whether Cronje can be 'headed.' Kitchener is after him along the north of the river, and we hear is in touch with his rear-guard. Tucker is keeping abreast him on the south bank, and, best news of all, French has relieved Kimberley and is coming down the Kimberley-Bloemfontein road, as fast as his worn-out horses can bring him, to try and prevent Cronje breaking away to the north'ard.

Food is very short, although there is only one brigade left round Jacobsdal—half rations of biscuit and three-quarters tea and coffee. Only three cases of jam are left at the supply *depôt*, though more expected tomorrow, if only the doubly worked oxen can crawl in from Modder Gamp. Meanwhile the North Staffords, not having had jam for days, 'bag' two cases. Our commissariat midshipman, a born diplomatist, happening to be on the spot, smoothes down the ruffled A.S.C. sergeant distributing food. A.S.C. sergeant, who hates being bullied, and everyone else tries bullying, says he may as well have the third case as anyone else. Midshipman and a couple of bluejackets manage to get it away between them—trust them for that.

Sergeant fancies there may be a 'tot' of rum left, just enough for our rations, so midshipman promptly annexes that too.

Sunday, February 18.—At dawn the headquarters of the Naval Brigade marched in with the remaining two 4.7's which had been hammering the Magersfontein trenches for so many weary weeks. Their carriages are not so good as ours, their wheels less broad, and they have no limbers, the ends of the trails being shackled to the rear of ox-wagons, and thus hauled along breech first.

At divisions the field-marshal's order against looting was read for the first time, and the men thought it a huge joke till the punishment to be awarded to transgressors—'the first man caught ... will be hanged'—sobered them, as well it might.

Quite unexpectedly, and whilst we were arranging for a good night 'in' orders came to march, and punctually at 9.30 p.m. the united Naval Brigade with its four 4.7's, its two 12-pounders, and its escort of marines, 'shoved off.'

Grant's guns led the brigade, following in the wake of our old friends the 82nd, and 5-inch howitzer batteries, whilst behind followed a huge convoy and the main ammunition supply column of the army.

The moon had not yet risen, and in the pitchy darkness we failed to strike the proper road, and were for a short time mixed up in apparently hopeless confusion, till away on our left a torch flared up; the column jolted across towards it, sorting itself as it went, found the right road, and marched steadily on, the moon rising later and giving a splendid light.

Just before midnight the column swerved to one side and met a long convoy of wagons captured by French, and now on their way back to Modder Camp to take the place of the wagons captured from us at Waterval. Over the first few flew the red-cross, weird in the dusty moonlight, and the huddled-up figures they bore were the men wounded during the running fight with Cronje's rearguard.

Midnight passed, and the dust grew almost unbearable, filling our eyes and nostrils, and parching our mouths and throats. As hour after hour went by, and still we went on and on, a great weariness seemed to come over the column, and, for the last three hours before daylight, men and beasts seemed to move automatically; men slept as they rode in saddle, on limber or wagon—many, in fact, as they even marched along.

In front of the naval guns, under the white dust cloud, were the two batteries, the rumble of their wheels, the jangle of harness and accoutrements, and the dull thud of hundreds of horse hoofs, half muffled in the soft sand, interminable and continuous. We could see the indistinct figures of men, with their great-coats turned up over their ears, and many with woollen nightcaps on their heads, nodding and swaying from side to side as they clutched reins or limber rails in their sleep. Our own long-chased guns, white with dust, rolled along two abreast behind the labouring oxen, their big wheels churning the dust like water-wheels. In front of each a bluejacket guide plodded wearily along, wading through the soft sand. These two might have been asleep, so apparently aimlessly did they stagger; yet ever and again they would, with a wave of a hand to right or left, guide the guns from danger, the little Bushmen leaders of the ox-teams following their every motion.

Behind the guns were the limber numbers, four on one limber pole—'Little Bobs'—for she was easy to steer, six on 'Sloper's,' much less handy, holding grimly to the cross-bars, and obliged to be awake, for at every yard an unevenness in the ground would jerk them from side to side as they clutched that steering-pole and steadied it amidships, and unless their attention was of the keenest, an unavoided obstacle might bring the gun to a standstill and break the trek-chain, or one wheel or both might sink into an unnoticed hole, and the whole column behind be stopped half an hour or more whilst it was being dug out.

Halts were called at intervals to close up the convoy, and, short though these were, every one slept, and, the dust-cloud blowing away, the huge convoy showed out clearly in the brilliant moonlight, with its motionless teams of horses, mules, and oxen, and the dark figures of the men sleeping on the ground on each side of it.

Silence, almost ghostly in its intensity, would be only broken by the screaming of some poor mule in the agonies of sand colic, or the jangling of a trek-chain as one of our oxen sank to the ground.

Five minutes of sleep—sometimes longer—would go by, and then along came the order to advance. Men climbed listlessly into saddle, the rumbling of the artillery wheels recommenced, along rolled our guns, and in a minute the column would be again shrouded in its pall of white dust, obscuring the moon, blotting out those in front and behind us, and making it, at times, extremely painful to keep our eyes open.

The column seemed to wake up as the sun rose, and pushed on with renewed vigour, halting eventually at Slip Vaal Drift, a sandy patch in an angle formed by the Modder, at 6 a.m., having marched for nearly nine hours. We were very tired.

Whilst at breakfast and sitting round our stretcher, Lord Roberts

'SLOPER'—ONE OF GRANT'S 4.7 GUNS,—'LIMBERED UP'

and his staff cantered up. He wanted the Naval Brigade to push on another ten miles, for, said he, 'I have Cronje surrounded, and want to give you a show.'

But though the men were extremely eager to push on, the oxen were unable to do so till they had fed—they were already grazing in the scrub—so we had to stay sadly behind whilst the infantry and artillery went ahead. At two o'clock, however, we were off, and behind us trailed the main ammunition supply column, with an escort of 250 details and the marines. These latter acted as right flanking guard, and though extended to a hundred paces, their number was inadequate to cover more than a small portion of the three miles of wagons.

Small parties of Boers were reported hovering on this flank, and as the convoy was so precious it only halted once during the first three terribly hot hours, and then only for ten minutes.

As we marched along the sound of guns in action kept the men 'going,' but as the afternoon wore on, and at last there seemed no prospect of getting up in time that day, the long march the night before began to have its effect on them. Thick though their straw hats are, the sun seemed to scorch their very brains. The sand and dust, the worst and the hottest yet experienced, were terrible. Underfoot their feet sank just enough to be conscious of the extra weight as they dragged them out, hot and burning. Above, it filled their eyes, nostrils, ears, and mouth.

Their voices so hoarse as to be unintelligible, their eyes bloodshot, and their lips swollen and bleeding, they could get no cool water to drink, only the little they had left in their bottles, and that as hot as the sand itself.

The limber numbers had the worst time of it, for the gun wheels threw the dust straight into their eyes, and the sun blistered their hands, yet they had to hold on to those cross-bars. Every movement of the gun jerked them from side to side; an awkward torn or a bigger stone than usual would make the gun swerve, over would swing the pole, and very frequently one or more, sometimes all, would be knocked off their feet; but they seldom let go, and were dragged along till they scrambled to their feet again, for, come what might, that gun had to keep her course, and that limber-pole had to be under control.

They were not marching, mind you, at three or three and a half miles an hour, but at two and often less, taking short steps to keep pace with the oxen, so tired were these poor beasts, and so slowly did they haul in the scorching daytime. The bivouac was not reached till eight o'clock, and, extremely weary, we soon were asleep.

We had covered twenty-seven miles in the last twenty-two hours—a very fine performance for guns of position—having actually been under way for fifteen hours of this period.

February 20.—We woke refreshed at sunrise, marched on at 9.30, and five miles further on swerved round the foot of a *kopje* and came into view of our own main camp and saw the long lines of wagons which marked the position of Cronje's *laager*.

Away went the captain and commander to report themselves at headquarters, and after them went the fat midshipman, bumping along on his white horse, to return in half an hour with orders for Grant's guns, another 4.7 and one 12-pounder, to cross the river immediately, take up a position and open fire on the *laager* as soon as possible.

'The Boers have three Krupps and a pom-pom,' said he, with sparkling eyes, 'and we have to get within 3000 yards of them—well within their range,' and as this news travelled along the brigade it was very pleasant to see the men's faces light up with eager expectation.

The four guns quickly began jolting down the rocky road leading to the *drift*, and to reach it had to pass through the main camp, the soldiers pouring out of their bivouacs to see the naval guns go by and pass the time o' day with Jack; for Jack was the man who could knock an enemy's gun 'out of time' 8,000 yards away, where they themselves could not see it, though it could reach them all right with its shells; and here was the long khaki gun Jack could do it with; yes, and had done it, up Ladysmith way, would do the same for them, and now just off to practise up a bit on Cronje. So why shouldn't they show Jack they were glad to see him?

And they did. '"Little Bobs," is it?' they sang out, seeing the name on the leading gun. 'He'll give 'em snuff,' and 'Eh! Jack, got some o' that lyddite stuff?' was their general query, and 'Give 'em lyddite. Jack,' their usual advice, passing the word and waking their sleeping messmates with 'Here comes the Naval Brigade.'

A royal progress indeed it was. Into the river, out of it, and up the opposite bank the guns were hauled, under the eyes of an admiring group of foreign attaches. The water was up to the men's armpits, but they took no notice of it, and when 'Sloper,' swerving violently, threw her limber numbers off their feet and several disappeared under the surface, they kept their hold, quickly regained their footing, and steered her triumphantly across.

A mile further on, and when close to the ridge on which we were to take up position, our excitement was increased by hearing, for the first time, the horrid noise of a strident pom-pom, and seeing its spiteful shells bursting in the plain on our left—300 yards away.

CHAPTER 3

We Fire Our First Shot

At half-past four on Tuesday, February 20, 'Little Bobs' fired her first shell. It burst among the wagons in the centre of the *laager*, and we waited for the Boer guns to reply.

Now it is a strange fact that though our guns were well within their range and made a comparatively big target, they never once fired at them during the following seven days of desultory bombardment. They fired at intervals, during the first four days, at bodies of infantry, convoys and batteries, but were never polite enough to pay us any attention.

The 4.7's fired thirty-seven rounds of lyddite and common shell that afternoon at a range from 2,300-2,800 yards, but all the enthusiasm of the men had vanished. They had come on shore for a picnic, not to do 'damned prize firing' at wagons with nothing to reply to them. Honestly they were terribly disappointed. The only people in a good temper were the conductors, for in the plains below there was very rich pasture, and our starving oxen would now be able to regain 'condition.'

There was nothing to do but make our bivouac as comfortable as possible, so the wagons were drawn up in line, in rear of the guns, and tarpaulins stretched from one to another. In this way most excellent shelter was obtained, and, in addition, a big sail, used as a screen and shifted to wind'ard as the breeze veered, made the officers' mess quite cosy during the cold wet nights which followed.

To keep time in camp the brass cylinder of a 4.7 cordite charge was hung up on a tripod in front of the wagons, and the hours struck on it as on board ship—a most excellent 'bell' it made, too—much to the amusement of any soldiers who happened to be passing.

Meanwhile headquarters camp, with the remaining 4.7 and three

12-pounders, had taken up a very exposed position on the south of the river and only 1,300 yards from the nearest Boer trench. They fired at intervals and quickly received attention from the Boer riflemen, who for the next seven days kept up a most irritating 'sniping,' and unfortunately killed one bluejacket and wounded another.

Next day we amused ourselves by trying to persuade the Boer gunners to cease firing at a large convoy, slowly trailing into camp, and a field battery on the march, both at much longer ranges than we were. They were using black powder, so the guns' positions were very conspicuous at the moment of firing. Each time the plucky gunners fired, we plumped a big shell apparently right into the middle of their white smoke cloud, or burst a shrapnel over it, yet, hardly had the smoke cleared away before they would fire again. It required several of these 'hints before they ceased to annoy our people with their shells.

[*These three guns were afterwards found in position just below the crest of the river bank and most admirably protected by the contour of the ground.*]

With nothing more exciting to do than this, our bluejackets relieved the monotony by paying casual attention to working parties, swarming like ants over a line of newly turned up ground, which marked a series of rifle pits, being extended into the open plain.

Once we fired a broadside—the little 12-pounder 'chipping in'—at a very energetic party, but they disappeared in their burrows directly they heard the shells coming, and long before they burst; after they burst, up would come their heads again, for all the world like rabbits in a warren. It was almost impossible to get at them unless a shell actually fell into one of their rifle pits, the chances of which happening were exceedingly remote.

Thursday, February 22.—At 8.30 a.m. a general bombardment took place and lasted during the whole day. All the naval guns (our three 4.7's being advanced to 2,200 yards), the 5-inch howitzers and several field batteries took part in it.

The lurid description of this day's work which we afterwards read when the English papers arrived, and which sent a feeling akin to repulsion throughout the whole civilised world, was rather more picturesque than accurate. Our guns were ordered to destroy one line of wagons, the 5-inch howitzers the other; two field batteries sprinkled the *laager* itself, and another battery turned its attention to the trenches on the banks of the river. There was no hurry, very little noise, and seldom did two big shells burst simultaneously.

As to the carnage among the huddled-up Boers, one bluejacket was shot through the head, and it is quite possible that this was the only casualty on either side. We, with our big ships' telescopes, could almost recognise the features of any man moving about among the wagons, and never saw a single human being till after the bombardment, for they and their women were snugly ensconced below the river banks, in pits amply sheltered from shrapnel and naval shells. The howitzers might have dropped shells among them if this had been desired, but no attempt whatsoever was made to kill men.

This, by itself, was not very interesting work, but the bluejackets added to their zest by making a match with the howitzers, whose target was a long line of wagons close to the trenches on the plain; ours another line of white-tilted wagons near the river.

They scored first—their shooting was marvellously accurate—setting fire to their line well to wind'ard, with lyddite. Our men, though handicapped by using common shell, did not care to have 'their eyes wiped' by mere 'shore-going gunners,' and were very delighted, a quarter of an hour later, to see flames burst out from the centre of a big group of wagons which they had been steadily plugging; and our flames and smoke soon made a braver show than the howitzers' fire. All the afternoon those two fires were kept going, the rivalry between the sailors and soldiers being very keen. If our fire seemed to be dying down, another 'common' would stir the flames to life again, and whilst they burnt fiercely an occasional shrapnel from the 12-pounder proved an effectual warning to prevent any efforts to extinguish them.

However, there is no doubt that on this day the howitzers won the 'rubber,' for they presently started another fire, lower down the line, and had two going at once, till the evening thunderstorm swept up the sky and put them all out. Then we 'piped down' and went to supper.

If any one person was to be pitied that day, it was the occupier of the sea-sick balloon which swayed and reeled incessantly all day long and 'flag-wagged' the results of the shooting.

All through the day the rest of the Naval Brigade were under a heavy 'sniping' fire, and, as previously mentioned, one man was shot through the head.

The water-question now assumed serious proportions. The river was our only source; and decomposing, swollen carcases of horses and oxen floated down interminably from the *laager*; we knew the Boers were defiling the river above us, and we also knew that enteric fever was raging amongst them. When drawn from the *drift*, water was the colour of, and almost as thick as, ship's cocoa, and of unpleasant odour. When boiled, with a pinch of alum to precipitate the mud, the comparatively clear water remaining gave to the tea or coffee it was afterwards used to make, only the taste of mud.

Food also was comparatively scarce, not fresh meat, it is true, but biscuits, sugar, jam, tea, and coffee, of which we received less and less every day. The fresh meat was trek-ox, and so unpalatable and hard was it, that we soon gave up cooking it in slices, and converted it into soup, after passing it through a mincing machine.

The Naval Brigade was, however, certainly better fed than the rest of the army, and this was due, not only to the smallness of our numbers, by which we often picked up tit-bits which would not be sufficient for a battalion or a battery, and so were not served out to them, but also to the fact that our men seemed to adapt themselves more readily to varying circumstances, to forage more for themselves, and to be better able to cook what they received than could the soldiers.

Every man in the navy has, of necessity, to be a sufficiently good cook, whilst a soldier does not have the same opportunity to learn, and therefore to gain experience in making a little go a long way.

Every day on the return of the wagon from the supply depot in the main camp, the first anxious inquiries were for the convoys expected from Kimberley, and our anxieties were much relieved when they gradually commenced to arrive. One of the first of these was the convoy we had met outside Jacobsdal, captured by French at Klip Kraal, and on its way with wounded to Modder Camp, now returning loaded with provisions from Kimberley. It arrived at Paardeberg on the 26th, and our wagon brought back that afternoon four days' rations in reserve, though these rations were calculated at half rations for biscuit and one-third for tea, coffee, and sugar, whilst the native drivers, who previously had received these 'groceries,' now only had a certain amount of flour issued to them. They accepted the inevitable with very little grumbling; in fact they behaved, all the time, most remarkably well, and their loyalty to us, their cheerfulness under fatigue, and their intense hatred of the Boers, were most marked. Whilst at Paardeberg they spent every day on the top of the *kopje* watching, in excited groups, the effect of our shells, and afterwards their evident enthusiasm at the prospect of our guns coming into action was most pleasing to see.

A large flock of sheep used to graze in the plain beneath, and the bluejackets kept a watchful lookout for stragglers. If one was seen to stray—though perhaps a couple of miles from camp—two or three would wander innocently in its direction, get between it and the flock and then commence to stroll back to camp. Naturally the sheep widened the gap between itself and the flock, till, self-evident fact, a time would come when it was so far removed that no one could suspect its ownership.

The guileless bluejackets (the stokers—good luck to them!—were the most successful criminals) seldom returned without it. Their invariable explanation was that 'it had followed them into camp,' but this was a very elastic term and included, perfectly correctly, those occasions on which the unwilling animal was towed in by a piece of rope; less accurately when it was pushed from behind by one and towed by the ears by another; and still less accurately, perhaps, when, as often happened, it was too dead beat from 'following' them so far, and was brought in on their shoulders.

Whilst at Paardeberg the days were generally cloudless and intensely hot, but, as the sun sank, thunder-clouds of inky blackness gathered all round the horizon, and, ushered by a cold breeze, spread rapidly over the sky. A few heavy drops of rain and then the storm would burst, circling again and again round the *kopjes* which surrounded the *laager*, thunder and lightning continuous, and rain coming down in sheets. Our tarpaulins and wagons were generally sufficient to defy the rain, but the cold wind could never be altogether excluded; still our condition was luxurious compared with that of most of the soldiers, who had nothing to protect them but '*tentes d'abri*,' made by lashing two or three water-proof sheets together and propping up the sides with sticks or rifles.

Our marines also had no wagons to shelter them, and each night had to be on trench duty in rear of the guns, for the Boshof Commando, a thousand strong, was hovering near and threatened to attack.

In the intervals of crashing thunder the sniping, down in the river bed, half a mile away on our right, could be plainly heard. The sharp spit of a solitary Mauser would be answered by a volley from our trenches, and the occasional boom of a Martini showed that some old-fashioned Boer, probably perched in a tree fork, was sniping our ever-advancing trenches.

If the night happened to be still, and even firing had died away, the eerie cries of the many wounded animals down in the river bed wailed out through the darkness, cries which made one shiver.

On two of these nights, to add to the gruesome effect, salvoes were fired at intervals from previously laid groups of guns, the flames of the bursting shells making a magnificent spectacle, though probably the Boers were too close to thoroughly appreciate the spectacular effect, and there is no doubt were much demoralised by them.

At daybreak the atmosphere was always exceptionally clear, and there was no mirage to disturb careful aim. On these occasions the Boers frequently sniped the men at the guns and telescopes, though the range—1,800 yards on our side of the river—was too long for accurate shooting, and they hit no one. Early Sunday morning they could be plainly heard singing hymns, but varied their religious observances in the afternoon with some very heavy sniping, one old gentleman, in particular, lying down behind a dead horse and showing great diligence in this matter.

On the day before the surrender, the first of our pom-poms (1-pounder Maxims) to arrive in camp came into action, and its moral effect was quickly demonstrated. A shell or shrapnel from the naval guns, howitzers or field guns, bursting close to a trench-digging party, never kept them under cover for more than five minutes, but when the pom-pom let 'rip' among them, they disappeared in their trenches for thirteen minutes—we timed them—and then they bolted behind the river banks.

To show our strength, three field batteries came across the river and lazily sprinkled the *laager* with shrapnel, whilst, later still, the four 6-inch howitzers—newly arrived in camp—fired two salvoes. The noise of the explosion was so great that we imagined a magazine had blown up, and went to the top of the *kopje* to see. The whole *laager* was filled with the oily green curling lyddite smoke, and when this blew away they let fly another salvo, the four shells falling in a line across the *laager* at regular intervals. The sun had just set, and in the gloom the flames of the tremendous explosions seen through the green smoke made it a most ghastly spectacle, and we felt, for the first time, exceedingly sorry for the foolhardy people below us.

On this night the final advance was made down in the river bed, and to the Canadians [1] fell the honour of finishing the eight days of dangerous sapping.

Intermittent firing used to go on every night, and always developed into a continuous crackle of musketry as day broke, owing to the

---

1. Sergeant (later Staff-Surgeon) G. M. Beadnell, R.N., accompanied them and was the first doctor to enter the *laager* and attend the Boer wounded.

dread the Boers had of being rushed from our trenches, at this time of day; but on this especial night a tremendous fusillade broke out at 3 a.m. down in the river, and the Gordons, extending in front of our guns, advanced towards the *laager* and fired volleys to distract the attention of the defenders.

Quickly the Boers replied, and every trench was outlined with little tongues and spirts of flame, and their bullets, badly directed at night, whistled over and among our guns and wagons in hundreds.

The firing died away as rapidly as it had commenced, burst out again at sunrise (when the Boers first discovered that the Canadians and sappers were almost on top of them), ceased, and white flags were shown as a token of unconditional surrender. The signalman brought the news down, and from the top of our *kopje* we saw a long column of unarmed Boers streaming towards the main camp. This was the anniversary of Majuba, and in honour of this curious coincidence and of our first big haul of prisoners Lord Roberts 'spliced the main-brace' throughout the whole army, issuing an extra 'tot' of rum.

Immediately after the surrender our four guns were ordered to recross the river. This was a longer task than we imagined it would be, for the river had risen and made our original *drift* impassable, and the *drift* in the *laager* itself, by which we had eventually to cross, was a very bad one with steep treacherous banks. Besides, the gunners had to secure the three captured Krupps and the pom-pom, and these blocked the way for a long time, and one of our ammunition wagons also capsized. We spent four or five hours in the *laager* at the top of the *drift*, and all the ammunition wagons did not cross till next morning. Those left in charge of them will not easily forget that night, for it was too cold to sleep and the stench was appalling.

To keep themselves warm, they buried a Boer whose body had been lying all day long above the *drift*—the first dead Boer they had seen—and this made them warm and good-tempered; but they could not get away from the horrible smell.

Dead horses, oxen and sheep, mangled in a ghastly manner, lay in hundreds on the ground, two and three deep in places; limbs and fragments hung from the branches of trees, where they had been caught when hurled into the air by the big shells.

There was scarcely an undamaged wagon remaining, so effective had been our fire, and many were simply represented by a blackened and twisted heap of ironwork. The ground was strewn with scattered clothes, saddles, harness, and cooking utensils, and the whole ghastly

75

evidence of destruction was so vivid that every one marvelled that the Boers had 'stuck it' so long. Rather more than four thousand had surrendered, the majority of them being Transvaalers. Cronje, his wife and staff, we heard, were to live on board the flagship *Doris*, and we were much amused to imagine how those on board would receive the news and their very unwelcome guests.

We claim to have put the pom-pom out of action, it having been disabled by a hole in its water jacket—too big to be made by a 15-pounder shrapnel bullet—and which must have been the result of one of our 4.7 shrapnels.

We joined Headquarter Naval Camp in the evening, and early next morning the rest of the wagons came across.

We had made good use of our time in the *laager* (trust sailors for that), and next day many things appeared in camp—saddles, two ponies, plenty of harness, spurs, bits and stirrups. A wooden table had been discovered by our stokers, brought along on top of a wagon, and made a splendid mess table for the officers. A couple of bentwood chairs also appeared, enamelled iron and even aluminium basins, a mincing machine, many rifles, carbines and *bandoliers*—even a tent. Some of the men's messes had well-fitted luncheon-baskets; most of them had rugs and pillows; our native boys went in half-naked or in odd bits of discarded uniform, they came out in European clothes, boots, cotton shirts, ties, collars and all.

Best of all, many sacks of flour were discovered, and, in fact, so many things useful or the reverse were obtained that for months afterwards something new was continually being discovered in the wagons, and at last, 'Oh, I picked that up in the *laager*' was the ordinary explanation to account for the otherwise unexplainable presence of many things. Three little chickens—little balls of yellow fluff—also had been found, and, being motherless, were taken care of by the bluejackets. They became great pets and went with us to Bloemfontein, being stowed in a kettle whilst on the march, hopping out directly we halted, and going chirping round the messes for food, returning to their kettle when tired, and waiting to be lifted back into it.

Our men had other pets: a wounded dog whom they carefully tended till he recovered and rejoined his proper master; another dog which had followed them from Modder camp and used frequently to catch hares and bring them back; a goat which lived on newspapers and tobacco; and a very wee, miserable lamb with sore eyes, which they used to bathe daily with warm water, and round whose neck they tied a *Doris* ribbon.

We bivouacked at Headquarter Camp, but even now the whole Naval Brigade was not united, for the two 12-pounders, previously mentioned as having marched with Kelly-Kenny, and which had sustained much damage to their carriages during the pursuit of Cronje, had been sent back for repairs under the orders of a very energetic lieutenant of the Victorian Navy.[2] Though ordered to return to Simonstown he, at his own initiative, went north to Kimberley, hurried through the necessary repairs and returned, having saved ten days at least, to rejoin the Naval Brigade before it left Paardeberg.

It was this same officer who, during the pursuit of Cronje, and when ordered to get his gun into position on the crest of a *kopje*, found that the sides were too steep and rocky to haul it up in the usual way, so, with the help of some infantry standing by, he dismounted the gun, lashed it to a pole and thus carried it to the top, where it eventually opened fire with effect on the retreating enemy.

---

2. Lieut.-Commander W. J. Colquhoun, eventually awarded the Distinguished Service Order.

CHAPTER 4

Battle of Poplar Grove

Thursday, March 1.—Two days after the surrender of the *laager* the whole army marched five miles to the eastward to get away from the appalling stench of decomposing animals and to be nearer a good water supply.

A halt was made for five days, during which time the Boer position, thrown across our road to Bloemfontein, was thoroughly reconnoitred, and all preparations were made for the general advance.

It was here that a congratulatory telegram from the Lords of the Admiralty was received and read at a special parade of the Naval Brigade. Another incident, much less pleasing, was the advent of an artillery staff officer, who took an inventory of our guns, ammunition, and transport, preparatory to the Royal Garrison Artillery, even now landing at Cape Town, taking them over. This event caused mach despondency. On several evenings severe thunderstorms raged, and on one occasion the thunder cracking and crashing over head, and the vivid lightning incessantly playing round the top of the *kopje*, above our bivouac, were very remarkable, if not awe-inspiring.

As our wagons were crammed with explosives, lyddite, cordite, and black powder, the approach of a storm always lent additional interest to the discussions as to what would happen if one was struck. The more 'scientific' assured the remainder that nothing *would* happen, but the 'remainder' nevertheless had an uncomfortable suspicion that the result would be a big hole in the ground, the sole remaining evidence of the Naval Brigade—despatched elsewhere.

On March 5, three 12-pounders were sent across the river to join the Highland Brigade on the north bank (the fourth had bulged and been sent back to Simonstown to be repaired), and the four 4.7's were ordered next day to take up a position on an isolated *kopje* 7,000 yards from the Boer centre. Grant's two were ordered to the summit, the other two to the right shoulder, none, however, to show themselves till daybreak next morning.

Several Boer guns had been located, and even now we could see, from the top of this *kopje*, the enemy's working parties swarming round several gun *epaulments* on a flat-topped hill in the centre of their position. We thought they were strengthening their defences, little dreamed that they were actually hastily hauling away their guns, and looked forward with great keenness to the morrow.

The first thing to do was to make a road up which to haul the guns, and our men quickly set to work with crowbars, picks, and shovels, undermining the bigger boulders and heaving them aside. They had been grievously disappointed with their Paardeberg 'show,' and now, with the hope of tomorrow's honourable duel, worked as few had seen bluejackets work before. By the time the sun went down they had made a road to the top, the big rocks rolled neatly to the sides and the big holes they left filled with small stones. In three hours a *kopje*, as typically rough and boulder-strewn as any, had a broad turnpike road running up it, conspicuous for miles.

'How about the blooming sappers now?' said a sweating bluejacket as he viewed his handiwork, whilst the sick-berth steward tied a bit of 'stuff' where four hundredweight of rock had 'jabbed a bit' out of his thumb.

The guns were hauled up just below the crest and our day's work was finished.

The guns' crews fell in at 4 a.m. and ran the guns into position as the sun rose, expecting to be very warmly greeted by the enemy directly they appeared on the sky-line; they were again disappointed.

Two hours later. Lord Roberts and his staff being close to the guns, one of the headquarters 4.7's fired a 'starting gun,' the signal for the cavalry to sweep round the Boer left flank, which rested on six little *kopjes* in front of us.

The shell burst halfway up One-Tree Hill below the *epaulment* and everyone waited anxiously for a reply. None came: their big guns had been taken away during the night.

'Little Bobs' and 'Sloper,' personally directed by the field marshal, then fired two shells at the ant-hills, and the second, going a little high, burst behind them. This was a lucky shot, for, helter-skelter, a couple of hundred Boers or more came racing along for dear life from among them, and disappeared over the ridge of some high ground in the rear.

79

The two guns followed them with a 'common' and a 'shrapnel,' bursting the last high up in the air to give it a chance, for the fuses do not act at such a long range.

'That will tickle up our mounted infantry,' smiled a staff officer standing by; and they no doubt 'heard it 'as they galloped in pursuit; but it did them no harm.

This was the last shot fired by the naval 4.7's, but the three 12-pounders on the other side of the river came in for a very warm half-hour. They were busily shelling the retreating Boer transport when a Krupp gun on the shoulder of One-Tree Hill opened fire, and, catching them in the open, drew their attention away from the wagons. Whilst they were engaged with this gun, another, on the top of a very high hill forming the extreme right of the enemy's line, began pitching segment shells into them; and in action, both on their right and left fronts, they were very busy. Though the Boer shells damaged a wagon, they neither killed nor wounded any one.

These two Krupps performed the only creditable action that day, for they kept up their plucky fire in face of tremendous odds, and, though eventually they had to abandon the guns, these artillerymen saved the whole of their transport.

The Presidents of both Republics were on the field, but, as is well remembered, even their influence and entreaties could not stay the flight of the commandoes.

The Battle of Poplar Grove was all over by noon—a magnificent spectacle, but almost bloodless till the evening, when some pursuing cavalry ran up against a pom-pom.

The Naval Brigade was promptly ordered to follow the army to Poplar Grove— twelve miles away, according to the map, but it took us eight hours to do it, under a broiling sun, progress being very tedious over the soft *veldt*, into which the gun wheels, broad though they were, continually sank, and the gun oxen, much distressed by the great heat, only managing a mile and a half to two miles an hour.

The heat was great, the pace irritating; and when it is remembered that we had been on our feet since 4 a.m. our fatigue will not be thought surprising.

The whole army marched in three columns till the second line of trenches the Boers had prepared was reached. Here the two columns, furthest from the river, had to converge into the track of the third, down rather a steep incline. Naturally at this point there was much confusion and a vast deal of cursing before we could all go on.

Grant's guns waited at the top, whilst we watched patiently for a gap in the road below in which to squeeze them; but in vain; so the order was given to run the first gun down—and run down it did, nearly lurching over its own oxen, and everything below scattering in front of it. A subaltern of artillery, very angry, rode up and motioned the gun back, shouting, 'Ho, there! You're blocking my ammunition column!'

'Blocking it?' said the *Barrosa's* lieutenant soothingly, 'I'm not going to block it. I'm only going to cut it.'

And cut it he did; and the poor young subaltern soon saw a quarter of a mile of Naval Brigade in the middle of his column.

He, however, learnt a lesson, and now knows that it is really useless to argue with five tons of 4.7 gun and carriage, bumping down a steep slope, and quite out of control. How the men stuck to the limber pole was marvellous. They were seldom on their legs, yet, directly the gun reached the road, they put the helm hard over and brought her round at right angles to her down-hill course. Failing this the gun would have trundled into a deep mud pool—and possibly stopped there.

Our tempers were terribly tried that day, for a little further on we came to a very soft patch in the road, in the middle of which a cursed foolhardy team of mules had obstinately stuck, and kept us waiting three-quarters of an hour, daylight gone, and our stomachs terribly empty.

At last the guns and wagons got over, fetched up somewhere, and we bivouacked in the dark, eased our bad tempers with sardines, biscuits, and the scrapings of a tin of jam, and soon fell asleep—for we were very weary.

We had been on our feet, in action with the guns or marching, nearly eighteen hours that day.

At Poplar Grove the army halted for two days, whilst forage came up for French's starving horses, and the dispositions for the march to Bloemfontein were being perfected.

There was good well-water to be obtained here, and we were much amused, whilst bathing in the exceedingly muddy Modder, to hear a conversation between two soldiers. One of these—a Highlander—having bathed, commenced to fill his bottle from the river, whereupon the other called out, 'Why, Jock, boy, there's any amount of good water, well-water, up there,' jerking his thumb in the direction of the water supply.

'Na, na, mon,' answered the Highland, 'this hae mair of a bite' and went off with his treasure.

Saturday, March 10.—At sunrise the great army commenced its march of seventy odd miles to Bloemfontein on sadly reduced rations, and at three in the afternoon the Naval Brigade followed in the wake of the central division (the 9th), having the 6-inch howitzers and the ammunition and baggage columns astern.

A most luxuriant grazing country was soon reached, and our half-starved horses revelled in it.

At nightfall we passed the first inhabited farm we had yet seen, and, as we watered our horses in the dam alongside, looked curiously and not without suspicion at the lighted windows of the farm, and the blinds every now and again half drawn aside for the inhabitants to peep out.

After marching for seven hours a halt was called; we had a hasty meal and slept till two in the morning, marching off an hour later, and finally reaching the camp fires of the division ahead of us at sunrise, stumbling along a very treacherous road in absolute darkness. This was Dreifontein dam, nineteen miles from Poplar Grove.

Sunday, March 11.—At 9 a.m., after a halt of four hours and with water carts replenished, the march was resumed. The Naval Brigade was in high spirits, for it was rumoured that two long Boer guns were waiting for us, and we were wanted, badly wanted, to be up in time to attend to them. There had been sharp fighting here before our arrival and, even as we marched off, ambulance wagons were still searching for wounded, and burial parties were still busy on the top of a ridge.

Doornboom was not reached till evening (5 p.m.); there were no Boer guns; the sun was excessively powerful, the road fearfully hot and dusty, and the only thing that prevented the Naval Brigade from being exceedingly bad-tempered was the fact that since leaving Poplar Grove, twenty-six hours before, we had marched thirty-four miles, and been actually under way for seventeen hours. Everyone imagined that this record for 'guns of position' was hard to beat.

At Doornboom, the northern and central divisions joined hands, and there must have been close upon eighteen thousand men gathered round the dam.

Monday, March 12.—At 5.45 a.m. all were off again in a great hurry, both Divisions and miles of convoys, and were overtaken half an hour later by Lord Roberts, clean and smart as a new pin, as he cantered past with his staff.

After five hours' trudging along, the Naval Brigade halted for two hours to let the oxen graze, and give them a rest in the hot hours of midday. They were very lazy afterwards, and very many times during the afternoon required the aid of the marines, hauling on the drag ropes, to pull the guns through soft places.

Whilst we halted, the army marched on, and battalion after battalion, battery after battery, and supply columns, miles long, went slowly past us.

The infantry were in a very ragged and weather-beaten condition. Their clothes in rags and their boots worn out, the soles tied on with string, and some even walking with their *putties* wrapped round their feet, they went limping by. Their faces were black with the sand and sun, bearded and parched; their lips were swollen, cracked and bleeding; their eyes were bloodshot; but their heads were held high, and they had that grim determined expression which success, and the knowledge of their power and strength, alone could bring, and carry them, with empty stomachs, through the terrible marches under the burning sun by day, and those as terrible bivouacs in the rain and cold by night.

Almost bringing up the rear of the army, our guns trundled over the *veldt* after them, and Venter's Vlei was reached at sunset after a most tedious day but otherwise uneventful except for the laziness and weakness of the oxen. The distance traversed was only thirteen miles.

Here all three divisions united, and the whole invading army with the exception of French's cavalry was assembled.

All along the line of march lay hundreds of dead and dying horses and mules. The latter would raise their heads with a piteous look at us as we passed, and too weak even to do this for many seconds their heads would fall back on the grass, and a shudder pass along their flanks, for they knew their fate as well as we did. One horse had damaged his back in a Boer trench. 'I've got orders to shoot him, sir, if he don't get up in an hour,' said the farrier.

'He's all right for a bit, when he gets on his legs.'

This was just the opportunity the bluejackets loved.

'Eh, Tommy, what's gone wrong with 'im?' they asked as they left the wagons and clustered round with an air of knowing all about horses.

'If he got on his feet we might get him on a bit,' they were told, so, off rifle and leather gear, and with ''Ere, mates, clap on; you and Bill, take 'old of 'is 'ed, and Nobby and me 'is tail, and 'eave all together.'

'Now lads, one, two, five! 'Eave!' and they put their backs into it, and nearly got him on his feet. Several times they tried with no better success, and by this time the wagons were a mile ahead, and they had to catch up with them; so, each man giving the poor animal a parting friendly pat on the head, they picked up their rifles and followed at the double. The pistol shot rang out before we had gone far.

On another occasion, whilst in camp, we officers noticed a blue-jacket discover an ox, sunk in the muddy river bank and dying of exhaustion, unable to move. He gave it a kick to see if it was alive and sauntered off. 'Cruel brute,' we said, 'he might let it die in peace.' Well, in a few minutes, back he came with a coil of rope and a few chums, and these four, and a soldier, worked hard for an hour, got the beast out, dragged it under the shade of a tree, and brought it water from the river in their hats. We were under a shady tree, and even then felt half suffocated by the heat. They were exposed to the full glare of the mid-day sun, had been working hard all the morning in the open, and were now supposed to be enjoying their hard-earned rest under a wagon.

Next morning the foreign *attachés* told us that Bloemfontein had been evacuated, that the line both north and south of it had been cut by General French, and that the two Republics were suing for peace. This news was not altogether welcome, for the great desire of every one was to give them a 'damned good licking,' and if 'it was to be all chasing, and no fighting, it might'—everyone said—'last forever.'

It was a magnificent sight to see this huge army of nearly thirty thousand men start the last stage of its march to Bloemfontein. They had twenty miles to go, and they stepped out with seemingly inexhaustible energy.

The Naval Brigade followed at nine o'clock in company with the 6-inch howitzers, 'horsed' by oxen, and a carious sight it was to see the Royal Artillery men and their ox-spans, though, no doubt, not more curious to us than we were to them. We ran away from them easily over the soft veldt.

There was one difference between the two batteries. Their men walked stolidly alongside the guns, each in his proper station. Our men didn't. They learnt to drive as well as the natives, learnt the names of the individual oxen belonging to their especial wagon or gun team, could crack a whip with the best, and were almost able to pick out any particular ox with the lash, without touching any other. They copied the unearthly noises with which the *Kaffirs* stopped and re-started them, with great skill, and not only that but they took great pains to teach these natives the most fearful and effective oaths they knew. Thus, whilst at the commencement of the march the *Kaffirs* had exhausted their vocabulary of expletives when they came to *'verdomde Roinek'* (not very complimentary to us certainly), they now had command of a vast store of ingenious combinations of oaths taught them by the bluejackets, which knowledge they were always proud of displaying, generally with the most incongruous effect.

In three hours' time the 6-inch battery was 'hull down' astern, and we halted to rest and feed the oxen, marched on again two hours later, and bivouacked at half-past nine that night close to Ferreira Siding, only four miles south of Bloemfontein, and having marched sixteen and a half miles during the day—all across country.

All day long the army had been marching parallel to a range of low hills about four miles to the north-east, sweeping southwards to avoid them. This was part of the great turning movement which made the Boers, heavily entrenched there, hastily evacuate this position, and removed the last obstacle to the triumphant advance to Bloemfontein.

Close to Ferreira Siding was a big farm, and it was not too dark nor our men too weary to go off on a foraging expedition, from which they returned loaded with potatoes, mealies, tomatoes, and huge pumpkins. We practically had had no vegetables since leaving the ship six weeks previously, so it can be easily understood how thankful we were to get these.

Wednesday 1 March 14.—By some mistake the arrival of the Naval Brigade had not been reported at headquarters, and we missed the promised honour of taking part in the ceremonial 'entry' into Bloemfontein. Orders were received to march there next morning, and a 'wash clothes' and 'make and mend clothes' day was spent in 'smartening up' for the occasion, several shaving off their beards, and all scraping and scrubbing off the sand which had accumulated during the last month.

It was most pleasant to be once more close alongside a railway, and to know that it would shortly connect us with our base and all that that meant of stores, clothes, and food, so badly needed by everyone. There it was, its rails glittering in the sun, going serenely southward, as if the life of an army was not entirely dependent upon it.

On leaving Enslin we had a certain amount of whisky in oar mess-wagon, and as we saw this rapidly diminishing would cheer each other with the prospect of reaching the railway in a week, four days, two days, and now we had at last reached it. 'Another week,' we said, 'and it will be opened up,' and discussed earnestly the chances a case of whisky would have in running the gauntlet up the line. so long as it got past the militia, we thought, it would be all right; but would it? and the doubt threw a gloom over us. As a matter of pure history our first case did not.

Thursday, March 15.—At 5.30 a.m., a beautifully cool, bright and refreshing morning, we inspanned and trekked the last four miles of our long march, going over the ground at a great rate; and when, on reaching some high ground, we saw the town of Bloemfontein at our feet, we felt most exceedingly proud.

We bivouacked late that morning on a plain, south of the old fort, and close to the lunatic asylum and the Free State Arsenal.

This asylum had already been partially converted into a military hospital, and one of our first duties was to send there an officer from the 12-pounder battery. Our next, a more pleasant one, to send a bluejacket to reeve halyards to the flag-staff over Government House, which he quickly did, swarming up the pole.

Our next, the most pleasant of all, was to dine at the English Club, and our first whisky and soda, and our first dinner, with its white cloth, clean plates, and abundance of food, will remain long in oar memories.

Bloemfontein.—The Naval Brigade quickly made itself as comfortable as sailors alone know how, and for the first few days we filled ourselves with good food, for the next two sorrowfully showed our tongues to the unsympathetic doctors, and on the seventh day—21st March—pulled ourselves together, painted the guns a most bilious and suggestive yellow, and were inspected by Lord Roberts, who, after thanking the Brigade for its services, called in front of him the doctors and their stretcher-bearers, and specially praised them—this proud distinction being probably unique in the history of the navy. Among the few spectators was Admiral Maxse, who had been present, in the Crimea, at the last previous occasion on which a field-marshal had inspected a Naval Brigade on active service.

Next day the seamen and stokers belonging to the *Powerful* left for home. The first fortnight was a very lazy time, with an occasional route-march in the early morning, to keep the feet hard, and plenty of football in the cool of the day, to fill up spare hours. Then, however, our dreamy security was rudely awakened by the Sanna's Post affair, within earshot of the camp, and immediately the 12-pounders were ordered to the north of the town, the rest of the Brigade following two days later, and placing the four 4.7's in position on top of a *kopje* two miles north of the town. This hill became known as 'Naval Hill,' a name which it will probably bear for all time. It commanded a great stretch of country, and formed an admirable camping-ground, on which once more we proceeded to make ourselves comfortable, and soon had all the paths approaching and running through it carefully marked off with whitewashed stones.

This whitewash brought great joy to the bluejackets, who described the camp as 'looking like a —— coastguard station,' and 'so homely.' Khaki serge was now served out, and none too soon either, for the nights had already become cold and our cotton clothes had worn out. The tattered ship's straw hats and battered marines' helmets were also replaced by soft felt hats, on the turned-up brims of which the bluejackets embroidered an Admiralty foul anchor, and the marines a bugle— these two badges now being practically the only marks which distinguished the Naval Brigade from the army.

On April 18 four 5-inch naval guns, on old army carriages—the 'Weary Willies' of Colesberg—manned by garrison artillery men, crawled up the muddy sides of Naval Hill and relieved us, our guns being brought back to the camp in readiness for the impending advance northward. Meanwhile the scourge of fever had not spared the navy, and the brigade had to be reorganised on account of the casualties from sickness. Seamen gunners and able seamen were only numerous enough to man three 4.7's and the 12-pounders, and to their intense delight the fourth 4.7 was handed over to the marine artillery, no more to be 'escort,' but now to be 'gunners.'

The first move was made on April 21, when two 12-pounders were sent off with a column to try and cut off the Boers, trekking back in hot haste out of the net spread for them round Wepener. They returned without having effected their purpose.

Three days afterwards Grant's guns marched eastwards with their old friends the Highland Brigade, and on May 2 the remainder of the Brigade marched northwards with Lord Roberts, leaving behind two 12-pounders to garrison Bloemfontein.

Our stay in Bloemfontein had extended over seven weeks, and few are likely to forget the long string of stretchers which morning after morning passed through the camp and wended their way down the hill to the field hospitals, with their burdens of fever.

Eighty-nine left the Naval Brigade in stretchers whilst at Bloemfontein, and no fewer than forty-nine of these were carried away during the last thirteen days, all suffering from typhoid, dysentery, or camp fever. The strength of the brigade was under four hundred officers and men, and the moral effect on those left, who saw their messmates daily taken to hospital, was very great. Can it be wondered that each officer and man longed for the order to 'get under way 'once more?

Whilst the dread of typhoid and the constant succession of funeral parties are now the most striking as well as the most dismal recollections of Bloemfontein, probably, in a year or two, the remembrance of our stay in this town will only conjure pleasant memories of many jovial dinner-parties at the club, followed, as we smoked afterwards in the moonlit verandah, by the nightly 'tattoo,' the skirling of the Highland pipers, and the 'Last Post,' in the great market square outside it.

MARCH FROM ENSLIN TO BLOEMFONTEIN

Date				Miles	Hours	
Feb. 13	Enslin	to	Ram Dam	9	4½	
„ 14	Ram Dam	„	Waterval Drift	15	6	Period of
„ 15	Waterval Drift	„	Wegdrai Drift	12	5½	25 hours
„ 16	Wegdrai Drift	„	Jacobsdal	5	2	

Enslin to Jacobsdal = 41 miles.

Feb. 18	Jacobsdal	to	Klip Kraal Drift	15	6	Period of
„ 19	Klip Kraal Drift	„	Clockfontein	12	5	22 hours
„ 20	Clockfontein	„	Paardeberg	4	2½	

Jacobsdal to Paardeberg = 31 miles.

Feb. 27–Mar. 6	Paardeberg	to	Osfontein	6	—	
Mar. 7	Osfontein	„	Poplar Grove	12	8	
„ 10	Poplar Grove	„	Dreifontein	19	10	Period of
„ 11	Dreifontein	„	Doornboom	15	7	26 hours
„ 12	Doornboom	„	Venter's Vlei	18	9	Oxen
„ 13	Venter's Vlei	„	Ferreira Siding	16½	8½	failing
„ 15	Ferreira Siding	„	Bloemfontein	4	2	

Paardeberg to Bloemfontein = 85½ miles.

Enslin to Bloemfontein—Total = 157½ miles.

CHAPTER 1

The Start From Bloemfontein

'An orderly for the captain.'

'All right! what is it?' came the captain's voice from the mess tent.

Orderlies were so numerous, and generally brought such uninteresting intelligence, that we were very agreeably surprised to hear an exclamation issue from our captain's lips on reading it—an exclamation which meant that the message was at least of some interest.

'We start to join in the advance at five this evening, and march to join the main body at Brandfort.'

Thank goodness! For six long weeks we had been stationed on a hill, some three miles to the north of the town, appropriately called 'Naval Hill,' and for that time had been fighting a much worse enemy than the Boers—enteric fever, which had devastated our ranks, and there was not an officer or man who was not delighted at the prospect of the move.

Two 12-pounders under the gunnery lieutenant and another lieutenant, assisted by a midshipman, had started off the day before, and we were left at Bloemfontein with two 4.7's, one manned by bluejackets, the other by marines, two 12-pounders, and all the headquarter staff of the Naval Brigade, which included the captain, the commander, the doctor, the major of marines, the paymaster, and numerous smaller fry.

It was one o'clock when orders were received, and in a few minutes the camp was in a state of confusion with preparations for starting. The two 12-pounders were to be left behind—who was to stay with them? They might be going on some more important business—though they did not as things turned out—so the junior major of marines was left in charge with the Scotch officer from the Victorian navy, a lieutenant R.N., and a subaltern R.M.L.I., the guns' crews, and half a company of marines. The remaining bluejackets and marines started packing their kits and loading the wagons.

By five o'clock everything was in readiness—oxen inspanned, wagons loaded, and kits packed up, all the heavy baggage being left behind to be stored in the town.

It was very nearly dark when the advance guard started, and nobody knew the way. However, with great confidence we commenced our march, and everything went well for about half a mile, when No. 1 gun endeavoured to take a short cut by jumping a deep *donga*, which delayed us about an hour, as we had to drag it out again backwards and get it on the main road. The main road ran round 'Naval Hill,' and we had to branch off across the railway over a siding. The unfortunate No. 1 gun missed the turning, and having made nearly a complete circle of the hill, at last got across the railway. After many inquiries from every one, we met on the road. No. 1 gun having gone some two miles out of its way.

Once with our heads turned in the direction of the Glen—which is supposed to be about fifteen miles from Bloemfontein, but distances are very elastic in South Africa—we went straight ahead, and marched on almost without a halt till 1 a.m., when we came across the remainder of our brigade drawn up by the side of the road, and were told that we were now within a mile of the Modder River, which we should cross at daylight; till then we could lie down.

It was very cold and the three hours' rest did none of us much good, and we were not sorry to get on the move again at 4.30, about half an hour before daylight.

Guided by two colonials with black feathers in their hats, we made for the Modder. How many times had we crossed and recrossed that dirty stream! Only once more should we cross, and that on our way home!

The *drifts* over the numerous rivers in South Africa were not made for spans of thirty-two oxen. An ox is not an intelligent animal even when everything is plain sailing; but when you are in difficulties his intellect vanishes entirely, and he becomes more of an obstruction than a help. Consequently we took some time to get the guns over, and the escort of marines, who facetiously called themselves the 'extra span,' did most towards pulling them up the other side.

We went on, rested for three hours, then on again, arriving at Karee Siding at 5 p.m. on May 3. Starting again at 4.30 the next morning, we marched on till 3 p.m., when we camped outside Brandfort. Here we found our two 12-pounder guns and the whole of the main force of Lord Roberts's army, which had occupied the village on the day before after a short but merry fight.

Brandfort is a small and uncomfortable-looking place—one main street, two hotels, and the usual large church placed in the centre of the usual church square, the church being the only building of any size.

We were naturally anxious to learn to which division we were to be attached, so our captain mounted his charger—named Charles I.; there was a Charles II., but he generally had a sore back— and started off to report himself and make inquiries. By a stroke of the best fortune he met on his way Lieut.-Gen. Pole-Carew, who was then in command of the 11th Division. The general accompanied our captain to headquarters, and, by insisting that his division sorely needed guns of a large calibre, got us attached to him. To say that we were pleased hardly expresses our feelings accurately. We had been with Pole-Carew ever since leaving Orange River, before he got command of the 9th Brigade, and the more we saw of him the more we liked him.

Early next morning, Saturday, May 5, at 4.30 we started off again, one unit of the army advancing on Pretoria.

Having got into our position we waited for the order to advance. Whilst waiting, the commander-in-chief, followed by the whole of the headquarter staff, passed by. No one could mistake him, dressed though he was in a 'coat, British warm,' and without a single medal ribbon on his khaki jacket, and no one could help feeling proud of serving under him. As he passed he stopped, inquired how the men were, made a cheery remark, and went on again. It was by small, thoughtful acts of this kind that he endeared himself to every officer and man in his command.

For seven and a half hours, in all the heat of a South African sun, we marched on, accomplishing about fifteen miles, and at 1 p.m. halted, outspanning our oxen to feed them. Both officers and men had dinner, and then, as we were not to move on till 3 p.m., disposed themselves for a short sleep. Our hopes for rest were, however, rudely dispelled by the appearance of a sergeant and two troopers from the provost-marshal—Major Poore, of cricketing fame. The sergeant asserted that the Naval Brigade had not only captured, but had moreover slain and eaten, twenty sheep which belonged to a neighbouring farmer, who, in a great state of ire, was demanding redress and compensation.

Our captain asserted that such a thing was impossible, and immediately started on a tour of inspection. Hard as it is to believe, the carcases and remains of seven unfortunate animals were found in close proximity to the wagons; thereupon, in the presence of the sergeant and the two troopers, the whole brigade was 'fallen in,' and the delinquents were requested to stand forward. No one moved. The captain then addressed us in scathing terms, and stated *inter alia* that it was his firm intention of requesting Lord Roberts to spare from his army such a crew as we, and of returning us without delay to our ships. For a monetary consideration of 10*s.* per sheep, however, the irate sheepowner was pacified, and the incident closed.

Hardly had we recovered from the effects of this accusation of sheep-stealing when the boom of guns was heard, and an A.D.C. came up to tell us to move forward as quick as possible, as the enemy were holding the Vet River about four miles to our front. We started off full speed (about three miles per hour) , and in spite of a limber being broken in crossing a *drift*— the said limber being full of most curious kinds of projectiles in the shape of jam, tinned milk, &c.—and one gun getting stuck in a morass, whence it was extricated with much difficulty and the help of nearly a whole regiment of Guards, we managed to get into action about 4.30. The artillery fire was very heavy—a battery of R.F.A. on our left having a most unpleasant time.

They are fine fellows, the Royal Artillery. There, with shells falling all around them, they stood and served their guns with as much coolness as if they were practising on the range at Lydd—an example of magnificent fire-discipline. It was only owing to the mercy of Providence that the whole battery was not exterminated, for the guns had been carefully placed close to a line of wire rails, the range of which the Boers had certainly fixed beforehand. We started firing at some opposing guns, which were very well masked, on the north side of the river, the Guards' brigade lying down in extended order in advance of the guns, ready for the signal to advance. Fortunately a general advance was not necessary, for towards sunset the enemy retired, as they found themselves in danger of being cut off from the flanks. We bivouacked on the ground for the night.

Starting again at 5 a.m., the whole of the army converged on one point—namely, the *drift* over the Vet River. Consequently we took till 1. p.m. to cross over. There is nothing calculated to raise anger in the breasts of staff officers more than getting a large army across one *drift*. Every unit wishes not only to cross among the first, but to get its baggage and impedimenta along with it, and the correspondents use every artifice in their power to prevail over the officer on duty to allow their Cape carts to cross over, out of turn. At this *drift* there was an officer who was the essence of good nature, but even his anger rose when one correspondent, who had managed to get his 'breakfast' Cape cart across early, then endeavoured to induce the officer to allow his 'luncheon' and 'dinner' carts to cross before all others!

Having arrived at the other side we marched on till we reached the small village of Smaldeel, a straggling hamlet, the only important building of which is the railway station. We were all fairly tired when we neared our camping-ground, but none more so than the major's horse, who showed such disinclination to proceed any further that at one point he slowly and gracefully subsided into a sitting position, leaving the senior officer of marines in a position at once undignified and untenable.

We stayed at Smaldeel two days—May 7 and 8—a halt made luxurious by the washing of clothes and persons. Here again the effects of the Bloemfontein enteric epidemic made themselves manifest, several men going to the field hospital, among them the lance-corporal of the officers' mess, who, to the regret of every one, died shortly afterwards.

Chapter 2

Kroonstad

Setting off again on May 9 from Smaldeel, we arrived next day at the Zand River. Here the enemy were again holding the passage, but again, on finding that their flanks were in danger, they hastily retired. Our large guns only fired half a dozen rounds apiece. The story reached us afterwards that the last two shells fired from them disabled one of the Boers' guns, killed seven men and wounded countless others. Unfortunately, we were never able to verify this or similar tales. Our 12-pounder guns crossed the river in hot pursuit—the mules keeping up a steady trot. This was excellent for the officers, who were mounted, and for the mule drivers, but for no one else attached to the guns, for they all had to run alongside, and a South African sun, together with a dense dust, are not calculated to improve anyone's 'wind.' Consequently they did not catch the enemy, or even get to sufficiently close range to open fire upon them.

After crossing the *drift* with the usual amount of annoyance and trouble at Virginia siding, we marched steadily on for the next two days.

It is easy enough to sit down and write now about marching 'steadily' on, but at the time one would often have given all one's possessions for one long drink, and it made one positively ill to consider how many unnecessary whiskies and sodas one had had, in the good days gone by, while now even the dirtiest water was at a high premium. We were unfortunate in one way and fortunate in another. Unfortunate because, owing to the necessity of our oxen having to be fed, we had to halt for three hours in the middle of the day, and consequently it was nearly always dark by the time we arrived at our camping ground—but fortunate because, during this three hours' halt, we got our dinners in comfort, and generally a wash for the cleanly ones. While talking of washing, due credit should be given to one of the senior officers. Hardly a day passed without his being able, by bribery or other means, to obtain a bucket of water and have his bath, and when in camp every morning he might be seen before breakfast, though there might be one of those cold, searching Transvaal winds, and the thermometer during the night had registered 15° of frost, stripped to the skin and enthusiastically soaping himself.

Until you, dear reader, have been obliged to have your bath in the open in midwinter, you will never realise to what extent an Englishman will sacrifice himself to cleanliness. This officer had an apparently sure antidote to pneumonia or other ills, in the shape of a small 'tot' of whisky taken internally before and after washing! We others, not sufficiently stimulated by the example of our noble captain, used to gaze at our water in disgust, and turn sorrowfully away, putting off the evil to a warmer day.

After two days' marching we arrived on Saturday, May 12, outside Kroonstad. For a long time we had heard alarming stories of the grand line of defence the Boers were making about six miles to the south of the town. We had ample evidence of their good intentions, in the shape of half-finished earthworks, tools left behind, &c., but no sign of a Boer. An incident occurred outside the town worth recording. As to who was in the right and who in the wrong, the author will not venture an opinion.

Strict instructions had been issued about looting. Consequently our gunnery lieutenant in command of the 12-pounders impressed on his men that they would be most severely punished for any misdemeanour of this sort. Now there were two innocent geese swimming about on a pond—no farm or habitation was near, and the men looked upon them with avaricious eyes. They were speedily caught and killed, one by the 4.7's and one by the 12-pounders. As the bluejacket from the 12-pounders was bearing off his prize, he was pounced upon by the lieutenant (G.), and, having received a severe address, was ordered to bury the bird. Another officer, who was of a more generous turn of mind in these matters, approached the man whilst he was in the act of covering the bird with earth, and, when about one inch of soil had been thrown on the carcase, suggested that it was buried sufficiently deep. As soon as the man's back was turned the corpse was promptly exhumed and carried off to the mess wagon.

If you wish to hear the opinion of the Guards' brigade as to how the Naval Brigade did their catering, make a few inquiries amongst a

THE MARINE'S GUN (4.7) MARCHING INTO KROONSTADT

certain regiment of Coldstream Guards. They once found a nice goose and hung it up. In the morning it had disappeared, but, marvellous coincidence, a goose (another one, of course), nicely plucked, was seen hanging on to one of the naval guns. The rage of the Coldstreamers was great, and they made many unkind insinuations.

On arriving outside Kroonstad we formed up for a procession into the town past the commander-in-chief, and our captain, assisted by the commander, the major of marines, and the midshipman A.D.C., entered the town at the head of the Naval Brigade at 3 p.m. One officer was so much occupied in responding to the acclamations of the English inhabitants on the left, on entering, that he very nearly failed to perceive Lord Roberts on the right. However, he did so just in time, but had to turn so quickly that Charles I., his warrior steed, was nearly the cause of an unhappy *contretemps*, which was luckily escaped by the presence of mind of the Major. We marched through and encamped about three-quarters of a mile north of the town, the officers luckily securing two rooms in a cottage for messing.

Kroonstad is quite a large town, with many large buildings. The magnificent railway bridge over the river had been blown down that morning—the handiwork of the Irish brigade, and a very good job they made of it, too. The hotels had been left intact, with much valuable whisky in them, which the owners kindly let us buy at the absurdly cheap price of 12s. 6d. per bottle. There were very few foodstuffs obtainable, and what there were were quickly commandeered at market price by the Army Service Corps, but we managed to make several additions to our mess stock all the same.

We stayed at Kroonstad for eight days—from May 13 till May 21 inclusive. None of us were sorry for the halt, and we spent a very pleasant time, having a roof over our heads for meals and a certain amount of sport—of shooting which was fairly successful, and of fishing which was entirely unsuccessful—to amuse us.

Three or four more men went to hospital here with enteric, and we lost our only remaining marine artillery subaltern, who also developed enteric and had to be invalided home. The marines' gun was consequently commanded by the major, with a subaltern, R.M.L.I., under him.

The sergeant-major of marines was an Irishman to the backbone, and a source of endless amusement to both officers and men; not that he was not an excellent non-commissioned officer—far from it—but he had the Irish knack of mixing up his sentences. One evening he approached the officer on duty in a great state of excitement. 'Now, hav' ye a gon, sorr? There's a great big burrd a-sitting on the telegraph wires, exactly like a eagle!' The officer on duty went forth to slaughter the eagle, but retired disconsolate, as the 'great big burrd' was an owl! On another occasion, that necessary parade known as 'feet inspection' was held. Several men absented themselves. Shortly afterwards, the stentorian voice of the sergeant-major was heard in the camp:

'All those men who were not present this morning will parade at 5 p.m. tonight with their feet!'

On the 20th the major, who had been left behind at Bloemfontein, arrived, bringing with him ammunition, much valuable whisky, and 60,000 cigarettes, the latter a present from some naval and marine officers in the Mediterranean. Needless to say they were much appreciated.

At 6 on the morning of the 22nd we started again. We marched twenty miles that day, halting at Honning Spruit for the night, seventeen miles the next day, and fifteen miles the next, when we reached Vredefort Road station; nothing of any interest occurred. The same can be said of the two following days. We went on with the same uninteresting marching and arrived on Saturday the 26th at the northern border of the Orange Free State. There is no doubt that the Free State is an uninteresting country. You may march for miles and miles without even seeing a *Kaffir kraal*, simply the same grassy undulating country; no sooner do you reach the top of one hill than another one, of exactly similar appearance, stares you in the face another couple of miles further on.

We had not even rumours of battle to stimulate us, but now that we were nearing the enemy's capital we hoped for, at any rate, the sight of our brother Boer, for we had not seen his back since we left Zand River, as he had not waited even for a rear-guard action of any size.

One source of amusement on the road was the chasing of any unfortunate hare which might get up and run for its life. Immediately, from every direction, dogs of every sort, size, and description appeared and started off in hot pursuit. We were very lucky in possessing a greyhound called 'Jack,' who was by far the fastest dog in the army; consequently many a hare found its way to our larder. Occasionally a buck would come running all through the column. Then helmets, rifles—anything—would be hurled at the unfortunate, terrified animal, who seldom got away.

We possessed another dog, by name 'Toby,' a black and tan terrier of sorts, who had been given to a midshipman by a barmaid, when the Naval Brigade was at Molteno. He followed us, attaching himself to the marines, every inch of the way, and was taken home when we returned to the base. He had a vast reputation for bravery—it was even said, by some, that he led the Naval Brigade up the hill at Graspan, others asserted that he always bolted two miles without stopping, at the first shot.

On Sunday, May 27, we started off, as usual, at daylight and marched four miles through loose sand, which was, at places, quite two feet deep, and consequently made the going very bad, and at 10 a.m. crossed the Vaal River at Viljoen's Drift, and were among the first of the British Army to set foot on Transvaal soil. We went on through the town of Vereeniging and camped the other side.

As it was early winter then, we all felt the cold at nights very badly. Every morning, on waking up, one found one's waterproof sheet covered with frost, and breakfast, an hour before daylight in the open, was a feast unpleasant in the extreme.

On Monday we thought that we were going to have a shot at the enemy, as he was in position on some ridges to our left, but, as had happened many times before, as soon as we had prepared for action we were told that he had hurriedly left. That day we marched twenty-two miles and encamped for the night on the south side of Klip River.

CHAPTER 3

Advantages of the Naval Brigade

In more than one respect we were more fortunate than other units in the army. For one thing, we never had, whilst on the march, any outpost duty to do, and consequently, except for the few sentries over the camp, every officer and man had his full night's rest. Few people can realise what a difference this means. The infantry, for instance, would march as we did all day, and then some would have to spend the whole night on outpost duty, marching again the whole of the next day. We were also most fortunate with respect to our baggage.

As our ammunition was of such enormous weight and took up so much room, not more than forty rounds could be carried in one bullock wagon, consequently when we had fired off forty rounds we had a spare wagon to use as we liked. By putting ammunition on every wagon, we were able to say, with truth, that all our wagons were 'ammunition wagons,' and, by reason of their being so called, they were never separated from us and put in the baggage train. Once, and once only, did we have trouble in this respect. It occurred when the army was approaching the *drift* over the Vaal River.

The order came for guns and ammunition wagons only to proceed across first. We, as usual, started off with all our following. A staff officer, seeing some doubtful-looking cases, stopped one of the wagons, and upon lifting up the hood of the tent saw numerous tables, valises, and other paraphernalia. Thereupon he remarked with wrath that this was not an ammunition wagon and could not proceed with the guns.

Whilst a heated argument was proceeding between him and our transport officer, our general galloped up and inquired the cause of the delay. On the staff officer explaining, the general said that all the Naval Brigade wagons went with the guns, whereupon the staff officer went off to report the matter to the chief of the staff, who evidently reported it to the commander-in-chief. The consequence of it all was that the latter held an informal review of our caravan as we passed along, with our general standing by his side explaining that all our fifteen wagons contained ammunition. All went well till the officers' mess wagon was reached. The tarpaulin had, unfortunately, slipped and exposed to view a large box labelled in unmistakable large letters 'Van Houten's Cocoa.' Lord Roberts perceived this, but, with a twinkle in his eye, merely remarked:

'Well, they mark it very funnily!'

It was a bitterly cold morning when we started off for the bridge across the Klip River. As there were prospects of fighting ahead, our heavy guns were sent on first after the advance guard.

There was only one bridge, and that a wooden one, of very ancient date, and it had not improved with years. However, it had been passed by the Royal Engineers as strong enough to bear our guns, and we started to cross without thought of any accident. The bluejackets' gun crossed first without mishap, though the ancient timbers gave forth an ominous groan. The marines' gun, coming next, had hardly got to the middle, when the left wheel disappeared completely through the bridge and the gun remained stuck fast, heeling over at an angle of forty-five degrees.

Everyone on the spot immediately offered suggestions, and at last the only possible thing to save the gun was started, namely, to cut away the remainder of the bridge and make a *drift* of the *débris*. Luckily there was a hard bottom, and we worked from 7 till 11.30, and at last succeeded, amidst much cheering, and with the aid of sixty-four oxen and several hundred men, in getting the gun out. Meanwhile the advance of the whole of the 7th and 11th Divisions had been delayed. Firing was heard ahead, and as soon as the way was clear we all hurried on as fast as possible.

Very few people knew the way, and still fewer our destination. Consequently we got lost many times, and at last, after a very long and tiring day, arrived in camp at Elandsfontein at 7.30.

Several other parties thought that we were already in possession of Johannesburg, and some made their way there. The enemy, however, considered this rather premature, and took those who had entered the town—amongst whom were two war correspondents—prisoners; but they did not keep them very long, as we found them again on entering Pretoria.

The bluejackets' gun, which had gone off to the front as fast as possible in hope of some fighting, smiled scornfully on the unfortunate marines' gun which they left behind them embedded in the remains of a bridge. They had to learn, however, and that day too, that there were worse misfortunes than that, for, after fruitlessly pursuing the enemy the whole day, they attempted to follow the field artillery back to camp at sunset.

Now the field artillery can go where a naval gun—which weighs nearly seven tons—cannot, and this they found out to their cost, for going over a softish piece of ground about three miles from camp, the gun sank deep in, and as it was found impossible to extricate it, the gun's crew had to remain there all night, without food or blankets, and wait for daylight and extra oxen.

The 12-pounders, as usual, had gone on ahead under the Gunnery Lieutenant, and, by the mercy of Providence alone, were restored to us intact in the evening, as after a most adventurous day they had finished up by returning to camp *viâ* the suburbs of Johannesburg, a town still in the hands of the enemy.

On Wednesday, May 30, we were all occupied till 11 a.m. in extricating No. 1 or the bluejackets' gun from its boggy resting-place. This having been done with much difficulty, we sat down to await events.

At about 10 a.m. some of the chief men of the town, under a flag of truce, came out of Johannesburg to interview Lord Roberts and ask his terms. He having responded that his terms were unconditional surrender of the town within twenty-four hours, the flag of truce retired, and we made preparations to bombard the town in case of refusal of our terms.

In the evening we heard that the town had surrendered, and we received orders to start at 10 next morning to join in the procession past Lord Roberts through the town. Accordingly at the time appointed we started off with only two ammunition wagons, leaving the rest of our impedimenta to follow on with the remainder of the baggage belonging to other units, in rear.

Passing along the Rand, we reached Johannesburg, after innumerable halts, at 2.30. On our way we passed several of the more important mines, all the *employés* of which gathered outside to look at and admire a spectacle the like of which they had never seen, and never would see again.

At 3 we marched past Lord Roberts, who had taken up his position, with the *burgomaster* of the town on his left, in the main square. A dense crowd of persons of every nationality thronged the streets, and we all met with a most hearty reception.

We marched drearily on and on, thinking that every minute we must be nearing our camping ground. Our captain had been told to follow the field artillery, but, unfortunately, we missed them, and at sunset found ourselves alone on the veldt without a notion where to go. There was only one thing for it—to draw up the guns where we were, and wait for information. This we did. The gunnery lieutenant went off, and after falling over two wire-fences with no damage either to himself or his horse, found the proper camp some three miles back, but our captain decided to stay where he was for the night.

Though we were well outside the outpost line, we found it absolutely necessary to make fires, searching the country all round for wood.

Our fires attracted other people, and by the morning we had quite a little camp of our own. We did not spend a pleasant night—it is very hard in South Africa in the winter to spend a pleasant night in the open when you have no extra covering and no food, and no one was sorry when day broke, and we made our way back to the main camp, some eight miles north of the town.

We stayed here that day and the next, during which time we collected many valuable mess stores out of the town at exorbitant prices, and a large quantity of badly-needed potatoes and vegetables from a neighbouring farm, also at a price.

Several of our officers visited Johannesburg, and all came back with magnificent ideas of the place, but with much more magnificent ideas of the excellent luncheon or dinner they had got there.

On Whit Sunday, June 3, we started on the last part of our march on Pretoria. Leaving at 7, we marched twelve miles and encamped for the night at what is called the 'half-way house' to Pretoria. We thought that the morrow would be the most important day of the war, with the whole Boer army holding its capital, and we hoped, on the surrender of the town, to find the President of the Republic standing on his *stoep*, ready to do homage to our commander-in-chief, and to acknowledge himself beaten. We were, alas! sadly disillusioned.

CHAPTER 4

In Action

Starting at 6.30 a.m. on June 4, we marched steadily on till noon, when we reached the Six-Mile Spruit, south-west of Pretoria. For some time we had heard the sound of big guns to our front, and we momentarily expected to come into action.

After proceeding for about another two miles, we came to the bottom of a steep hill. At this point all transport, and all the units ahead of us, stopped, and we went up the hill at our best pace, with the guns and two ammunition wagons. On reaching the crest, our two 4.7 guns were ordered into action, and hardly had we moved outwards to allow room for the oxen to sweep round when we were greeted with several pom-pom shells from the enemy's position. One looked round to see what damage had been done, and to one's surprise saw, apparently, none; but our commander, who was mounted and placing the guns, came riding back and called out to two men to help him off his horse—then we saw that he had been badly hit in the foot with a pom-pom fuse.

The guns got quickly into action with no more casualties, and we started firing at our opponents. From the top of the hill we had an excellent view of all the surrounding country, a long, low range of hills on our left on which the Boers had several guns, and two of the far-famed Pretoria forts to our right front.

For the first hour we were very much annoyed by several 'zarp' or Johannesburg police, who had stationed themselves behind a stone wall some seven hundred yards to our front and were sniping us continually, but luckily doing no damage except to two of the 12-pounder mules, who were hit. A few rounds of shrapnel from our guns and a battery of Royal Artillery soon, however, sent them away.

The Boer artillery fire now got rather heavy, but all their shells, luckily for us, passed over our heads and buried themselves among the great mass of ambulances, baggage wagons, &c., which were behind us. We kept replying, but it was very difficult to fix the position of the opposing guns.

One fort was well within our range, and several well-directed shots sent columns of sand flying out of it. The Boers had, however, carefully removed all their guns and ammunition, and had evacuated it. We found this out afterwards. One of our principal endeavours was to hit the railway station and thus stop any trains. This was extremely difficult, and it would have been a very lucky shot to have been successful, as we had no knowledge of its whereabouts except that it was somewhere some two thousand yards behind the nearest fort! We ascertained afterwards that we very nearly accomplished our object, several shells just going over and burying themselves in some gardens beyond, much to the surprise of the inhabitants.

On the enemy's fire slackening, our infantry advanced, and our 12-pounder guns also started to take up a position under cover of the stone wall lately occupied by the Boers. Here they proved most useful, entirely silencing the guns from the range of hills on our left. The infantry advanced steadily, and by sunset had gained a great advantage. We all bivouacked in the positions we occupied at dusk.

It was a curious thing, but our guns, especially the large ones, always offered, apparently, a most tempting bait to every owner of a cinematograph or camera. Whenever we were in difficulties, if we were fast in a bog, or delayed in a *drift*, or had broken a bridge, then was the moment for every camera within a range of two miles to make its appearance and fix its penetrating eye on us. The same happened when in action, but one bold photographer at least got more than he bargained for this day. He had arrived, early in the fight, with a cinematograph, and requested the officer in charge of the marines' gun to let him know when he was going to fire, as he wanted to take the gun firing. The officer gave some orders and then turned round to the photographer. Meanwhile some Boer shells had come whizzing close over our heads, and all the officer saw was the photographic machine standing disconsolate and the operator in full flight to the rear of the column!

At 10 o'clock that night Pretoria surrendered, and we all made preparations for a triumphant entry into the town next morning. We heard, also, much to our disgust, that Botha, the Boer commandant, had managed to effect a retreat from the town with the larger part of his army, and a large supply of ammunition and stores.

During this short fight we had ample opportunity of observing the effect of the Boer shells. It was just the same as we had found before. They were nearly all segment shells with a very small bursting charge, and therefore did nothing but bury themselves in the ground when they landed in sand or other soft substance, but when they fell on stony or rocky ground used to scatter their segments in every direction.

The Boers had the great advantage of nearly always knowing the accurate ranges, and their shooting should without doubt have been better. We never had any range finders with us, and used to fire two or three trial shots to ascertain the distance. With practice we found we could judge within about two hundred yards of our proper range by the first shot, and always managed to go very near our mark by the third.

On our way to the town next morning, we passed over a large portion of yesterday's battlefield, strewn with empty cartridge-cases and other evidences of the fight. Our way lay through a most picturesque valley, with the great fort 'Klapperkop' towering over us on our right, and an immense range of hills on our left, features of the ground which showed us how strongly Pretoria was fortified by nature, and what a tough job we should have had if the Boers had attempted to hold their capital.

We neared the outskirts of the town at 1 p.m., and then the Naval Brigade made ready for the march past the commander-in-chief. On our left, as we went along, we passed the large artillery barracks, which had been so recently evacuated by the enemy that some of the first of our troops to enter them found dinners half-cooked on the fire; then our way took us past the Model School, for so long the undesired abode of many of our officers.

Well-built houses, with charming gardens, lined the streets, and a flowing stream of water ran down both sides of the roadway.

We were sadly delayed on the way by several of the oxen striking altogether, lying down in the road, and refusing to get up again. Consequently there was a large gap between ourselves and the troops who had preceded us. On reaching the market-square we were greeted with the strains of 'A Life on the Ocean Wave' from the drums and fifes of the Guards, and all the released prisoners and other spectators who lined the streets or crowded the balconies of the Grand Hotel gave us a most hearty reception. The streets were kept by the Grenadier Guards, and Lord Roberts had taken up his position opposite the government buildings and underneath the usual church. It was a dirty, dusty crew which represented the navy at the entry into the capital of the Transvaal. None of us had had the chance of a wash for some time, and among us all there was not a single suit of clothes that even a tramp would have condescended to accept as a gift. Our number was very small We had lost very many officers and men since the start from Orange River, in action and from sickness, and all that remained at this time, at the front, were roughly, a hundred bluejackets and seventy marines, with ten R.N. and four marine officers.

Having marched through the town, we encamped some two miles outside to the west. Our first want on arrival was food; our second, water. Having fed and washed ourselves, some of us went forth and inspected the town we had marched so far to take. So many descriptions of Pretoria have been written that it would be useless and out of place to attempt another; suffice to say, some of the officers managed to get as far as the Grand Hotel, where, having found a white tablecloth and inferior champagne at 25s. per bottle, they rested content.

The major of marines, who had been left behind at Kroonstad to bring up ammunition and a company of marines, arrived next day; and three days after our entry we moved camp to Silverton, some eight miles to the east of Pretoria.

The Boers, meanwhile, having evacuated Pretoria, had retreated along the railway line in this direction, and occupied the range of ridges which encircled the town at a distance of some twenty miles. Our camp was about seven miles by the railway from the opening or 'poort' in the hills through which the railroad ran.

On the day after our arrival here we were considerably surprised to hear the boom of a big gun about 11 o'clock, and to see a shell fall a hundred yards short of the Guards' camp, sending up volumes of dust and stones. Another and another succeeded, none luckily reaching the camp itself, but all falling about the same distance short. We hurriedly inspanned our oxen and got into position, but before arriving there, the enemy's gun, which had come out of their lines on a railway truck, had retired. Several alarms occurred in the next two days, but nothing came of them. However, by their endeavouring to shell the camp they were unpleasantly close the whole time, and we were not sorry to receive orders on Sunday night—June 10—to make a night march that night or early next morning, to get into position unobserved, preparatory to a combined effort of the whole army to surround the enemy and cut off their retreat.

Accordingly at 2.30 next morning, in inky darkness and cold unspeakable, we set off. The guns were bad enough to move by day, but when one could not see one's hand in front of one's face, the difficulties very nearly became impossibilities. We marched for three hours at the rate of nearly one mile per hour, and at 5.30 a.m. reached the ridge we were to occupy, and early in the morning commenced the engagement commonly known as 'Diamond Hill.'

CHAPTER 5

Effects of Our Fire

At daylight we found that the ridge on which we had been placed was nearly eleven thousand yards distant from the enemy's position; and as our extreme range with the field-carriages was only 9,500, we were of hardly any use the whole day—in fact, we only fired five rounds, and those at some snipers who had come down to the bottom of the hills and were firing at our mounted infantry, who were occupying Marks's Farm.

During the whole of the two days the engagement lasted we saw very little of the fight itself, as our division was engaging the centre of the enemy's position and the main attack was on the flanks. But the Boers, knowing Lord Roberts's tactics and wishes to surround them, also had very few men in their centre, which was practically unassailable, and had massed their main body on their flanks.

Having camped on the ridge for the night, early next morning we moved to another one, which was only about seven thousand yards from the range of hills. Here we opened fire, and, if report can be believed, did considerable damage amidst the enemy's *sangars*, the station-master who lived at the 'Poort' railway station telling as afterwards that he himself saw seven dead and several wounded taken out of one *sangar*, the effects of one lyddite shell.

Our principal endeavours were to prevent the big gun, which was trying to come out along the railway and return our fire, from doing so. At last a lucky shot tore up a piece of the line, and all danger from that quarter consequently disappeared.

During the day we fired fifty-seven rounds from the two guns.

We encamped where we were for the night, and were up at the usual hour before daybreak next morning, anxiously awaiting news, as we knew nothing of what had been happening on the flanks. At 10 a.m. Lord Roberts rode up with his staff, and smilingly remarked that our last shot had cleared the Boers out altogether, and that they had gone on further east. He stayed talking some time with our captain, and made some very complimentary remarks about our work.

That evening we got orders to 'trek' back to Koodoospoort, and sorrowfully thought that this retiring on the town was a sign that we were not amongst those who were to follow up the Boers further east; fortunately we were mistaken.

While at luncheon, a photographer, belonging to a well-known firm, photographed the Naval Brigade; and not only us, but he also photographed our Highland escort, in a most wonderful selection of striking attitudes—'Charging a *Kopje*' (enemy left to the imagination), 'The Last Cartridge,' 'The Last Bugle-Call,' 'Carrying off the Wounded' (who were specially bound up for the occasion in handkerchiefs dipped in mud and wound round their heads)—altogether a magnificent and true series of pictures of the war!

Moving on the next day, we halted at Koodoospoort, which was only two miles east of Pretoria; and spent here a peaceful time till the 21st. We replenished our larder as best we could from the scanty resources offered in the shops in the town, for, as most of the useful stores had already been taken by the Boers and no fresh supplies were allowed up yet, there was very little left, and the little there was, was sold at exorbitant prices. Postage stamps were, of course, the great rage, and every one hoped to make the fortune he had omitted to make at Bloemfontein, where one bought, one day, a 'sixpenny red' for sixpence, and found to one's delight that it was minus a D or had an extra dot, and was consequently worth fifty pounds, the next. The Pretoria stamps were, however, uncomfortably devoid of errors.

On the 21st we again moved camp, to Marks's Farm, some sixteen miles east of Pretoria. Here we stayed till the 24th. Our mess stock was greatly replenished on the first day of our arrival here by a party of officers, who, going out shooting, came across some coverts full of guinea-fowl, and proceeded to beat them. Hundreds of apparently confiding birds arose, some of which were promptly added to the game-bag, as many more would undoubtedly have been, had it not been for a lack of cartridges, and a message from the general, that they were not to shoot Mr. Marks's *tame* guinea-fowl.

On Sunday 1 June 24, we moved our camp again about half a mile, so as to get our guns into a position commanding the *poort* in the hills.

Here we remained till July 22. Nothing exciting occurred during this time. We occasionally were ordered to fire some rounds at the *kopjes* to our front, as we were given to understand that there were Boers there; but we did not do much damage, only setting the furze alight. On one occasion, after some firing a witty officer asked our captain why he had expended quite thirty rounds of lyddite when a half-penny box of matches would have done as well.

We were given large quantities of corrugated iron and wood, and made huts for officers and men. The mess hut was a great masterpiece, and although the wind—an uncommonly cold one—would whistle through it, it was a great improvement on biscuit boxes on the open *veldt*.

We bought a certain amount of cricket gear in Pretoria and played several matches; but the pitch could hardly be called a good one, and the scores were consequently small; however, it helped us to pass the time away. We also made several excursions into Pretoria in search of food, &c., by the train which ran in and out with stores. Going in was quite easy work, but coming out was more difficult, as the engines had seen their best days and used to jib at the steep inclines when they had a large load behind them, and often it was necessary to get out and help the engine do its work.

The nights were bitterly cold while we were here, but the days were very fine—a warm sun and a cool breeze, and the air magnificently fresh. The climate played havoc with the oxen and they lost condition rapidly, giving us much trouble when we eventually moved on. During our stay the senior major of marines was sent to hospital and invalided.

On the morning of Tuesday, July 22, we received orders to 'trek' again in the afternoon, so at 1.30 we started off, leaving behind us the huts we had built with such skill, for some other fortunate persons to use.

We marched that day as far as Donkershook, about seven miles off, and encamped there for the night. On the following morning we were ready to start by 6.30, but did not move till 10, as the enemy had hastily retired, and instead of surrounding them and cutting off their retreat eastward, we were left again in the unfortunate position of having to follow after them as fast as possible. Our hope that they would stand and give us a fight was not fulfilled; but there must be, we thought, an end or corner to the country, where at last we should bring them to bay, so we cheerfully plodded on after them.

On Tuesday, the 24th, we marched fifteen miles, and arrived at Bronker's Spruit, the scene of the disaster to an English regiment, marching in to garrison Pretoria, during the first Boer war. We saw the graves of the men who had been killed. They were sadly in need of repair, and this has since been done.

The next day was one of the most unpleasant we . had ever experienced. All went well till noon, when the wind got up and rain commenced to come down in torrents. We marched on and on in the blinding rain and against a howling wind, until we came within a stone's-throw of our camping-ground. It was nearly dark then, and our tempers were not improved by getting one of the guns stuck in a small *drift*. After half an hour's work we got it out and started to bivouac for the night. The ground was like a snipe-marsh, and torrents of rain still fell. However, we got fairly comfortably settled under our tarpaulins, and changed our clothes, if we could find any to change into, and retired between blankets, the officers' mess wagon being also the shelter for our favourite ox, an animal called 'Bantam,' who was extraordinarily tame, and would answer to his name and follow you like a dog (if you had a biscuit in your hand).

The captain, however, was not so fortunate. He had the luxury of a tent—the only one we carried with us. Perhaps on this night it had not been pitched with as much care as usual, owing to the wet and the men being very 'done up.' Anyhow, the whole thing blew down, and our C.O. was suddenly awakened by finding the tent-pole pinning him to the ground. He crawled out, clad in a shirt, having taken his breeches off to dry, and called for men to pitch the tent again. No one heard him, and so he had to pull the wet canvas over him and sleep like that for the rest of the night; but, marvellous to relate, he was not a bit the worse afterwards.

The next day turned out bright and sunny, and we were given till noon to dry ourselves, and then only marched four miles. Most people had come off worse than we had, and we heard afterwards that it was daring this night that the young officer in the Argyll and Sutherland Highlanders and three men had died from exposure.

On the 26th the gunnery lieutenant, who had been detached with two 12-pounders, rejoined. He had been away a month defending the north-eastern portion of the outer range of hills surrounding Pretoria, and had had only a few opportunities to do a little long-range shooting—mostly without much result.

112

CHAPTER 6

The Battle

On Friday, the 27th, we had a long day's march and encamped at Brugspruit, a station on the Delagoa Bay Railway. We heard that our stay here was likely to last some time, and were rather disgusted, as we were very anxious to push on eastwards as quickly as possible. We had an excellent camp here, and a very fine, commanding position for our guns, overlooking the colliery owned by Mr. Howard, who had been so instrumental in assisting the officers, who had escaped from Pretoria, to make their way to the coast. We were also rather lucky in making large additions to our mess stock, for the paymaster—always an energetic officer—discovered a small store some five miles off, where beer and other useful and scarce commodities could be purchased.

We were the first to find the store, and bought the goods at extortionate prices; the next day, some other officers discovered the place, and also discovered some ammunition hidden in it, so they took as much beer, &c., as they could find, and only had to pay less than English prices for their stock to the provost-marshal, as the store had been taken over by him, and the owners made prisoners for having contraband goods in their possession. However, we did not grieve much, for beer, even at 3s. a pint, was cheap then. Some of us went out buck shooting while at this camp, but with very little result, except that once we were mistaken for Boers, being some way outside the lines, and nearly shot by some Australian mounted infantry.

On Friday, August 3, we were off again, marching that day to Oliphant's River, and then on again to Middelburg next day, a distance of about twenty-five miles in all. On arriving there we encamped one mile to the east, but moved our guns into position next day on a *kopje* about four miles north-east of the town. The position was a very good one, as we had a good commanding view all round, but it was not the most comfortable place to live in, as the cold wind—there always was a wind up there, and it always was cold—blew sand and dust in every direction. While we were here, a mounted patrol was told off for scouting purposes, and put under the command of our captain. They were consequently known as 'Bearcroft's Horse,' and an adjacent fort will also carry his name down to posterity, for the party of Guards who built it put on the outside in large white stones—'Fort Bearcroft.'

The town of Middelburg was about the same size as an ordinary English village, and, in common with nearly all the other towns we had passed through, contained nothing worth buying or stealing. There was one large store, the owner of which rejoiced in the name of 'J. Chamberlain,' and this had been looted by the Boers (perhaps on account of the name!) and the owner had fled for safety. There we found many useful cooking utensils, musical instruments, linoleum, knives, forks, &c., which we made use of; also a complete cooking range, which was a great luxury to us, as we were able to roast our joints for a change, instead of the eternal boiling in a pot. We continued our cricket here to wile away the time, and had many exciting and successful matches, our pitch being the high hard road to Lydenburg, which was not at all bad, but the outfielding was a little trying among tropical ant-heaps and large stones. However, we defeated a company of Scots Guards, our Highland escort several times, and many others.

On Friday, the 17th, we were ordered to move one gun to a position west of the town, so the marines' gun went. Here they found a nice sheltered camp, and an old magazine, which was promptly turned into an officers' mess and was most comfortable. On Monday, the 20th, both guns were relieved by 5-inch siege guns, and we went back to our old camp and waited for orders to 'trek.'

Those orders arrived on the Wednesday, and we left at 7 a.m., extremely glad to be once more on the march, for, at every halting-place, rumour had it that the Naval Brigade would go no further, and we feared that one day rumour would speak the truth.

On Wednesday we marched to Rietpan, a short march of only ten miles, and next day reached Wonderfontein, so-called from a large pan which was always dry; but then most names of places in South Africa end in 'fontein,' and it does not necessarily follow that you will find water there.

Here we picked up the Guards' Brigade, and early next morning advanced slowly on Belfast, which position, commonly known as

Dalmanutha, Bergendal, or Belfast, the enemy were holding in force. Unfortunately, at about 8.30 a.m., No. 1 gun got stuck in a bog. It was really remarkable, but if there was a soft piece of ground anywhere for miles round, one of our guns was certain to find it, and stick in it. No. 2 gun luckily escaped, and as no amount of whip lash, or *Kaffir* bad language, would induce the oxen to move the gun, which was gradually sinking lower and lower, No. 2 gun went on and left a party of engineers, the captain, commander, and gun's crew to solve the difficulty of getting the other gun out of the mud.

At 11 a.m., we reached the position on top of the hills overlooking Belfast, and here found that the enemy were in strong force, the mounted infantry in front of us having to retire hastily. On the advanced posts of the enemy retiring on their main position, we moved on to the railway station, where we met our other gun, which had been extricated with much difficulty, and encamped there, in biting cold weather, for the night.

Next morning. Lord Roberts arrived at Belfast Station, by train from Pretoria—the railroad having been repaired as we advanced—at 10 o'clock. We had been 'standing by' since early morning, with oxen inspanned and everything ready for a start, but shortly after his arrival received word that no further advance would be made that day.

Early in the afternoon General Buller galloped in, having moved up in a northerly direction from Natal, and having just come within signalling distance of our column. General French arriving soon after, a conference was held in the saloon railway carriage, the headquarters of our commander-in-chief, to decide how to attack the apparently very strong position of Dalmanutha, held by the enemy. Roughly, the scheme was for our column to push home the attack from the centre, while General Buller operated on our right flank, and General French made a wide detour round the left flank of the enemy's position and endeavoured to cut off their retreat further east, and, at any rate, prevent them retiring on Lydenburg.

In the evening we received orders to be ready to move next morning. Accordingly at 8.30 a.m. next day we moved off and put our guns in position on the hill known as Monument Hill—so called from a monument erected on its highest point—which is supposed to mark the highest spot in the Transvaal. This monument, by the way, might have been with advantage destroyed by us, as it afforded an excellent mark for the enemy's fire, and during the next two days' engagement a hail of bullets fell continuously all round it. No. 1 gun was placed facing due north, while No. 2 gun faced due east and commanded the railway. Towards noon we were heavily engaged, but owing to the smokeless powder used by the enemy, it was extremely difficult to fix the position of their guns; also they, in a very wily manner, it is said, used to explode a pan of black powder in one place and fire their guns from a different position. Pom-pom shells and bullets were falling very thickly all round No. 2 gun, and it was very hard to retaliate for the reason stated above, also for the fact that the gun had to be fired from below the crest of the hill, for, had it been put in position on the top, the gun with its gun's crew would have offered such a large target to the enemy, that very few of the crew would have been left alive. At 3.30 p.m. orders were received for No. 2 or the marines' gun to move to the east of the railway; it accordingly moved off, but hardly had it gone half a mile when such a heavy shell-fire broke out, sending shells right into our wagons and camp, that General Stevenson ordered it to turn back and try to silence the fire.

On returning it opened fire again at the enemy's guns in the hills to our front, and the opposing guns soon were silenced. As it was now getting dusk and it was no good throwing away shells, both guns were ordered to cease firing, and the guns' crews were ordered to lie down under cover, for the bullets from the enemy's trenches were still flying about in rather an uncomfortable manner. It was while lying down like this and waiting for further orders that the subaltern of marines, who was in charge of the marines' 4.7, was severely wounded through the upper part of the thigh. Luckily the fleet surgeon was quite close, and he was bound up and carried to the ambulance wagon. Shortly after this the guns were taken back to camp, and we bivouacked at the base of Monument Hill for the night.

Next morning the bluejackets' gun crossed the railway and took up a position three-quarters of a mile south of the railway station, where it was greeted by a few bullets from some Boer snipers. Towards 10 a.m. firing commenced on our right, and our captain, seeing that the guns under General Buller were shelling Bergendal Farm, ordered the gun into position and fire to be directed on the farm.

After a short time we noticed a heliograph flashing a message in our direction from behind Buller's batteries, and received orders not to shell the farm any more, as his infantry were advancing on it. Meanwhile, however, the Boers were dividing the attentions of one of their 'Long Toms' between General Buller's troops and ourselves, but without any effect, as all their shells fell about five hundred yards to

TYPES OF ARMS—12-POUNDER NAVAL GUN ON IMPROVISED CARRIAGE

TYPES OF ARMS—4.7-INCH NAVAL GUN ON IMPROVISED MOUNTING

our right rear.

During this time the marines' 4.7, under command of the major, was having a duel with another 'Long Tom.'

Towards 2 p.m. the enemy who had been occupying Bergendal Farm, and who mostly consisted of *zarps* or Johannesburg police, driven off by the magnificent advance of our troops, rode away as hard as they could—as many as were left. Instantly a scathing fire from our guns, some R.H.A. batteries in front of us, and all Buller's guns, was directed on them, and as long as they remained in sight a concentrated fire was poured in. Then the mounted troops advanced, and the battle of Belfast, as far as we were concerned, was ended.

'Toby,' the terrier, whose pluck had been often called in question, seemed intuitively to understand that this would be his last opportunity of forever silencing traducers, and, to show his absolute contempt of danger, spent the day chasing shells. He would dash at the place where one had buried itself and excitedly, commence to dig it up from the soft ground. His surprise at burning his paws with the hot pieces was most comical to see, but experience did not damp his ardour in hunting for 'curios.'

On August 26 the gunnery lieutenant and his two 12-pounders were again detached, advancing with Pole-Carew's division.

CHAPTER 7

Several Adventures

The next few days were employed by the crews of both guns in building gun emplacements, and by some officers in journeying to Waterval Boven in search of stores to replenish our almost empty larder The latter were very successful, securing Quaker oats *chianti*, and butter—the latter a great luxury which we had not seen for some considerable time. On their journey back from there, they travelled with our prisoners escaped from Nooitgedacht, several of whom were clothed in all sorts of weird costumes. To one of the latter, dressed in short knickerbockers, a sweater, and socks, a sergeant called out, 'What time's the kick-off?' The ex-prisoner did not appreciate the jest.

On the morning of September 5, orders were received for No. 1 gun to trek to Carolina. No. 2 gun and crew, under the major of marines, remained at Belfast, taking up a position and entrenching themselves on Monument Hill. Here they remained until the gun was turned over to the army, and the Naval Brigade returned to Pretoria *en route* for Simonstown.

Starting on the morning of the 5th with No. 1 gun, we were given an escort of Brabant's Horse, in addition to our own escort of Black Watch, which had been with us since Johannesburg, and marched to Van Wyk's Vlei, where we joined Colonel Spens's battalion and a squadron of the 18th Hussars.

On reaching Carolina, we found it a small town, much the same as Middelburg and others, and boasting a doctor, two or three stores, a bank, a good water supply, and the usual church in the middle of the usual square.

On Sunday, September 9, having repaired the brake-blocks, which sadly needed it, we were on the move again, being under the command of General French, with the 1st and 4th Cavalry Brigades, Mahon's brigade, and an infantry brigade under Colonel Spens. Early in. the day we were in difficulties, as we missed the right road and got into a dense fog, which, besides keeping us in semi-darkness, was exceedingly cold. We also did a thing we had done before occasionally—namely, got held fast in a bog, which delayed us half an hour. However, we picked up the main column in safety and at 11.30 a.m. outspanned.

Shortly after noon the R.H.A. battery became engaged with the enemy, but our infantry brigade advancing soon drove them off, with only one casualty on our side. At 4 p.m. we moved on and occupied the hill lately occupied by the Boers, and here encamped for the night.

Next day we moved on again and crossed the three *drifts* of Buffelspruit, and on the following evening encamped opposite Taval Kop, where the Boers were supposed to be in force.

Next morning, September 12, Gordon's 1st Cavalry Brigade, with 100 mounted infantry, worked down to the south of the enemy's position, whilst the remainder of the force threatened from the southwest. The 4.7 was brought to a small *kopje* and laid for a *nek* where the Boers were reported to be, Gordon meanwhile attacking from the south-east.

General French, who was on our *kopje*, at 7.45 a.m. received a message from General Gordon that he had captured one of the enemy's *laagers*, and at eight o'clock we were ordered to advance. At 10.30 we came to a small *kopje* and found a battery of Royal Artillery firing at the *nek* occupied by the Boers. The infantry advanced shortly afterwards, and the Boers, as usual, vanished. We saw, however, several of their wagons slowly trekking up a steep hill, unfortunately out of range; they had, though, to abandon about half a dozen of them later on.

The road up the *nek* was so steep that only treble-spanned ox-wagons could go up, so that it took some days to get the whole force to the top. General French and the 1st Cavalry Brigade went on ahead into Barberton, where he liberated several captured officers and some men of the Duke of Cambridge's Own Yeomanry, and found fifty-two locomotives, all in fairly good condition. The whole of the little column halted at Nelsburg, at the top of the *nek*.

Starting from here on September 19, we came in for some very troublous times. In the forenoon the top of the 'chute,' which is very steep, was reached. On going down, several Gape carts capsized, and one of the wagons 'took charge' for twenty or thirty yards and three oxen had to be shot in consequence—one poor brute having a horn torn off, another a leg broken, and a third his hind foot crushed. One gun wheel also gave us considerable anxiety. The next day the gun wheel broke down completely. However, necessity is the mother of invention, and an ingenious officer suggested using a spare wagon wheel; so after a short interval the gun made its way into Barberton, the largest town, outside the capitals, we had come across. We encamped two miles outside.

Several Scotch residents welcomed the advent of the British troops into Barberton with enthusiasm, and all sorts of entertainments were got up in their honour—dances, at which several officers and some charming Dutch ladies assisted and no introductions were needed, musical evenings, and a hunt.

The gun wheel, meanwhile, had been repaired, and the gun remounted, chiefly owing to the energy and resource shown by our armourer.

On Monday, October 1, orders were received to turn over the gun and ammunition to Major Taylor, B.A.; this was done, and on October 2 we bade farewell to Barberton on our return journey. We left by train, but on reaching Avoca had to walk a couple of miles, transhipping our gear, as the bridge had been blown up, and a new one had not yet been built. More troubles awaited us, as before we had got halfway to Kaapmuiden in the new train, the engine broke down, and we had to wait there till the morning, during the night being drenched to the skin by a bad storm. We reached Kaapmuiden in safety next morning, and breakfasted there. Going on, all went well till Witbank was reached. From here the engine-driver hoped to run through by night to Pretoria; but was stopped at the next station, Brugspruit, as the commandant there had received information that the Boers were going to cross the line from north to south that night between Brugspruit and Balmoral.

Our captain wished to prevent this, and at 9.30 p.m. we left accompanied by a few mounted infantry and one company of the Buffs, and preceded by a ganger and trolley. After proceeding slowly for about three miles, we came to a ganger's cottage, and left here fifteen men under a N.C.O. Here the ganger, for some inexplicable reason, took the trolley off the line, and after proceeding about one hundred and fifty yards, there was a loud explosion and the engine was thrown off the line. The fireman was hurled out of the engine into a ditch, but only sprained his ankle slightly. On this happening, the ganger was sent back to Brugspruit to inform the commandant and to ask for a gun, men were placed along the line in pairs on either side, and our sergeant-major with a party of marines was sent on ahead to establish communication with the company of Buffs in front. Next morning the breakdown gang arrived, and the engine was raised on to the rails again. Some Boers attacked the mounted infantry, but on being fired on by a 15-pounder which had been sent out, retired hastily. The overseer of the line (late of the CI.V.) had gone on to Balmoral on a trolley and reported the line clear, but the train had hardly proceeded two hundred yards when it was blown up again. This time, luckily, no truck was derailed, and, after a new rail had been laid, it went slowly on again, but not before the overseer and the engine-driver (the latter very reluctantly) had gone over part of the line with the engine.

After spending a miserably wet night at Bronker's Spruit we reached Pretoria next day at 10 a.m., and were joined by the major of marines with No. 2 gun's crew from Belfast, and by the gunnery lieutenant with his 12-pounder detachment from Komati Poort, the Naval Brigade being once more complete, but without its guns.

That afternoon, drawn up outside the railway station, we were inspected by Lord Roberts, who made a pleasant little speech of fare-well. The officers were then introduced to him, and the brigade gave him three rousing cheers as he rode away with his staff. More cheers were given for General Pole-Carew, who was also present, and bade us goodbye; he was immensely popular with us, and, indeed, with everyone else.

We left Pretoria at 12.45 that night, and proceeded on our journey back to Simonstown. We passed through Kroonstad next night, and at Bloemfontein picked up a large load of stores which had not yet been sent up to us. General Kelly-Kenny came to the station to say good-bye, and we passed quickly down the rest of the line.

At Wellington the men were entertained by the ladies of the town to breakfast, and at 2 p.m., October 12, we reached Simonstown, be-ing received with great enthusiasm.

WINBURG: 4.7 GUN, WITH HALF THE TEAM, DRAWN UP IN FRONT OF THE OFFICERS' MESS

CHAPTER 1

Join 9th Division and March to Winburg

Before leaving Bloemfontein the Naval Brigade was divided into two sections.

Grant's two 4.7's formed one of these, and at daybreak, April 23, we descended Naval Hill—the guns being lowered down by hand—and marched due east in the wake of the Highland Brigade. We bivouacked at Klip Kraal (21½ miles), trekked again at 6 a.m., crossed Koorn Spruit, and had a very stiff pull up the steep and stony sides of Mamena Kop, at the top of which the two guns were placed in position about three hundred yards apart.

De Wet, after his failure at Wepener, was being hustled northward, and we hoped to be able to bar his retreat or damage him as he broke through the Bloemfontein-Ladybrand line.

Four days later the doctor was ordered by telegram to return to Simonstown. The propriety of this move was hardly apparent to the uninitiated, as it left us without either doctor or medical staff of any sort. However, there was no help for it; so the medicines and medical comforts were turned over to another officer, who received them with some misgivings, but with a perfectly open mind as to their various uses, and we were left doctorless.

On the 30th the guns were lowered down the hill again—we were becoming quite adept at this—and marched ten miles to Waterval Drift. The road led along a razor-backed ridge which sloped sharply away on either side to a depth of fifteen to twenty feet. The road itself was in places only nine and a half feet wide, and the gun wheels spanned seven feet; so there wasn't much 'to veer and haul on.' However, this was safely passed; but, unfortunately, in crossing the *drift* the

Cape boy leader, instead of taking his oxen straight on, followed the curve of the road. The result was that the bight of the team was pulled out straight, and, in spite of the helm being hard a-port. No. 1 fell into a deep ditch and capsized on to the near wheel. With the assistance of the Royal Engineers and our escort of the Argyll and Sutherland Highlanders it was again on the march in twenty minutes.

The Naval Brigade halted at this *drift* for two nights, and, as the guns were in position, of course it necessitated sleeping at them; and very cold work it was.

On May 2 we moved off at 6 a.m., and marched to Fairfield (13 miles) in company with the 9th Division, under Sir Henry Colvile, which formed the eastern column in the advance northward from Bloemfontein.

Shortly before arriving at Fairfield a considerable rifle-fire broke out, and a scout galloped in to report that the right flanking party was engaged. Two battalions were extended, and the two naval 4.7's' stood by.'

However, it turned out to be a spirited engagement between our mounted infantry and a patrol of the 21st Brigade. The former claimed the victory, having killed a horse belonging to their temporary enemies.

Found here the 2nd Cavalry Brigade, 19th and 21st Infantry Brigades. These all moved off next morning, as did the field battery. We marched at 9.30 a.m. ten miles to Papjei's Vlei.

On the 4th we marched at 6 a.m., and at 9 came up with the advance guard and scouts, who had located the enemy in position on a very large and steep *kop* known as Baboon Kop, which lay just to the right of the line of march. This position the Highland Brigade attacked under cover of our fire. We shelled the position heavily, and, from information gained from prisoners, got pretty well among them (one shell was said to have killed and wounded thirty odd). The Highland Brigade were delighted at the slight loss sustained, as the place looked like another Magersfontein. We bivouacked for the night, having marched ten miles.

Marched on the two following days eleven miles and thirteen miles to Winburg, crossing some nasty *drifts* on the way. Here the guns were placed in position to the north-east of the town. We remained here fifteen days until May 22, on which day we marched with two battalions (the other two having preceded us to Ventersburg) and the divisional troops. The strength of the naval detachment and its belongings was now as follows: Officers, 3; seamen and stokers, 60; conductors, 3; natives, 42; wagons, 13; carts, 3; guns, 2 (4.7); horses, 7; trek-oxen, 290; ammunition (4.7), 570 rounds.

We marched nineteen miles to Zand River, and on the 23rd fifteen and a half miles to Roode Kraal, where the other two battalions rejoined. On the 24th and 25th we marched eighteen and sixteen miles respectively. A certain amount of opposition was encountered on these days, but as the 4.7's did not actually come into action it is not necessary to go into details. On the 26th we marched at 6.30 a.m. along a bad road with numerous *spruits*. (The small *drifts* through these *spruits* were always more troublesome than the larger ones through rivers.)

At about 10.30 the enemy were found to be in position on a high ridge lying right across our front, which we proceeded to shell at 3,700 yards. The infantry made a turning movement, and this, in conjunction with our fire, proved to be too much for the Boers' nerves, and away they went. The Eastern Province Horse suffered some loss, as on the previous days, and there were some casualties among the infantry. We then resumed the march to Lindley, the enemy engaging us on the right flank for the greater part of the day. Bivouacked to the north of the town, after marching sixteen miles.

May 27.—A very cold and windy day. The rearguard were engaged immediately on leaving Lindley, and were so for most of the day. Just before sunset we crossed Rhenoster Spruit, about two and a half feet deep and icy cold—rather a bore just before getting in. One of the ammunition guard, an A.B., was this day run over by an ox-wagon. It was loaded to about five thousand pounds with ammunition, the road was hard, and the front wheel passed over his right ankle and left leg below the knee, yet without breaking any bones!

The morning of the 28th was very cold; ten degrees of frost at 8 a.m. Got under way about 9, and marched till 10.30, when we were ordered to come into action on the left of the road. Had a great race with the field battery. Our way of taking the gun's muzzle first saved a great deal of time when coming into action. The '*voorloeper*' understood the order 'Action front' as well as anyone, and was taught to turn his leading bullocks sharp round and double (in both senses) the team back. As the last pair turned the wire span slackened and was unshackled. The gun, being already pointing in the desired direction, was all ready for action when unlimbered. The enemy were holding a high ridge on the opposite side of a valley. We shelled this heavily and drove them out, the infantry then advancing over it.

We were told to bring our guns on as quickly as possible, which we did. Just as we topped the ridge (the first Boer position) shell began falling pretty thickly all around us from two guns down in the valley beyond. After about a quarter of an hour of this we got their range and cleared them out, moving No. 2 gun four hundred yards to the front. Fighting was by this time pretty general round all points of the compass. The Highland Light Infantry were engaged in front, and the Seaforths were moved to the right flank to resist a considerable body of Boers who were trying hard to get in from that direction. The latter were very determined, and the Seaforths had to be reinforced.

The rearguard (Argyll and Sutherland Highlanders) were also heavily engaged, and keeping up a tremendous rifle fire. Half a battalion Black Watch were engaged on the left flank, the remaining half being with headquarters and naval guns. Even the Royal Engineers company were acting as infantry, and were engaged on the left rear. The 4.7's were in action up to 4.30 p.m., firing as opportunity offered, though not as freely as we should have liked, the G.O.C.'s orders as to economy of ammunition being most stringent. At 6 p.m. we bivouacked for the night, much in the places where we finished fighting. Things were looking rather queer, as we were practically surrounded, eighteen or nineteen miles from our objective (Heilbron), and on one-third rations. Our oxen were showing signs of the heavy marching and insufficient food, poor brutes!

The next morning was again extremely cold. We marched at 6 a.m.. No. 1 gun remaining in position while the column crossed a *drift*, and moving on with the rearguard. No. 2 gun was advanced about three miles, and was then placed in position until No. 1 came up. The guns were moved alternately all day (a plan which proved most effective in keeping the enemy at a respectful distance), coming into action several times. About 10 a.m. the enemy opened with three guns from the right flank, throwing shell with considerable accuracy among the transport and right flank-guard. Both naval guns came into action, and silenced the opposing guns temporarily. They did not open fire again until 3.30 p.m., by which time the transport had crossed the dangerous open ground. We did not get into camp until after dark, the last few miles being weary work, a thick cloud of fine dust which hung to a height of five feet above the ground making the march very distressing for man and beast.

We lost fifteen oxen from our guns and wagons on this day alone, and forty-two since leaving Bloemfontein, replacing them as opportunity offered. Bivouacked at Heilbron at 7 p.m., having marched eighteen miles or over. This made 128½ miles in eight days, with fighting on five days, three being general engagements. Our 'marching in' state was the same as on leaving Winburg, with the exception of the one injured man.

On June 2 it was decided to dig pits for the guns. This work was carried out by the Royal Engineers, the pits being respectively thirty and twenty-six feet in diameter (No. 2 gun, having a wooden trail, required a larger space than No. 1). The bluejackets were started digging 'ready magazines,' two in each pit. This was done by cutting down through the ground to the floor of the pit for a distance of three feet at right angles to the circumference; then, taming at right angles, a further cutting of three and a half feet was made. The cutting was roofed over with railway sleepers sunk below the level of the berm and covered with earth. The work was very laborious, as the ground was extremely stony, the picks having to be reground twice a day.

Blistered hands became universal; but the sailors worked with a will, and in two days the guns were in their new position and forty-eight rounds in each pit. The pits were connected by a trench ninety yards in length and four feet in depth. By this time the enemy were entrenched on the surrounding heights, but did not make any more actively offensive movements. This was probably due to the fact that they could not open fire on any portion of our force without risk of damaging the town—a proceeding from which they have always been averse.

On June 20 No. 2 gun was moved out in company with the Seaforths, two companies Highland Light Infantry, two guns Royal Field Artillery, and mounted details, to cover the entrance of a convoy escorted by Lord Methuen. After marching three and a half miles to the north-west we sighted Methuen's force about twelve miles off, and between us and them we saw a considerable force of Boers in position on two steep *kopjes*, between which the road to Heilbron ran. The ridges of these were lined by Boers, who appeared to be watching the convoy so intently that they were quite oblivious of what was going on behind them. We were at very long range, but could not get closer, as the ground fell away sharply in front of us, and we should have lost sight of them by going on; so tried a round of common at 9,000 yards, which appeared to land fairly in the middle of them.

The scene for the next few minutes was most amusing. They mounted and galloped to the right, but another shell scattered them in all directions. If we had only been close enough to use shrapnel we could have inflicted heavy loss. They were more numerous and closer together than we ever saw them in the open, either before or after. However, we kept them moving and accounted for a certain number, and the much-needed convoy marched in without opposition amid the cheers of the rather hungry garrison.

During the remainder of the halt at Heilbron nothing of special interest occurred. Various reports as to the movements of the enemy (usually accompanied by corroborative details *re* De Wet with x men and y guns) kept us fairly busy, a gun being always moved out to cover troops going in or out, convoys, &c.

On July 27 orders were received to evacuate Heilbron. The job of entraining our guns, wagons, bullocks, &c., was fairly arduous, most of it being carried out through a dark, cold night. The Naval Brigade was spread over several trains, as the trucks were not always of a suitable description. Meanwhile the enemy were closing in, and when the last of the Naval Brigade left (the last train but one), were not two miles away. They did not molest us, the fact of our having a 'leading resident' on each train perhaps accounting for this policy of non-interference (the one on our train was praying aloud when it started). A most unpleasant journey brought us to Krugersdorp. It rained and blew and was very cold. An open bogey-truck, with an inch or so of coal dust in it, which gradually turned into a black mud, cannot be recommended as a comfortable conveyance.

Chapter 2

250 Miles in Fifteen Days

We had only just settled down after twenty-four hours at Krugersdorp when, about midday on July 31, orders arrived to entrain guns and wagons as rapidly as possible, but to leave the oxen behind. The last part was a blow, as we had utilised our long stay at Heilbron in perfecting the teams, and they were just about as good as they could be. We were 'all aboard' by 6 p.m., and started off shortly after, arriving at Kopjes Station, south of the branch line to Heilbron, at 11 a.m. the following day. The new oxen arrived that evening, and were a poor lot compared with those we had left behind. Grossed the railway and camped near to the 2nd Batt. Marched at 6.80 a.m. on August 2, fifteen and a half miles to Wonderpeusal, where we bivouacked between the 6th and some cavalry (13th).

De Wet was holding a chain of *kopjes* running across a bight of the Vaal River, roughly from opposite Vredefort on the east to a big *kop* called Rhebok Kop on the west. On the following day, about 8 a.m., the Boers opened fire, with a 16-pounder, on the camp of the 1st Sherwood Foresters. As our oxen were grazing at some distance, five companies of the 6th were sent to drag the guns up to the top of the ridge. This they did at the doable, passing through a soft mealie-field on the way. After a little trouble in finding the range we burst a shell (shrapnel) right on top of the Boer gun, killing or disabling four of the gun's crew and smashing one wheel. (This we heard from an escaped prisoner.)

On the night of the 6th De Wet broke away, crossed the river, and trekked off along the road to Zeerust. Away we all went: two cavalry brigades, one mounted infantry brigade, and the infantry. This was the beginning of a very heavy and trying march. On August 7 marched ten miles to Bloemfontein. No. 2 gun (which had been detached on the 4th) rejoined here. Shortly after bivouacking the armourer reported that one of the wheels of No. 1 gun was showing signs of weakness. After careful examination it was found that the web of the wheel was sheared at the point where it entered the boss for a distance of some two or three inches.

This accident will be, perhaps, better understood if the wheel be considered as an ordinary wheel, the *inner* ends of the spokes of which had broken just where they enter the hub. It will be easily seen that, in the event of this shearing continuing right round, there would be nothing to prevent the whole wheel from falling over. The various bumps and strains incidental to trekking on South African roads would naturally tend to increase the damage.

After consultation with the Royal Engineers, Royal Artillery, and Army Service Corps, it was decided to try and screw bolts into the boss on either side of the web to minimise the lateral motion. Our appliances were limited, but we borrowed a ratchet drill and a set of tape and dies from the Royal Artillery and set to work. Four bolts were put in and we marched at 6 a.m. on the 9th, fifteen miles through Parys to Modderfontein. On August 10, at 5 a.m., marched five miles to Lindeque Drift (Vaal River), where we were obliged to halt to allow the 2nd Cavalry Brigade baggage to cross. The river here was quite pretty, but we were more inclined for rest than scenery. Eventually the *drift* was clear at 1.15 p.m., and the guns crossed.

The road down to the river was very steep, rough, and winding, and the first eighty or ninety yards of the river bed was dry, but very rough and stony; which did not tend to improve the damaged wheel. Several of the bolts (of which we had put in eight) worked out, and the opposite wheel was found to be going in the same way. The last fifty or sixty yards was through three or four feet of water—the men steering being frequently *towed*. One of them was heard to remark that 'it was about time they piped "Leadsman in the chains!"' Then came a long and weary pull up a hill for over a mile. We bivouacked at Losberg, in all nineteen miles. The country for as far as one could see was all burnt. Put three more nuts in the gun-wheels, the armourer working till after 2 a.m.

Marched again at 6 a.m. on the 11th. This was a day to be remembered. A strong head wind (force about 6-7) would have been sufficient by itself to make marching rather heavy work, and when this was accompanied by a steady stream of dust and the ashes from the burnt grass, it became almost intolerable. By the time we got in (3.30 p.m.)

eyes were smarting, streaming, and almost closed, and the skin round both eyes and nostrils cracked and bleeding. However, it was eighteen miles more put behind as. Our troubles were not over for the day, as, when we were settling down for the night, most of the men's bedding, &c., being on the ground, we were warned by a cloud of smoke and a loud crackling that the grass (which just here was long and thick) had been fired to windward of us.

Turned the weary sailors out, with bags, overcoats, &c., but the wind was too much for them, and the fire swept through the bivouac, much of the bedding being destroyed, and an ammunition wagon set on fire. This was extinguished before anything serious occurred, but the loss of bedding and partial destruction of leather gear was a nuisance.

All the bolts on the wheels were found to have sheared or drawn, and the unfortunate armourer again spent a night at work, assisted by the gun's crew in spells. The bolts had to be taken from wagons or anywhere they could be found, and a thread made on them. An angle-iron was made after a fashion, by bending a bit of iron tyre in the cooking fire, and was bolted to boss and wheel. Captain Grant's reference to this indefatigable man may well be quoted here. Extract from Letter of Proceedings. Naval Brigade, Krugersdorp, August 28, 1900:—

I must bring to your notice the zeal and energy displayed during the march by Joseph Tuck, armourer's mate, of H.M.S. *Barrosa*. It was due to his exertions that the guns could be taken along; every halt, day or night, being utilised by him, aided by the guns' crews, to repair, replace nuts, &c. . . .

A general order, complimenting the troops on their marching, endurance, and general conduct, was issued this night (11th), and a special issue of rum ordered. Great joy, which was somewhat discounted by the final paragraph:—

Reveille will sound at 2 a.m., the force will march at 3.

12th.—Marched at 3 a.m., arriving at Welverdiend (on the Klerksdorp line) at 9.45 a.m., fourteen miles. Found here the cavalry, Mounted Infantry, and Smith-Dorrien's brigades, so we had come along a steady pace. No. 1 gun was now staggering like a drunken man, the wheels describing a sort of figure 8 in the air. It was decided to leave it with a Gunner, R.N., and seven men, for repairs, which

132

were carried out at Pretoria. The remainder of the brigade moved on to Blaauwbank, six miles.

August 13.—Marched five miles, crossing the Mooi River (four feet deep and very cold), and bivouacking at 8 a.m. To our horror No. 2 gun was found to have taken the same complaint in the wheels as No. 1, and was accorded the same treatment. The G.O.C.'s only comment was, 'You've *got* to bring it on.'

Marched again at 11 a.m. to Schoolplaatz, in all fifteen miles. We were still pretty close behind our friend De Wet, in spite of sore feet and weary animals. He was engaged by Lord Methuen only twenty miles away, and we continually passed indications of his being hard pressed, in the shape of abandoned transport, dead beasts by the score, &c.

August 14.—Resumed the march at 7.30 a.m. fifteen miles to Klip Krantz, arriving at 3.45 p.m., and marching again at midnight, thirteen and a half miles to Rietfontein, where most of as went to sleep on arrival. De Wet, who was for the *nth* time supposed to be absolutely cornered, had escaped through Oliphant's Nek. Shifted camp in the afternoon, two and a half miles, to better water. On the morning of the 16th received orders to go to the relief of Colonel Hoare's force, which was held up on the Eland's River. Marched at 8 a.m., but, after going three miles, intercepted a cyclist orderly (C.I.V.) who was taking orders to the various columns to go to various places, some to Pretoria, us to Krugersdorp, and so on.

We accordingly returned to Rietfontein, but apparently were wrong in so doing, as we started off again at 1 a.m. (17th) along the same road. Halted at Tweefontein at 9.45 a.m. after covering twenty-one miles. Marched again at 2 p.m., but, after three miles, were ordered by heliograph to proceed to Krugersdorp. Bivouacked at Tweefontein, having marched twenty-seven miles since 1 a.m. The left gun-wheel was now sheared for all but about two inches. Captain Grant was obliged to tell the general that it was unsafe, and to ask permission to place the gun on a wagon.

After some consideration this was agreed to, on the understanding that we were to mount and fire the gun inside of an hour, if required. This was a great relief, as the last few days had been like a bad dream—one had been so constantly on the lookout for even small stones and holes, which might make the damage worse. Marched on the 16th six miles to Leeuwfontein. On arrival the trail of the carriage was sunk about a foot. A wagon was emptied and backed over the trail with the wheels on either side of it. A purchase was hooked to a strop round the dessel-boom of the wagon, and to a pendant toggled through the gun; a few rollers on the floor of the wagon completed the arrangements, and the gun was drawn out of the cradle and on to the wagon without difficulty.

August 19.—Marched at 6 a.m. seventeen miles to Vlakfontein. The mounting, thus lightened, got along very well, the men steering reporting that she was 'rather quick on the helm.' There were many jests from the soldiers about 'guns with sore feet riding on wagons,' and so on.

August 20.—Marched seventeen and a half miles to Cypherfontein. The enemy annoyed us a little this day on the right flank and rear, and on the left front.

August 21.—Marched nineteen and a half miles to Rietfontein, and on the 22nd eleven miles to Krugersdorp, arriving about noon, very glad too. This completed 250 miles in fifteen consecutive days.

On arrival at Krugersdorp No. 2 gun was placed in the hands of a local firm for the necessary repairs, which consisted of casting new bosses and placing a circular plate on either side of the fractured webs. Bolts were then placed through bosses, plates, and webs, and riveted over. No. 1 gun had, in the meanwhile, been repaired at Pretoria, and rejoined on August 28. The number of oxen lost on the above march was sixty-one (several more never recovered), but there was not a single case of sickness among officers or men.

On August 29 General Hart's column again started on the trek. No. 2 gun, being still under repair, was left behind with a lieutenant, thirteen men, four wagons, 280 rounds, and the necessary oxen, boys, &c. The repairs to the wheels of this gun being completed, the carriage was brought up to the camp on the afternoon of September 3, the wagon containing the gun being placed in the same relative position as described when dismounting. A pickaxe was buried and 'backed 'by another at some twenty yards from the mounting; the purchase being hooked to these and to a pendant through the gun, which was mounted and ready for firing in seventeen minutes, the only people employed being the men and 'boys' attached to the naval detachment.

This operation was watched with great interest by officers and men of the garrison. The gun was then placed in position, covering the heights to the north of the town. A few minor operations took place near this post during the time that the gun was attached to General Barton's force, but not of sufficient importance to be worth describing.

CHAPTER 3

The Potchefstroom Column

On the afternoon of August 29, No. 1 gun ('Little Bobs') of Grant's Brigade with 300 rounds of ammunition left Krugersdorp with General Hart's Potchefstroom column, composed of two and a half battalions of infantry, a composite company of mounted infantry, and a field battery.

By the evening of the 30th the force had only marched ten miles, rain having delayed the start each day and the roads being very bad. The gun 'hung up' once in the soft ground and was dug out with difficulty.

August 31.—Marched ten miles to Waterpan and found the enemy holding a position near the Johannesburg waterworks, which they had unsuccessfully attacked during the morning. They were dislodged without difficulty, the 4.7 firing two rounds at short range.

On September 1 we marched to Jackfontein, halted there for three days to clear the district of all food stuffs, wagons and cattle, and marched through the night of the 3rd to Leeuwport. Arriving here at daybreak news came that some Yeomanry were in a tight place four miles to the west, so No. 1, the field guns and some infantry moved out at 1 p.m. to relieve them. Thirteen rounds were fired, the enemy driven off, and the little force returned, bat the Boers came back again, on some ridges to the north, and had to be cleared off, camp not being reached till the evening. No. 1 had fired twenty-four rounds during the day.

On the 5th we marched eight miles to Woolstadt, the gun being in action off and on for the greater part of the day. Fired fifteen rounds and found a few Boers dead, including their commandant Theron.

The force arrived at Welverdiend on the railway early September 7

after a long night march, drew fresh supplies and left again the following night, clearing the country round Klerksdaal.

September 9.—At dusk the force split up into three sections and,
marching by different routes and at different speeds, started off to
surprise Potchefstroom. B column, to which the naval gun was attached, marched thirty-seven miles during the night, the bluejackets taking turns to ride on the ammunition wagons, and arrived off
Potchefstroom at 8 a.m., finding the more mobile A column already
surrounding the town. They had reached their destination before daylight and posted pickets round it. At daybreak the enemy tried to
escape, a few managing to run the gauntlet successfully. Of the remainder some were wounded and the rest turned back into the town
and surrendered.

Our gun having been placed in position to command the town,
the infantry advanced and took possession of it, capturing about eighty
prisoners besides a quantity of arms, &c.

The 11th was occupied in a house-to-house search, and all people having any munitions of war were made prisoners and their
places confiscated. The bluejackets took part in this proceeding and
enjoyed it immensely. The following night, leaving a small garrison,
we marched along the Ventersdorp Road, but halted soon afterwards,
for Boers were ahead. Starting off at daylight, we soon sighted them
and fired eleven rounds after them at long range. They bolted, and
we marched on into Frederickstad—sixteen miles—and halted for a
week, transferring prisoners and captures to the railway, getting provisions from Welverdiend, and fifty rounds of ammunition from No. 2
gun at Krugersdorp.

The gun was in action on two occasions whilst here, firing three
rounds on the 14th, and thirty-five rounds on the 17th. On the latter
afternoon, the enemy got a gun up behind a ridge, nearly four thousand yards off, and began dropping shells among the transport. We
found great difficulty in locating it, but eventually saw the flash of the
discharge, quickly got the range, and dropped a lyddite shell almost on
top of it. The gun (or guns) shortly afterwards bolted, leaving behind
many empty brass 12-pounder Krupp cases.

On the night of the 19th we marched westwards, twelve miles to
Witpootje. Boers were swarming all round, and before getting into
camp in the morning the 4.7 fired seventeen rounds, was at it again
after breakfast, moving out to help some Yeomanry in a difficulty in

a wood, and again in the afternoon helped turn the enemy out of a comparatively strong position, punishing them severely as they fled. Seventy-one rounds were fired during the day.

Next morning the Boers had come back to the ridges, but fled in front of the force when it advanced.

In the afternoon we came across quite a number of Boers in an open plain, but unfortunately, when hastening to take advantage of their exposed position a shell jammed in the gun after the second round, and by the time it was shifted the opportunity was gone. The Boers retired slowly in front of us all day.

On the 22nd great efforts were made to surprise a *laager*, but it succeeded in getting away. We fired five rounds, and one long shot was said to have killed and wounded twelve; marched thirty-seven miles in twenty-five hours and had only a few prisoners to show for our labours.

On the 25th the little column returned to Potchefstroom, which the Boers had reoccupied after the withdrawal of our little garrison. As we neared it we saw them leaving, and hauled down their flag which they had left flying over the court-house.

Orders were then received to return to Krugersdorp, which was reached after four marches on September 30.

The Potchefstroom column had marched 310 miles in twenty marching days, and No. 1 gun had fired 187 rounds, 22 common, 64 shrapnel and 101 lyddite. Only one man had fallen out and gone sick during the march.

On October 2 'Little Bobs' and 'Sloper' were turned over to the Royal Garrison Artillery, and by 3 p.m. all that was left of Grant's brigade—the men and their personal equipment—was entrained and left for Simonstown, arriving there without incident on the 7th.

In transmitting the field marshal's orders, General Hart wrote wishing Commander Grant and the little brigade goodbye, adding:

> . . . Well assisted by your subordinates, you have overcome serious campaigning difficulties with a ponderous gun which has deservedly become the terror of the enemy.

So ends the story of our performances, which cannot be finally concluded without a few remarks. As to the general behaviour and deportment of our men, the extract from Captain Grant's despatches given below is almost sufficient. It is enough to say that the hardest work and greatest discomfort count for nothing when one remembers the cheery spirit in which the work was always carried out. The men never forgot what service they belonged to.

Extract from Commander Grant's final despatch:

> ... I have much pleasure in reporting that the spirit, endurance, and behaviour of the officers and men throughout the campaign has been beyond praise. Work, often under conditions of great hardship, requiring endurance and spirit to a very high degree, has been met throughout with the greatest spirit and cheeriness, and the smartness, discipline, and soldierly qualities displayed will, I am sure, be ever remembered to their credit and to that of the Naval Service. In no single instance has Lieutenant Fergusson ever had to bring a man before me for any crime, neglect of duty, slackness, or any other offence whatsoever, and this for a period of nearly nine months. The marching powers displayed by the men have been to me a revelation. ...

Finally it must be said that the discomforts and annoyances incidental to any campaign were minimised as far as possible by the extreme kindness we met with from the sister service; in which remark everyone who was with our guns will concur.

SUMMARY OF MARCHES, ETC.

	Days.	Miles.	Av. per day
From Bloemfontein to Winburg	8	95½	11.94
From Winburg to Heilbron	8 (cons.)	127	15.9
After De Wet	17	265	15.6
Potchefstroom Column	20	310	15.5
	53	797½	15

In the De Wet chase 250 miles were marched in fifteen consecutive days, giving an average of 16.7.

The longest marches were	37 miles in 13 hrs
	,, ,, 25 hrs
Three marches were between 30 and 40 miles.	
Five ,, ,, ,, 20 ,, 30 ,,	
Twenty-eight ,, ,, ,, 15 ,, 20 ,,	

On the twenty-five occasions on which these two guns were in action (counting the whole of Paardeberg as one, though it extended over eight days) between 500 and 600 rounds were fired.

PART 5

From Belfast to Komati Poort

From the Diary of Lieut. E. P. C. Back, R.N.

After the occupation of Belfast, and the arrival there of the Naval Brigade under Captain Bearcroft, extensive operations were put on foot for driving the scattered remnants of the organised Boer forces, still holding the remainder of the Delagoa Bay line, either into the mountains or across the Portuguese frontier.

To effect this the 11th Division (Guards' and 18th Brigades), being the centre of three columns, commenced the eastward march on August 26, and was accompanied by a small, highly mobile Naval Brigade, consisting of two 'long' 12-pounders under Lieutenant Back, of H.M.S. *Monarch*.[1]

The Mounted Infantry and the Guards pushed forward that afternoon from Belfast, and hardly had debouched from Monument Hill when they were received by a heavy rifle and pom-pom fire from ridges in their front and a rooky valley on their right.

The two naval guns, waiting behind to protect the rear of the column, were hurried forward to support the 85th Field Battery; but the range of the hollow below, whence came the firing, was so short that they were of little use, with their flat trajectory, and fired but few rounds. Bullets were flying very thickly. By dusk the Guards had made but little headway, and all night intermittent sniping went on, under cover of which, however, the enemy slipped away.

At daybreak a Boer 6. 2-inch commenced dropping his big shells with great accuracy on the ridge occupied by the division, and the

1. This brigade consisted of Lieut. Back, R.N., Lieut.-Com. Colquhoun, Royal Victorian Navy, Mr. Cunningham, midshipman, and thirty-six men. The transport included three mule- and three ox-wagons and a water-cart, fifty-eight moles, and fifty-four oxen. To look after these was a Colonial conductor (Mr. Duggan), and twelve 'Cape boys.'

two naval guns were 'called away' and advanced half a mile to help the 5-inch battery keep him quiet. This they presently managed to do, after expending forty-one rounds, fired at extreme elevation at a range of 9,000 yards, and thereby straining their improvised carriages considerably.

The enemy showed every sign of stubbornly contesting the advance, till the sound of heavy firing to the eastward indicated that Buller was in touch with them and fighting his way toward Machadodorp. With their left and rear thus both threatened, they gradually commenced to give way along their whole line, and the advance was resumed, the naval guns at first covering the rear and the long baggage train, and afterwards pushing ahead and occupying a commanding position to cover the advance.

Finally the division halted at Eland's Kloof for the night. An early start was made next morning, and, after a most remarkable and memorable march through the mountains, clothed in mist, and along steep and very rocky roads cut out of the steep sides, Helvetia was reached at noon and a junction with Buller effected.

Range after range had to be crossed; and it was an exceedingly striking sight, when at the summit of one of them, to see the road winding along the valleys and up the opposite mountains, covered, as far as eye could reach, with the snake-like, crawling supply columns.

Broken-down wagons and refractory or worn-out teams caused frequent obstructions; but the naval guns, with their powerful teams of ten mules, travelled at a great pace, and, helped frequently, both up and downhill, by the escorting company of Guards, managed to keep up with the head of the column.

In fact, so well to the front were they that when during the march a pom-pom suddenly opened on French's cavalry,[2] they were able promptly to silence it and compel the Boer rearguard, retiring sullenly on Lydenburg, to give ground.

After arriving at Helvetia the division was left in comparative peace, and the following day marched southward to the railway again, and bivouacked on the high ground overlooking Waterval Onder station.

From Nooigedacht (the next station along the line) the British prisoners were already streaming over the hills towards the camp, and the little Naval Brigade was very proud of having taken even a small share in their release.

---

2. *French's Cavalry Campaign: a Special Correspondent's View of British Army Mounted troops During the Boer War* by J. G. Maydon also published by Leonaur.

For eight days the division remained here whilst Buller was completing his turning movement to drive the Boers towards the frontier, and during this time one of the 12-pounder carriages, strained by the stress of high-angle firing and the wear and tear of rough roads, was replaced by a new one sent from Belfast. The wooden portion was 'sprang' close to the axle. It might have lasted, but it was safer to replace it; so the armourer 'took off his coat,' and in a few hours had fitted the old wheels and axle to the new carriage and remounted the gun. Armourer's Mate Smithfield (his name deserves recording) was simply invaluable. On one occasion he reforged a gun axle. He repaired wheels, wagons—even mended railway tracks; and whether as armourer, blacksmith, wheelwright, or carpenter, there was nothing he could not do, and do well.

It was from a saloon carriage in the siding here that Mr. Kruger had issued his edicts, paper money, and unstamped gold discs—'damps,' they were called. Several of these were obtained; and the simple (or wily) Frenchman, who kept the hotel, also parted with a few 'bluebacks,' which he felt sure 'would be paid in full.'

Meanwhile Buller had cleared the country to the north, and French was scouring the mountainous district to the south of the railway. So, the flanks being secured, the division and the naval guns advanced along the railway on September 11, reaching Godwan's River, twenty miles to the east, two days later, though not before the railway bridge had been destroyed.

Leaving the railway next day and marching south-east along the Barberton road, an exceedingly arduous climb of ten miles brought the division to Kaapsche Hoek, a little village perched in the mountains, where a welcome supply of bread was obtained, and from which a magnificent panorama of the combined operations could be seen.

To the north-east, fifty miles away, Buller's heliographs were flashing among the Lydenburg mountains, whilst to the south-east, where lay Barberton, nestling at the foot of the Swazi mountains on the other side of the Kaap valley, French's columns could be seen winding their way through the passes.

The 18th Brigade were left behind, and, with the Guards, the only infantry remaining with Pole-Carew, the march into the valley was resumed.

It was all downhill that day; and very trying it was too, for the bluejackets had to be on the drag-ropes nearly all the time, in several places the road being so steep that in spite of drag-ropes, brakes, and drag-shoes the guns and wagons skidded down.

The main road was left two days later, and, marching nearly due east and cutting a road through thick bush, over ground very rough and strewn with boulders, the Barberton branch line was reached at North Kaap station. Avoca was reached next day, a large number of locomotives and rolling stock being captured; and two days later, after difficult marches of ten and seven miles along disgusting roads, and after crossing numerous bad *spruits*, which tried the gun-wheels severely, the little force bivouacked at Kaapmuiden Junction, the Naval Brigade sharing the capture of more rolling stock and vast quantities of flour—most of which, however, had been saturated with paraffin and burnt; some was still on fire.

In nine days the naval 12-pounders had marched ninety miles, traversing a series of mountain ranges, and requiring constantly the most careful seamanship to get them safely up and down the steep roads. They had 'shown the way' to the heavier 6-inch guns, and even kept ahead of their old friends the 85th.

So good had been the pace that the supply column had dropped far astern, though the few naval ox-wagons, acting independently, generally managed to crawl into bivouac in time to replenish the small amount of mule forage carried with the guns. The naval mules thus received full rations up to the last day of the march, and reached their destination in capital condition. The oxen, however, did not fare so well. Excessive heat and scarcity of pasture killed a third of them.

After only one night's rest the column pushed on twenty miles towards Komati Poort through the Crocodile Valley—a wide, open valley, hot, stifling, and suggestive of malaria, covered with thorn, scrub, and occasional bright yellow fever-trees. On each side were ranges of low-lying hills, their outlines blurred and indistinct in the stifling mirage—altogether a most undesirable country, and almost waterless.

The naval guns happened to be leading the artillery, and to the bluejackets fell the work of clearing the thick thorn bush from the track, which had probably not been used for twenty years or more. To make matters worse, many *spruits* had to be crossed, and it was frequently necessary first to fill these with stones—a job sufficiently arduous under a hot sun. Everyone was pretty well fagged out by the time the bivouac was reached.

A march of seven miles brought the column to Hector Spruit station next day, and the first traces of the utter disorganisation of the Boer army were found here, for in the river bed were many damaged guns and vast quantities of abandoned stores.

Leaving the river the following morning (September 23), and striking right across country, Komati Poort, twenty-six miles away, was reached at 10.30 a.m. on the 24th.

The last fifty-four miles from Kaapmuiden had been done in four days, the 144 miles since leaving Waterval Onder in thirteen—splendid going, when the difficulties of road and climate are considered; and the travel-stained guns and their crews were only too glad of a rest.

The great railway bridge was intact, and for miles on each side of the line leading to it were scattered the abandoned and partially destroyed stores, arms, and ammunition of the main Boer army, which the previous day had fled over the Portuguese border.

An enormous amount of rolling stock blocked the line. Many of the trucks, filled with mealies, flour, sugar, and coffee, had been burnt or were still burning, and the heat thrown out by these made the atmosphere almost intolerable.

Here, also, damaged and useless, was the 'Long Tom,' which had so persistently harried the advance, and which certainly deserved a better fate.

For six days the little Naval Brigade remained at this sultry place, and then camp was struck for the last time, the transport handed over to the Army Service Corps, and the guns and ammunition stowed safely on trucks down by the station.

A half-drunken man who described himself as an engine driver raised steam in one of the captured engines, and at noon, October 1, after taking leave of General Pole-Carew, the Naval Brigade, which had the honour of helping to cut off the enemy's communication with Delagoa Bay, and had brought its guns further east than any other naval guns, started on its way back to the sea.

The funny little train, with six oddly assorted trucks and its dilapidated, crazy engine, had only crawled three miles before it came to a standstill, as steam could not be kept up.

The stoker stretcher-bearers, glad of an opportunity for displaying their professional knowledge, quickly discovered that the tubes wanted sweeping, manufactured substitutes for brushes, swept them clean, and after a time on went the engine again.

But a steep gradient proved too much for it, and, to the amusement of the soldiers in the train, the Naval Brigade, 'as one man,' jumped overboard, and with a shout of 'Shove her up, mates!' literally pushed the train up that hill.

A more serious accident occurred later on; for, whilst rounding a very sharp curve near Hector Spruit, another train was seen shunting in the station, and the engine-driver, knowing he had to do *something* in emergencies like this, opened out full steam and released the brakes, instead of doing the very opposite.

There was a crash. Several trucks were telescoped, and another, up-ending, fell back on two men (Royal Engineers), killing one and badly injuring the second.

It took two hours to clear the line, the never-failing drag-ropes proving most useful, and then the journey west was resumed.

Pretoria was reached at 9 a.m., October 5, without further incident, the little train jolting along by day and resting at night.

At Pretoria the brigade was absorbed into Headquarters Naval Brigade, recently recalled from Barberton and Belfast.

CHAPTER 1

Ordered to the Cape

On September 22, 1899, just as affairs in South Africa had reached a critical stage, H.M.S. *Powerful*, homeward bound from the China station, arrived at Singapore. Here, much to the satisfaction of all on board, she received orders to proceed home *viâ* the Cape, and, after coaling, sailed on the 24th.

Calling at Mauritius, she found there a half-battalion of the King's Own Y.L.I., thirsting for active service, obtained permission from London to embark them, and with this large addition to her complement thrashed across to Durban and Table Bay, disembarked the soldiers on October 13, and later that day cast anchor in Simon's Bay, where she met her 'relief' and sister ship, the *Terrible*.

Seven days later, her marines, and two 12-pounders, with their bluejacket crews, were sent ashore to join the first Naval Brigade landed daring the war, formed from all the ships lying in the bay, and placed under the command of Commander Ethelston, of the *Powerful*. They left immediately for Stormberg.

Then came Sir George White's urgent appeal for naval guns, and, when it was known that the *Powerful* was to carry the guns to Durban and send crews to fight them upcountry, the delight of her officers and men was unbounded.

The rest of the squadron lent a hand to fill her up with coal once more, and the day after the order was given she shipped two 4.7's from the dockyard with their stores and ammunition, and rushed back to Durban, no one perhaps realising that the fate of Ladysmith depended on her speed. Durban was reached two and a half days later (October 29), and in this short space of time wooden field-carriages were constructed by the ship's own skilled men for three long 12-pounders; crews, also, for the different guns were 'told off,' and two small-arm

LADYSMITH: CONNING TOWER OF THE NAVAL BRIGADE.
CAPTAIN LAMBTON OBSERVING BULWANA AND 'PUFFING BILLY'

companies, of fifty men each, were paraded in fighting trim, khaki clothes having been obtained from the military authorities.

By 5 p.m. all the paraphernalia of the brigade had been safely stowed in lighters, and was on its way ashore.

Then came the hurried goodbyes as the men filed down the gangway. 'Goodbye, Bill; shall I bring yer some o' Kruger's whiskers?' says one; 'None o' your carrying on with them Boer girls, Tommy,' is the parting advice of an unfortunate chum left behind. With suchlike chaff and banter they left their ship. The band played 'Auld Lang Syne,' the inconsolable ship's company left behind, swarming up the rigging and on the nettings, gave three vigorous cheers, and the *Powerful's* Naval Brigade 'shoved off.'

Directly after landing the work of loading the trains with all the 'gear' was hurried through, and by seven o'clock in the evening all were *en route* for Ladysmith and that mysterious locality known as the 'front.'

Loyal Durban turned out 'as one man 'to watch the landing of the men and their guns, and cheered again and again as the snorting engines steamed slowly away with their heavy loads. Once the open country was reached the bluejackets started singing popular songs, the strains of 'Jolly young Jacks are we,' and 'We've got a long way to go,' waking the echoes of the bleak and rocky hills, round the sides of which the Natal Railway winds its ever ascending way.

Sleep was impossible, for the men, at any rate, so tightly were they packed, so cold the night, and so 'wobbly' the permanent way. Pietermaritzburg was reached at 1 a.m., and, late though the hour, the harassed governor, Sir W. Hely-Hutchinson, met the two trains. He had grave doubts whether Ladysmith would be reached in time for the great and decisive battle, which was hourly expected to take place there, and feared that the railway line might be already torn up.

On went the trains, however, reaching Estcourt at dawn, and Colenso, only twenty miles from Ladysmith, at 8.30 a.m. Here it was found that the line was still clear, and that the big fight was even now proceeding, and an already intense excitement was raised to a still higher pitch by hearing the distant booming of guns.

With a full head of steam the remaining distance was ran without further incident, though all precautions were taken, and a Maxim gun rigged to fire out of the guard's van, in case it should be necessary to force a way through any small bodies of the enemy.

CHAPTER 2

Under Fire

'Hullo, who are you chaps?' said a hard-worked sergeant of the Army Service Corps, as the truck-loads of strange-looking khaki-clad figures, with their straw hats enveloped in brown-stained linen covers, drew up near the detraining platform.

'Oh,' answered the loquacious yeoman of signals, 'don't you know who we are? We're the Naval Brigade from the *Powerful*,' with a 'and-don't-you-forget-it' kind of air.

'How's the fight going?'

'Oh, we're knocking spots out of them, and our cavalry are chasing them round the back of that hill,' pointing to a long flat-topped mountain to the eastward. 'Didn't you see any of them running away as you came along?'

One had to acknowledge missing the entertaining spectacle, and further conversation was put a stop to by the trains moving on into the station.

The arrival was heralded by a few shells from what was afterwards ascertained to be the Boer 6-inch gun, the same weapon which had played a prominent part in forcing our troops to evacuate Dundee a few days before, and which had already been christened and soon became celebrated as 'Long Tom of Pepworth Hill.' The shells, with a sickening scream, passed close over the railway station, causing a universal 'ducking' of heads amongst the officers and men who were hurriedly detraining, and it was with curiously inquiring expressions on their faces that they watched these deadly missiles burst a few hundred yards away in an open space where there was no chance of their damaging anybody. 'That's all right,' said one of the midshipmen, with a smile of satisfaction upon his youthful countenance; 'we've been under fire and we shall get the medal anyhow! '

The general feeling manifest amongst the towns-people, with whom one entered into conversation appeared to be one of the utmost astonishment and surprise, that a lot of farmers should have the supreme audacity to actually bombard the town. They were so astonished as to be almost amused, and seemed quite confident that the advent of naval guns was just the one thing necessary to put a stop to such a foolish 'error of judgment' on the part of the enemy.

The detraining platform was quite close to one of the main roads through the town, and if the previous information was correct, it appeared to the 'simple sailor,' from the continual stream of ambulance wagons and *dhoolies* full of wounded coming down this road from the fight, that if a victory was being won, it was at a somewhat heavy price.

This was no time, however, to stand still and talk and be fired at, and in a very short time definite orders were received, and three 12-pounders were unloaded from the train and sent out into the midst of the fight which was proceeding on the northern side of the town, a boy on a bicycle going on ahead to show the way. The wooden trail of each gun carriage was lashed to the back of a wagon drawn by sixteen oxen, the wagon thus occupying the position of the limber of an ordinary field gun. With the ammunition following in other wagons, this curious-looking procession proceeded rapidly along the Newcastle Road for two miles, amidst a continuous roar of musketry in the distance on their left front (the Gloucesters and Irish Fusiliers in their disastrous position at Nicholson's Nek), the din of the artillery firing shrapnel shell at 'Long Tom,' and the still greater din of 'Long Tom' returning their fire. Finally the guns arrived at a position on the southern side of Limit Hill, where they 'unlimbered' and prepared to engage 'Long Tom,' over the crest of the hill.

No sooner were they ready to fire, than up dashed an A.D.C. from Colonel Knox, under whose direction the guns were being advanced, to say that as the Boers were threatening the town on the left, a general retirement of our troops had been ordered and was already in progress, and on somebody venturing to doubt this hardly credible intelligence, he remarked, 'Well, we are only waiting for our right to retire.' The right *did* retire a few moments afterwards, rather hurriedly, with 'Long Tom's' 94-lb. shells bursting amongst them, so there was nothing for it but to attach the trails of the 12-pounders to the wagons again and retire also, the ammunition wagons being sent on ahead and one company of bluejackets, under Lieutenant Hodges, covering the retirement.

The guns came under a heavy and accurate fire from 'Long Tomas they got into the open, and the foremost one was overturned by a bursting shell, one wheel being knocked off the carriage, and three of the bluejackets wounded. 'Where are the gun's crew?' asked Captain Lambton, as he came galloping up amidst the smoke and dust of the shell; 'have they deserted their gun?'

'I am afraid they are all badly wounded, sir,' said the gunner.

'Good,' was the answer; 'that is better than running away from their gun.'

Fearing it would fall into the hands of the enemy, steps were immediately taken to render this gun useless, and the 'striker,' by the action of which the cartridge is exploded, was taken out of the breech-block, and an attempt made to damage the screw threads inside the breech with stones (they were luckily easily repaired afterwards). The oxen which had been dragging this gun had bolted in the general excitement, but a fresh team was procured, and with the assistance of the company who were covering the retirement, the gun was righted, the wheel put on the carriage, and the whole dragged to a place of comparative safety on Gordon Hill.

The other two 12-pounders had meanwhile unlimbered and come into action on the level plain in front of Gordon Hill, and had opened such an accurate fire on 'Long Tom's' position with common shell that, at the third shot, the officer in the war balloon, who was watching the progress of the battle, reported that the enemy's gun was 'knocked out,' and that the gun's crew had taken to their heels. The range was between 6,000 and 7,000 yards, and the honour of laying and sighting the guns so accurately belongs to Mr. Sims, the gunner of the brigade. A few more shots were fired at 'Long Tom' without eliciting any reply, and the fight practically ceased with the silencing of this gun.[1]

Sir George White appeared on the scene as the damaged 12-pounder was being dragged to a place of security, and congratulated Captain Lambton on the splendid practice made, thanking him, saying that the navy's opportune arrival had saved the situation. Though it was late in the progress of the fight, and the general retirement had actually been ordered when the naval 12-pounders arrived upon the scene of action, there is no doubt that the sudden appearance of long-

---

1. Whatever damage was done to this gun it could not have been considerable, as, though silenced for the remainder of the day, it opened fire again early on the following morning.

range guns capable of paying the enemy back in his own coin, and of reaching with common shell a gun position, where he imagined himself to be out of range, caused him to reflect and pause in his intended swoop on the town.

The second company, under Lieutenant Halsey, ran out the naval field gun past Junction Hill and along the Newcastle road, but had not gone far when they were informed that they were 'running into the Boers,' so this gun also retired to Gordon Hill, and, being a gun of shorter range than the 'long' 12-pounders, did not come into action on that day.

While these exciting events were happening a few miles to the north of the town, the gunnery lieutenant had been taken out by the officer commanding R.E., and shown the position in which it was proposed to mount the first 4.7 gun, on a hill known as Cove Redoubt, a mile to the north-west of the town and occupied up to this time by the Natal Naval Volunteers with a 7-pounder; whilst down at the station the two engineer officers, assisted by the 4.7 guns' crews, the gun-mounting party of stokers, and a yelling, chanting mob of *Kaffir coolies,* were employed the whole of this 'mournful Monday,' as the day was afterwards known, in getting the guns, gun-mountings, and the gear for building up the gun platforms, &c., &c., off the trains and into their respective wagons.

By 4 p.m. the two 4.7 guns and their mountings, ammunition, &c., occupying altogether eleven bullock- wagons, were ready to move off, but orders were received to wait till darkness set in to obtain greater security from the enemy's fire, and to move only one of the guns to its position that night, for no spot had yet been selected on which to mount the second. Lieutenant Hodges and his company, who had by this time come back from the fight, were left to guard the second gun; and as soon as it was dusk the first and its gear, filling six wagons each drawn by sixteen oxen, started off for Cove Redoubt under the guidance of the gunnery lieutenant and a Colonial conductor, with a small party of bluejackets as an escort.

The gun was not destined to get to its position that night, however, for the string of wagons had not gone very far when the foremost of them stuck in a very narrow passage across a gully, the efforts of the oxen to extract it proving useless, despite the frantic wielding of the long whips, and the abusive language of the *Kaffir* boys, whose final and most withering form of vituperation was to stigmatise each bullock separately as a '*Verdomde Doschman*'—had they been working for the Boers under a similar condition of things he would have been called a '*Verdomde Rooinek.*' The way for the remaining wagons being thus blocked through the sticking of the one in front, they were taken back and placed out of sight of the enemy under the friendly shelter of Gordon Hill for the night, the wagon which had caused all the trouble being left where it was, till daybreak and a double team of oxen enabled it to be moved away.

The two 12-pounders which had so successfully engaged Long Tom were dragged at dusk to the top of Gordon Hill, where the other 12-pounder, the field-gun, and the four Maxims had already been placed; and behind this formidable array of weapons of war, tents were pitched by the tired and travel-stained sailors; bread, tinned meat and coffee were served out, and, with the exception of the numerous sentries, all were soon asleep.

As the brigade had brought no tents with it, it had to take what could be had on arrival at Ladysmith, and be thankful for them, though many were so thin and worn, and others so full of holes, that they were very little protection either from the sun or bad weather.

A rather amusing incident happened when the tents were ready to be served out to the men, who were somewhat scattered and hard to get together in the dark. One of the buglers who was gifted with exceedingly powerful lungs was ordered to sound the 'Assembly' so as to bring the men together, which he did with somewhat startling results, as not only did the bluejackets collect, but, in a few minutes, mounted officers and orderlies came galloping up from far and near with concerned expressions on their faces and anxious inquiries as to why 'the Alarm' had been sounded. 'Alarm be damned,' said the lieutenant who had ordered it; 'that's what we call "the Assembly" in the navy.'

The sentries on the camp and guns had to be particularly vigilant all through the night, for, apart from the fact that there were known to be many Boer sympathisers in the town, who would do any damage to the guns they possibly could do, if they only got the chance, it was thought very likely that the Boers after their success of the previous day might attempt to rush the town during the night. 'Powerful' and 'Terrible' were the password and countersign, and all night the sharp challenge, 'Halt! who goes there?' kept ringing out as one or other of the bluejackets who had formed the escort for the 4.7 wagons, and had lost his way in the dark, came tumbling into camp.

'Halt! Who goes there?'

'Friend.'

'Halt, friend, and give the password.'

'Powerful' comes the weary reply.

'Advance, "Powerful," and give the countersign.'

Up the slope of the hill comes the sailor, falling over rocks and boulders in the darkness, growling out as he rubs his injured limbs, 'Terrible, Terrible; all right, Jerry, can't yer see it's me?' With one keen look at his face 'Jerry' passes him on to the next post, till he finally staggers into camp, as yet hardly appreciating the joys of war, and swearing softly to himself as he mutters, 'Terrible? I calls it 'orrible!' sinks down in the first convenient spot, and, with his straw hat for a pillow, sleeps the sleep of a tired-out man till daybreak.

★★★★★★

The guns brought up to Ladysmith by the Naval Brigade:

Two 4.7 Q.F. guns, to be mounted on wooden platforms.

Three 12-pounder (weight, 12 cwt.) Q.F. guns on Percy Scott's field carriages.

One 12-pounder (weight, 8 cwt.) naval field gun.

Four Maxims, three mounted on field carriages and one on a tripod stand.

Ammunition.

For 4.7's—

Common shell, Lyddite and Shrapnel—each	200	rounds.

For 12 pounds —

Common shell	788	,,
Shrapnel	396	,,
Case shot	24	,,
Lee-Metford ammunition, besides the 150 rounds carried by each man	39,000	,,
Maxim gun ammunition	64,000	,,
For revolvers	5,400	,,

CHAPTER 3

Surroundings of Ladysmith

By the time the Naval Brigade arrived in the straggling little town, names had already been given to the principal hills and positions in the lines of defence.

Gordon Hill, a piece of high ground in the centre of the northern line of defence, was the first position selected for the naval 12-pounders, and to this hill they retired after the action of October 30, the four Maxims also taking up positions on the same hill. From here they had full command of the open plain in front of Gordon Hill, and would have been able to concentrate a terrific fire on any advancing enemy, had they thought fit to follow up the advantage gained by their success, in the battle of Lombard's Kop, and attack the town on the northern side—a plan of action which it was thought quite possible they might attempt to carry out during the first few days of the bombardment.

The two 4.7 guns were also mounted on the northern line of the defences, principally to engage 'Long Tom' of Pepworth Hill; the first one on Junction Hill, about half a mile to the north-east of the main naval position on Gordon Hill, and the other on Cove Redoubt, a hill five hundred feet high, and three-quarters of a mile to the west of the main position, from which commanding altitude it could fire in any direction, and was in a fairly concealed position, some way back along the flat crest of the hill.

This latter gun remained in this same position during the whole four weary months of siege; but the one originally placed on Junction Hill was dismounted and moved away to be mounted in a position on the southern line of defences, on Wagon Hill, a few days before each of General Buller's three unsuccessful attempts to relieve the town, in order to cover the advance of a flying column intended to effect a

155

junction with his forces if possible. It was only actually mounted in its new position once, however, just before the Battle of Colenso, on December 15, the enemy on the second occasion unfortunately selecting the same night—January 6—for their big assault, as had been chosen for mounting this gun on the hill they assaulted; while the third attempt at relief and the operations round Vaal Krantz had actually been abandoned when it was decided to move this gun once again.

After each retirement of the relief column across the Tugela the gun was remounted in its old position on Junction Hill again, till this unfortunate 4.7 came to be regarded as a sort of bird of ill omen, and faces fell directly there was the slightest suggestion of moving it. Finally, however, it was taken across to the eastern end of Caesar's Camp, just before the end of the siege, with the intention of harassing the enemy in their retreat; and there it remained till the Naval Brigade left, worrying the gunners of the Bulwana 6-inch gun all through the night of February 28 in their attempt to get this gun away, though, much to the disappointment of the whole garrison, and the Naval Brigade especially, without success.

The four 12-pounders were far too useful weapons to retain all together on Gordon Hill, and, with the exception of one of them, which remained on this hill during the whole of the siege, were moved from place to place, as the frequent shifting of the besieger's guns made it necessary. Thus, one was sent over to the west of Cove Redoubt to engage the guns on Surprise Hill and Rifleman's Ridge, and another to Caesar's Camp to try conclusions with the Boer 6-inch gun on Middle Hill and the field-pieces on the other ridges to the southward; while the naval field gun was thrown out with the advanced post on Junction Hill, so as to cover the approaches to the 4.7 gun, across the open plain.

One only of the Maxims was used at all, the other three being merely ornaments to the earthworks on Gordon Hill. This one was fired under the command of Midshipman Stokes, also with the advanced post in front of Junction Hill, and was of great service in keeping down the fire of the snipers, who often secreted themselves at early morning in a farm known as Brooks's Farm, about two thousand yards to the northward of the hill.

At the end of the siege all these guns, with the exception of the naval field gun and the four Maxims, which were taken back to H.M.S. *Powerful*, were turned over to the Royal Garrison Artillery, with many a fond word of farewell from their crews, so sad were they at parting with them.

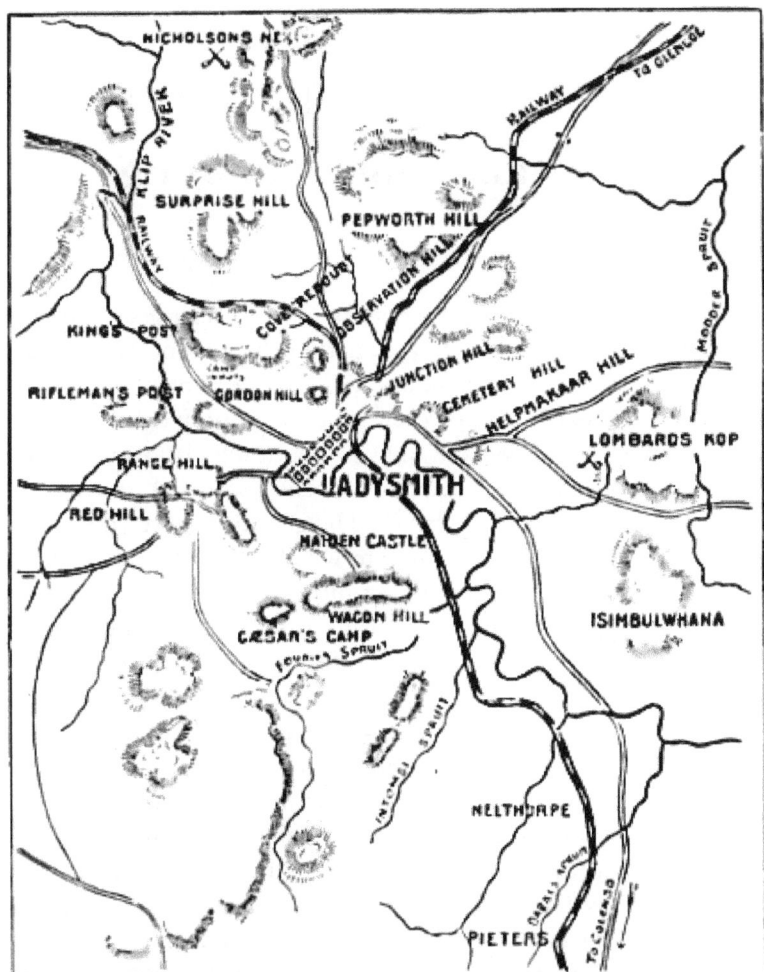

MAP OF LADYSMITH AND SURROUNDING HEIGHTS

CHAPTER 4

Guns and Gun Mounting

Of the guns taken into Ladysmith by the Naval Brigade, four were able immediately to come into action, three being long 12-pounders, on Scott's improvised field mounting, and one a naval 8-cwt. field gun. Not so the two 4.7's, however, which were supplied merely with platforms in an unfinished and unfitted state, each platform consisting of four heavy baulks of timber twelve inches wide and twelve inches deep and about fifteen feet in length. The guns themselves, the 'cradles' in which they recoil, the mounting to which the cradle is secured, the 'base plate' to which the mounting is fitted in such a way that the gun can train laterally, and finally the baulks of timber for the platform, were all entirely separate on arrival in the town, and before either gun could be used each part had to be fixed in its correct position.

In the case of the first gun, this was carried out on the night of Tuesday, October 31, the day after the arrival of the brigade, when the platform was constructed and the gun mounted on the top of the gentle slopes of Junction Hill, a party of sappers digging out a pit in which to embed the platform, while the hills around echoed to the blows of the naval blacksmiths' hammers, as they drove in the long steel bolts, and the flames from the forge threw a red glare over the sky and lighted up the tired but eager faces of the men.

How it rained, and how cold it was! None of the officers or men had any warm overcoats and consequently worked all the harder to keep themselves warm. By seven o'clock next morning they had the satisfaction of seeing the platform and base plate in position and ready for the mounting and the gun. These were put into their places, after considerable labour, during the day, by the gun's crew, assisted by a party of fifty men from the Liverpool Regiment, all working under the direction of the gunner of the brigade. Then the sappers finished bedding down the platform, and, a light sandbag parapet being thrown up during the night, the first 4.7 was ready to fire, in any direction, by daylight on the morning of Thursday, November 2, three days after arrival.

Though this gun was mounted in full view of the enemy from their positions on Pepworth and other hills to the north, it is curious to relate that not a single shot was fired at it or at the working party till the gun commenced to bombard their 6-inch gun position early on the Thursday morning, when the return fire mortally wounded Lieutenant Egerton, the gunnery lieutenant. Similar methods were followed out in the case of the second 4.7 gun, which was mounted in a commanding position on the crest of Cove Redoubt during the nights of November 1 and 2, and was protected by a formidable parapet and ready to take its part in the defence of the town by daylight on November 3, four days after arrival.

The efficient protection of these two guns and their crews, and of the 12-pounders and Maxims as well, occupied a considerable portion of the time and attention of all hands during the earlier days of the siege, and early every morning and late at night, when even the sharp-sighted enemy could not see them, bluejackets and stokers were busily employed in throwing up parapets and traverses, working away with pick and shovel at deep cuttings, or struggling with crowbars and ropes to remove some refractory rock which always seemed to crop up in the very place where it was not wanted. The parapets round each of the 4.7 guns gradually grew into huge structures, as will be seen by the photographs. Sandbags (?) filled with earth were used three or four rows thick in the inner part of the parapet and piled up to the height of a man's head. Outside these were several feet of loose earth, and all round the face of the structure were stacked heavy boulders and stones, the object of these being to burst any shell striking them before it actually entered the parapet.

Near each gun, twenty yards away, hollowed out in the side of a convenient hillock, was built a magazine for stowing the bulk of the ammunition, and this was connected to the rear of the gun emplacement by a narrow, deeply-cut trench in which men could run along with shells and cartridges, without their heads being visible above the ground, whilst in another secure position nearer the gun was cut out a 'ready' magazine containing a few shells of each kind for immediate use. The men took the greatest interest in the construction of these magazines and passages—possibly because the work was so novel to them—boarded them up internally with wood, and kept them always as spick and span as possible, with ammunition carefully separated and ready for use at a moment's notice.

In the early days of the siege, twenty or thirty rounds would be fired from the 4.7's every day, at the enemy's gun positions, but, the vital necessity for strict economy in ammunition soon becoming apparent as the days went by, very often these guns would not be fired for a week at a time—in fact, the 'Lady Anne' on Junction Hill was silent for six whole weeks during the latter part of the siege. When it is considered that 200 rounds of lyddite, 200 of shrapnel, and 200 of common shell, with 600 cartridges, constituted the total available supply of ammunition for these guns on arrival in the town, it will be seen how necessary it was to fire only on the most favourable occasions.

The appearance of these gun positions is well shown in the photograph, representing 'Lady Anne' on Junction Hill, with the crossbeams forming the platform for her mounting, imbedded in the earth, behind the sandbag emplacement. This was the gun which afterwards 'knocked out' 'Long Tom of Pepworth' and sent him back to Pretoria for repairs.

In the photograph her sights are laid on this gun, and the captain of the gun, a great bearded petty-officer, stands by with the firing lanyard in his hand.

The lieutenant in command, with glass glued to eye, is watching 'Long Tom' and waiting till he elevates his muzzle and long chase and presents a more favourable target. The moment comes; 'Long Tom' is getting his sights on something, a convoy of wagons or a line of cavalry tents, maybe; sharp comes the order, 'Fire'; down comes the horny hand on the lanyard; click goes the 'striker'; the gun flies back and forwards again with a deafening crack, a little acrid yellow haze comes floating in through the embrasure, and one of those 200 precious khaki-coloured lyddite shells is speeding its way to the Boer gun, nearly four miles away.

The breech is swung open, the empty cordite cylinder pulled out, the man crouching with the shell in his arms jumps to the gun and shoves it well home through the smoking breech, another jambs in a fresh charge; with a bang the breech is closed, the gun is ready again, and there is still plenty of time to see what the first shell is going to do.

Every one cranes eagerly forward; over on the Boer ridge, close to

'LADY ANNE' 4.7 ON JUNCTION HILL.
HER SIGHTS ARE TRAINED ON 'LONG TOM OF PEPWORTH'

'Long Tom,' comes a splash on the brown slopes, a great yellow-grey cloud shoots up, and the shell has done its work.

'Good shot—by Jove! right on top of him;' 'A bit short, give her a little more elevation;' 'Over, I'm afraid—hope we hit some of the ammunition people coming up the hill'—such were the various remarks to be heard at either of the 4.7 gun emplacements, as one watched the crew of six bluejackets loading, laying and firing, and the ammunition party of four stokers hurrying silently to and from the magazine along the deep connecting trench.

The lines of defence encircling Ladysmith were so extensive that connecting telephones were absolutely essential. These were rigged up by the Royal Engineers, and as the siege advanced became very elaborate. From the 'conning-tower,' the central position of the Naval Brigade on Gordon Hill, one could talk to headquarters, to the naval camp, and to the 4.7 gun on Cove Redoubt. Later on, as the value of Cove Redoubt as a post of observation became greater, direct connection was made from this position to headquarters, and proved of great value.

The naval signalmen kept up communication, between Junction Hill and Cove Redoubt, with their signal flags or flashing lamps.

Besides the numerous earthworks, parapets, &c., thrown up by the Naval Brigade during the first few weeks of the siege, a most elaborate and complicated system of wire entanglements was rigged in front of each gun and well round the main position on Gordon Hill. These wire mazes were, like all other means for defence, gradually improved as the time wore on, till they were almost unnegotiable by the blue-jackets even in broad daylight, and would have rendered it impossible for an attacking party to approach without being heard. Luckily for them they never attempted an attack on the guns, though it was rumoured at one time that General Schalk Burger had called for volunteers to attack the naval guns, and, out of a surrounding force of about twenty thousand men, managed to secure *two*, so gave up the project!

Picket duty at night was another form of campaigning work in which the Naval Brigade took part, till its numbers were so reduced by fever and dysentery, that all hands left were required for manning the guns and entrenchments. Midshipmen were in command of these pickets, and considerable amusement, not to mention admiration, was caused by the easy and self-confident manner in which these boys, some of them fresh from the *Britannia*, took charge of their men.

[*On the investment of Ladysmith, the water mains were destroyed by the enemy, and the Klip River, that very muddy tributary of the Tugela, became the sole source of the water supply.*

The alum in store was soon exhausted, and the few Berkefeld filters were inadequate, so, as enteric fever was increasing at an alarming rate, the construction of extemporised distillers was decided on, and the design of these was worked out by Mr. Sheen, one of the engineers of the Naval Brigade.

A large corrugated iron tank used for storing mealies was obtained, and inside it were fitted three spiral coils of ordinary water-piping, bent into shape and the sections screwed together. The three coils were nearly five hundred feet long.

Steam was forced into these from the boiler at the repairing shop down by the railway station, and condensed by pumping river water through hoses leading into a large drainpipe, which opened near the bottom of the tank, the water overflowing at the top.

The whole condenser was constructed in the repairing shop in three days by the railway fitters and by the naval engine-room artificers and stokers, and was so efficient that it was capable of producing fifteen hundred gallons of condensed water daily.

So successful was it that two more were made and supplied with steam from two locomotives.

These three supplied the whole garrison with condensed water from December 11 to January 25, on which date no more coal could be spared to work them.

This work, in the design and superintendence of which Mr. Sheen took a leading part, was not the least important contribution by the navy to the defence of the town. (Original) Ed.]

CHAPTER 5

Site of the Camp

The first position chosen for the naval camp was on the summit of Gordon Hill, in the northern line of defences, and this ground was occupied till an objectionable 4.5 howitzer, mounted on Surprise Hill, four thousand yards away, forced us to seek a more favourable spot. This gun, which fired a slow-moving shell of about forty pounds in weight, after trying for some time without much success to get the range of the small group of white tents, finally found it, and, putting two or three of its lolloping' projectiles right into the open space in front of the cook's galley, so interfered with the prospects of lunch that on November 19 at dusk the tents were struck and all the paraphernalia of the camp moved to a safer position behind the hill and at the foot of it, where meals could be taken with less fear of interruption.

The bombardment of the camp by this howitzer brought out one of those amusing incidents which tend so much to enliven a campaign. It was a few minutes before noon, and the officers' cook was preparing lunch, standing with a frying-pan held over the fire, in one hand, and a large spoon in the other, frying an appetising-looking dish of onions, when one of the shells was heard coming in our direction. Nearer and nearer it came, and officers and men rushed and scrambled for the nearest cover, or laid flat on the ground wondering where they were going to be hit.

Only the cook remained, and he, with an interested expression on his face and a curious look in his eye (he squinted), calmly went on frying his onions, till the shell dropped into the soft ground a few feet in front of him, and, after a fizzle, finally burst, scattering shrapnel bullets and mud in all directions. Then he emerged from the *débris* with a look of grave concern on his mud-bespattered face, and remarked in serious tones, 'I do believe they're trying to hit me, sir, and spoil your dinners.' He felt highly pleased that the enemy had picked him out as a target, but rather annoyed about the onions.

The new position chosen for the camp was partly in the garden of a tiny cottage, occupied by a Johannesburg refugee, with his wife and family, who had stayed in Ladysmith too late to catch the last train to Durban. Fruit trees, gums, and cactus bushes abounded in the garden; and though no fruit ever appeared, it was pleasant to imagine what a charming spot it would have been in times of peace. The gum trees were full of the hanging nests of the weaver-birds, or South African canary, as the inhabitants called them; and the presence of these pretty little birds in the camp seemed to lend an air of security and peace to the surroundings, in spite of the incessant scream and splash of the shells, as they passed, sometimes close over the camp, sometimes a few yards away on the road in front of it, according as they were directed either at the 4.7 gun on Cove Redoubt behind us or at the convent on the hill in front.

In the midst of this pretty garden the officers' tents were pitched. Spars lashed together and wagon-covers spread over them, made an excellent ward-room, whilst chairs (taken from a chapel) and tables (from the local school) made the place quite comfortable. The midshipmen had a gun-room of their own, constructed and supplied with furniture in a similar manner; and the usual service hours with regard to meals were observed in both messes, even 'seven-bell' tea being gone through in the customary way, though in later days there was more imagination than reality about it.

The Naval Brigade was exceptionally fortunate in having Fleet-Paymaster Kay—an old campaigner who had seen fighting in Abyssinia, up the Nile, and in Burmah—as its commissariat officer. To his powers of organisation and to his forethought the absence of much unnecessary discomfort was due, and he played the part of father to all. In the last few weeks of the siege he performed the duties of field-paymaster to the army, and unfortunately contracted enteric fever, dying on the voyage home, most sincerely regretted by his messmates, and was buried in the quiet little cemetery at Ascension.

Foreseeing the prospect of a prolonged siege, even on the day of arrival in town, he bought up as many of the necessities of life as were obtainable, one little 'item' being thirty pounds' worth of draught beer, nearly the last in the town, the possession of which helped to make the naval camp quite a popular resort.

There were few amusements to wile away the monotony of camp

life, a dozen books or so, including a well-worn copy of Shakespeare, being the sum total of the literature available; whilst 'Patience,' played in its many forms with old packs of cards—their faces so covered with mud and rain as to be hardly recognisable by the end of the siege—occupied many a weary hour.

Football, too, was indulged in till the ball gave out from sheer over-work; and an occasional Sunday game of cricket or evening concert helped to pass the time away. *The Ladysmith Lyre*, a local sheet which was produced five times under the editorship of G. W. Steevens, also helped to raise a laugh and stimulate conversation for days.

The principal form of amusement, however, was 'lie swopping,' as it finally came to be known. One only had to start a vaguely possible story, and in sundry and various forms it was all round the garrison by the end of the day; so that it was a very difficult matter to know how much to believe of anything one might hear. Old South Africans say that everybody in South Africa becomes an expert at truth perversion if he stays out there long enough; and the want of news, combined with the anxiety for it, daring a siege are particular incentives to the working of a fertile imagination.

The sailor's well-known liking for dumb animals caused the Naval Brigade camp and gun positions to be quite a fashionable resort or residence for many of the dogs in the place. Quite early in the siege a stray fox-terrier bitch, of apparently rather mixed ancestry, excited the compassion of some of the officers, who rigged her up a comfortable resting-place, and were rewarded in a few days by being presented with a litter of seven pups, five of which survived, and grew and flour-ished on siege rations, rejoicing in their mere existence and in such appropriate names as 'Cordite,' 'Lyddite,' 'Shrapnel,' &c. They finally came to be quite well known, and were at once the pride of their owners and the envy of other camps. In addition to these, the 'pack' consisted of an underbred mastiff, with a horror of shell fire, a black spaniel, a black-and-tan terrier, a wheezy-looking mongrel, which wisely attached itself to our commissariat officer, and occasionally a pointer or two, and a three-legged animal wounded in action thrown in. It was quite unusual to see a naval officer or bluejacket without a dog of some sort following in his wake.

Dinner parties, events as occasional as they were important, were great features of the siege, and all the resources of the commissariat and all the somewhat forgotten skill of the cook were called into play. How does this menu sound for the seventy-fifth day of the siege,

when the officer commanding the Royal Artillery, his staff, and others
dined with the brigade?

Soup.
Stock pot.
Fish.
Tinned salmon fishcakes.
Joints.
Roast lamb (mutton?) and mint sauce.Vegetable marrow.
Sweets.
Tapioca and tinned apricots.
Rice and peaches.
Savoury.
Pâté de foie gras sandwiches.
Whisky and soda. Brandy and soda. Rum.
No smokes.

The sheep was obtained through the prayers of the fleet paymaster, and the mint sauce made from some herb picked up by one of our *Kaffirs* on the wayside. This glorious feed, however, represented days of saving of stores, and was the last 'flash in the pan,' the remainder of the whisky and brandy being kept for medicinal purposes, and the food from that time forward consisting mostly of horse in one form or another and ration biscuit in very small quantities.

Many were the appetising dodges resorted to to make the food palatable. A mincing machine was of the greatest use, as it rendered eatable meat which otherwise it would have been a physical impossibility to get one's teeth through. The genius of Lieutenant MacNulty of the Army Service Corps gave us the poor starving troop and artillery horses in a variety of forms, and horse soup (*chevril*), horse sausage, potted horse-tongue, and cow-heel jelly were amongst the numerous productions of his factory in the railway-station yard; whilst occasionally some herbs gathered by the *Kaffirs* would be made into a semblance of spinach and supply the want of fresh green food—a want very keenly felt.

CHAPTER 6

The Big Fight of the Siege

As during more than two months' bombardment the enemy had made only one half-hearted attack in force, the general opinion was that they had abandoned the idea of taking Ladysmith by storm, and would endeavour to starve out the garrison. Everybody was therefore greatly surprised when, on the morning of January 6, it was realised that the enemy had really 'come on' at last, and that they were bent on 'coming in' if possible. All day raged a desperate fight for the possession of Wagon Hill and Caesar's Camp, points in our lines absolutely vital to the safety of the town.

The part played by the Naval Brigade in repelling this fierce attack consisted principally in keeping down the fire of the opposing siege-guns, but a small party of bluejackets happened to be in the brunt of the fighting and took a not inglorious part in the successful defence.

The presence of this small party was due to the fact that, on the night of January 4, an attempt had been made to shift a 4.7 gun from Junction Hill to Wagon Hill, for the same purpose as it had been previously mounted there, *viz.* to cover the advance of a column intended to effect a junction with Buller's forces in his second attempt to relieve the town. A heavy thunderstorm, however, had made the ground so soft that the transport of the heavy gun had to be deferred till next night, when it was successfully accomplished under the occasional glare of a searchlight from Bulwana Hill.

The working party consisted, as usual, of a detachment of infantry, larger this time than before, for short rations were beginning to tell on the men's strength, and their lifting power was considerably diminished. As a result it needed all the gunner's 'endearing epithets' to get the necessary work out of the men. 'Now then, men, it's got to be done, you know,' said he, as he harangued them from the top of the parapet. 'Spit on yer hands, grind yer teeth, now! all together! lift her! &c., &c.' And weren't they all glad when the final "Vast 'eavin', lads!' was shouted, and the gun and all its gear was safely stowed in the wagons and set off on its jolt across to Wagon Hill. The string of wagons, with an escort of Gordon Highlanders, arrived at the foot of this hill about 1 a.m.

Two wagons, one with the great platform beams, the other with tools, &c., were hauled up the steep slippery sides to the rear of the old gun emplacement, and the bluejackets and Highlanders started work with a will, under the persuasive and by this time well-known eloquence of the gunner, and in a few minutes had got the platform halfway off the wagon, when the harmony of the proceedings was rudely disturbed by a sudden and unexpected splashing and pinging of bullets on the rocks and boulders forming the crest of the hill.

For a few moments it was thought that the clatter of the wagons, the light from the swinging lanterns, and the yelling of the *Kaffir* drivers had drawn the fire of a few Boer snipers, more courageous than usual; but it was quickly realised that this was something far more serious, and the garrison of the hill, now augmented by the seventy Gordons, thirteen bluejackets and thirty Royal Engineers, at once seized their arms, and, extending along the crest of the hill, fired down through the darkness in the direction of the attack.

The *Kaffirs* had bolted at the first shot, and it was with great difficulty that the oxen were cut adrift from the two wagons by the bluejackets and driven down the hill, though it was impossible to get the last few of the tired animals away, and they remained browsing on the scanty tufts of grass during the whole of the terrible struggle, and were nearly all wounded and had to be killed at the end of the day.

The Imperial Light Horse pickets were driven in, and twenty or thirty plucky Boers—picked marksmen all—gained a position on the crest itself and remained there, till the Devons cleared them out in the evening.

The bluejackets and a few Gordons and sappers manned the empty gun-emplacement, the gunner of the Naval Brigade taking command of them and directing their firing with such an easy flow of drill-book 'lingo' that one might almost have imagined he had that precious manual in his hand. 'Number,' he shouted in his best fo'c'stle voice as he appeared through the darkness in the midst of an erratically firing mob, with their rifles poked over the top of the earthwork round the empty 12-pounder emplacement on the extreme end of Wagon Hill.

'One, twa, three, vower, voive,' up to fifteen, came a curious mixture of west-country and Gaelic pronunciations. 'Nos. 1 to 8 will be the right half-section; Nos. 9 till 15 will be the left half-section; the right half-section will fire a volley while the left half-section loads, and *vice versa*. Now then, men, are you ready? Bight half-section, ready, present, fire!!!' and so on till in the growing dawn smiles could be seen on all those sunburned, weather-beaten faces, whose owners seemed to be vaguely wondering whether they were on the drill-ground fighting an imaginary foe, or really taking part in what turned out to be one of the most important fights of the present campaign.

Meanwhile the attack thus commenced on Wagon Hill was extending along Caesar's Gamp, and heavy fighting was taking place at the eastern end of the ridge, where the enemy had come along as quietly and as determinedly as at the western end, and had rushed the pickets of the Manchester Regiment, most of the men being shot down almost point blank, those who survived the first onslaught retiring on their main position.

As soon as it began to grow light, the Boer 16-pounders on Middle Hill and along the ridges to the eastward of it started a heavy bombardment of the crest of Caesar's Camp, and the naval 12-pounder there was busily engaged in returning the fire, first of one, then of another, with common and shrapnel shell, at a range of about four thousand yards. Discarding their khaki tunics, and working away with their short-sleeved service 'flannels' flapping in the wind, and showing the various devices tattooed on their sunburnt arms by Japanese artists in more peaceful times, the three bluejackets and three stokers who comprised this gun's crew, cheered on by their young midshipman, got their gun, the 'Lady Ellen,' loaded and fired so rapidly that the Boer gunners had some excellent practice at 'shell-dodging,' and often one or other of their guns on those southern ridges with muzzle raised ready for another shot was quickly lowered, and the gunners rushed for cover as they realised that a shell from one of the 'long' 12-pounders was coming in their direction.

With daylight, it could be seen that the enemy was being rapidly reinforced by mounted men riding across the plain, out of range of rifle fire, from the direction of the Colenso Road, and from behind Rifleman's Ridge; these men went round the back of Mounted Infantry Hill, and while some took up positions on the crest of this hill, the others rode across through the thorn bushes in the direction of Caesar's Camp, posting themselves in the *dongas* and behind the low

THE 'LADY ELLEN,' 12-POUNDER, IN THE REDOUBT ON CAESAR'S HILL

rocky ridges on the level ground to the southward of our positions. The sappers and bluejackets on Wagon Hill West kept up a heavy magazine-rifle fire on these men as they advanced at a range of about a thousand yards, and emptied a few saddles.

A battery of artillery now came out, and burst shrapnel over Mounted Infantry Hill from the plain near Range Post, being in turn subjected to a heavy fire from the Boer 16-pounder on Rifleman's Ridge; the naval 12-pounder on Cove Hill did its best to keep down this fire, but was not particularly successful.

Meanwhile Major Abdy's battery of artillery shelled the Boers who were attempting to take the eastern end of Caesar's Camp, and did terrible execution amongst them, though under a terrific fire the whole time from the 6-inch and other guns on Bulwana Mountain. The big gun alone fired 103 shells, and, marvellous to relate, never killed or wounded a single man; this was, without doubt, principally due to the very rapid, accurate and disconcerting fire kept up on this gun by Lieutenant Halsey from the 'Princess Victoria' on Cove Hill.

The Boers who had gained a footing on the eastern crest of Wagon Hill had found splendid cover and were causing much loss among the Imperial Light Horse. An attempt to turn them out failed, but in other parts of the hills the enemy were gradually forced back below the crest line and the fire slackened considerably later in the forenoon, and, though it never ceased entirely, there were hopes that the attack was being abandoned.

This was very far from being the case, however, for shortly after 1 p.m., a fresh assault was made, with great suddenness, on the extreme south-west point of Wagon Hill.

The 4-7 gun crew, with Gunner Sims and Mr. Sheen, engineer, were at this time somewhat in rear of the crest of the hill, having been relieved at noon from their positions on the gun emplacement by a fresh detachment of Gordons, and had at great risk managed to secure some food and water from one of the naval wagons. The 'inner man' being more or less satisfied, this little party were vaguely wondering what was going to happen next, when suddenly there was a great increase in the firing and a loud yelling and shouting on the top of the hill, and, turning to look up, they saw a confused mass of men rushing helter-skelter down towards them, shouting that the Boers were on top of the hill and up to the gun emplacements.

The gunner at once grasped the fact that it was only a momentary panic, and, shouting in a loud voice, 'Naval Brigade!' (there were only thirteen of them) 'extend in skirmishing order to the right and left—forward-d-d!!!'—led them up the few yards which separated them from the crest of the hill, the men fixing their bayonets as they advanced and expecting every moment to see a row of hairy faces appearing over the crest. As the top was reached. General Ian Hamilton was to be seen pointing his revolver at a grey-bearded Boer only a few yards distant and shouting at the same time: 'Come back, men, for God's sake—it's all right. Send up the reserves as quickly as possible.'

As a matter of fact, the men who had started to run away had turned round after going a few yards in their first alarm, which was almost excusable, for the small attacking party of the enemy had got right up to the gun parapets and shot down some of the men inside, point blank, yelling out 'Retire!' at the same time, another little ruse which came near to being successful.

By this time our men were on top of the hill again with fixed bayonets, a huge Gordon Highlander, as he jambed his bayonet home in its socket, shouting out in broad Scotch: 'Come on, boys, let's have another —— Elandslaagte!' But there was no necessity to use cold steel, every Boer who had gained the crest line having been shot dead.

One of the 4.7 ammunition carriers, a stoker, was shot dead and an A.B. was badly wounded, and shortly after this attack the 'high velocity' gun on Rifleman's Ridge enfiladed the hill, and Mr. Sheen was slightly wounded by a shrapnel shell in the face, the gunner's rifle being blown out of his hands at the same time.

An hour or so afterwards it came on to rain, and under cover of this the enemy made another attack on the south-west comer of the hill, but were again repulsed, and at 5 p.m. three companies of the 1st Battalion Devonshire Regiment under Colonel Park, with a magnificent charge, cleared the hill of the enemy under a terrific fire and brought the fierce day's fighting to an end.

The losses for the day were very heavy, fourteen officers and 135 N.C.O.'s and men being killed and thirty-one officers and 244 men wounded; while the Boer loss was probably even heavier, seventy-nine dead bodies being actually found within our lines, and natives reported that their casualties were at least 700.

Chapter 7

A Boer Tribute to the Naval Guns

The siege had its bright times, days of success, of good news from the relieving column, or of sadden finds of some welcome addition to the commissariat; but on the other hand there were the dark days, days when the news was bad and everything seemed to be going wrong for oar arms, or when some comrade or friend fell in the forefront of the fight or succumbed to the ravages of fever or dysentery. Darkest of many dark days to the Naval Brigade was Thursday, November 2, the first day of the real siege, when communication with the outer world was practically cut off by the enemy, and when Lieutenant Egerton lost his life.

The first 4.7, the one on Junction Hill, had just been mounted and early in the morning had fired her first shot at 'Long Tom' of Pepworth Hill, 6,500 yards away, the preliminary to a fierce duel between the two guns which lasted some hours. 'Long Tom's' fire was terribly accurate and our defences at that period of the siege not very strong, the parapet of the 4.7 having been purposely kept low to give the gun an 'all round' fire.

About 9 a.m. the flash of the discharge, and the cloud of white smoke, were seen on Pepworth Hill, and there followed the twenty-five seconds of suspense as the 6-inch shell sped on its way to our position. Everybody who could be spared was ordered under cover, Egerton and two or three of the gun's crew being left alone inside the light sandbag parapet round the gun; he stood on the left of the gun looking down anxiously at the wooden platform, which seemed inclined to jump very slightly, when the shell came crashing into the embrasure, just touching the top row of sandbags, missing the gun itself by a few inches, and striking poor Egerton in the legs.

Burgeon Fowler was on the spot and did all that was possible—

not much, for his wounds were terrible— and then the bluejackets tenderly picked him up and laid him in a *dhoolie*. His only remark was, 'This will put a stop to my cricket, I'm afraid,' while, on the way down to the hospital he stopped his bearers to get a light for his cigarette. He died that same evening, never having recovered from the shock and loss of blood. Conscious almost to the end, he fortunately suffered little pain.

His death, the first in the brigade, had a very sobering effect on both officers and men, who were perhaps inclined to look upon the whole 'show' as a sort of land picnic.

November 9, the Prince of Wales's birthday, was ushered in by a very vigorous firing at dawn from the enemy's guns, which by that time had considerably increased in numbers. This was followed by an attack, on the part of their infantry, on Caesar's Camp to the south, and Observation and Devonshire Hills to the north, the fire of their big guns being kept down as much as possible by the two 4.7's. A hot action lasted till noon, though the enemy never came to very close quarters, their nearest approach being at Caesar's Camp, where they were held in check by the Manchester Regiment.

At noon the guns of the Naval Brigade thundered forth a royal salute of twenty-one shotted guns, the crash of the artillery being followed by three terrific cheers for His Royal Highness which were probably heard in the enemy's camp. The correct interval between the rounds was given by flag signal from the 'conning tower,' the two opening and the two closing shots being fired by the 4.7's, and the remainder by the 12-pounders. When the cheering was over the Prince's health was drunk in champagne in the Naval Brigade's mess tent, Sir George White and his staff being present, and a pigeon, which it is happy to relate, arrived safely at its destination, was despatched to Durban, offering the congratulations of the garrison, the message being cabled thence, and duly received and acknowledged by His Royal Highness.

The casualties in the brigade, during this first organised attack on the part of the enemy, were 'one sucking pig,' the barrel in which it reposed being struck by a 12-pounder shell, and the pig so seriously wounded that it had to be put out of its misery!

During General Hunter's magnificent and successful sortie on December 7, which resulted in the destruction of the Boer 6-inch on Gun Hill, the lower part of Lombards' Kop, a letter from a Boer gunner to his sister was picked up and brought in; it was written in Dutch, and as it gives what one hoped was the general opinion of the enemy with regard to the naval guns, it is inserted here as a 'special event.' It ran as follows:—

> My dear Sister,—. . . It is a month and seven days since we besieged Ladysmith, and don't know what will happen further.
> The English we see every day walking about the town, and we are bombarding the town every day with our cannons. . . .
> They have erected plenty of breastworks all round the town.
> It is very dangerous to attack the town. Near the town are two naval guns from which we receive very heavy fire, which we cannot stand. I think there will be much blood spilt before they surrender, as Mr. Englishman fights hard and well and our *burghers* are a bit frightened.
> I would like to write more but the sun is very hot, and still further the flies are so troublesome that I don't get a chance of sitting still. . . .   I remain, &c.

It was a matter of supreme satisfaction to the brigade to know that the enemy objected to our gunfire, and there was almost equal rejoicing to know that flies were as annoying to them as to us.

On Christmas Day, contrary to most people's expectations, the usual daily bombardment had to be put up withy and athletic sports, projected for the afternoon, had in consequence to be abandoned. The commissariat officers did all in their very limited power to make the day seem as much like Christmas as possible, however, and extra rations of jam, and tobacco and materials for making plum-puddings were served out.

During the forenoon a message was received from Her Majesty the Queen, transmitted by heliograph from Weenen, 'wishing a happy Christmas to her brave sailors and soldiers'; this considerably cheered everybody and made all realise that they were not forgotten by the outside world.

All the tents were decorated for the festive occasion with what green stuff there was to be found, an extra coat of whitewash was put on the stones which marked the various pathways, and all hands did their best to realise that it was actually Christmas Day, and vaguely wondered what their friends and relations at home were thinking of them and envied them a little, perhaps, their comfortable dinners, though in that line, bluejackets would not have kept up their reputation, if they had not managed to provide some little luxury for such

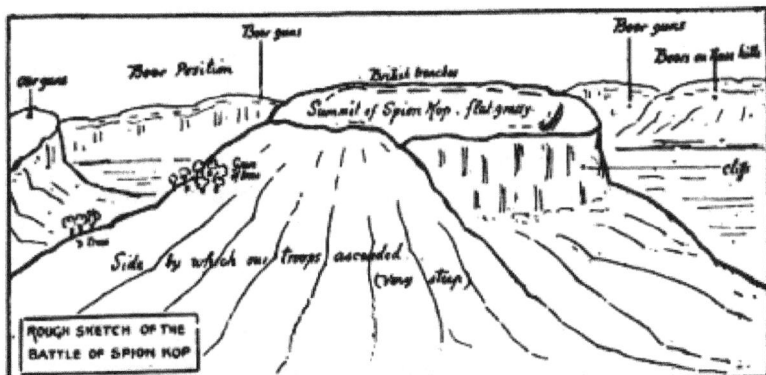

Boer guns   Boer Position   Boer guns   British trenches   Boer guns   Boers on these hills

Summit of Spion Kop. flat grassy

cliff

Boer guns

Side by which our troops ascended. (Very steep)

ROUGH SKETCH OF THE
BATTLE OF SPION KOP

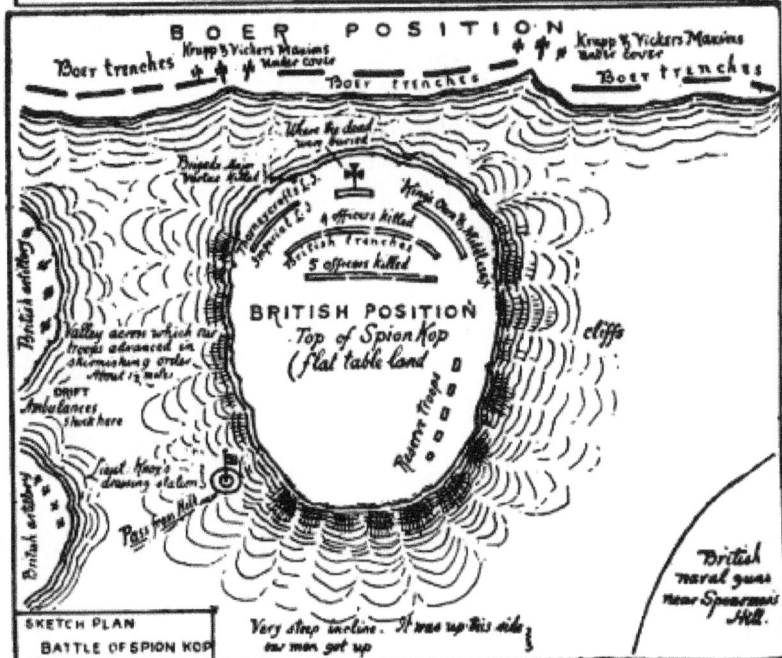

B O E R   P O S I T I O N

Boer trenches   Krupp & Vickers Maxims Under cover   Krupp & Vickers Maxims Under cover

Boer trenches   Boer trenches

Where the dead were buried

Brigade Major Morris killed

Scharpshooters (?)   King's Own & Middlesex

Imperial (?)   4 officers killed

British trenches
5 officers killed

BRITISH POSITION
Top of Spion Kop
(flat table land

British artillery

Valley across which our troops advanced in skirmishing order. About 1½ miles

DRIFT
Ambulances stuck here

cliffs

Reserve Troops

British artillery

Lieut. King's dressing station

Pass from Hill

Very steep incline. It was up this side our men got up

British naval guns near Spearman's Hill.

SKETCH PLAN
BATTLE OF SPION KOP

a day. The men had roast pork, some of it presented by the officer of the Remount Department, the remainder the product of a few midnight raids on the part of the guns' crews; while the officers managed to 'commandeer' a turkey in addition to a very tasty sucking pig. The enemy, too, sent in their contribution to the commissariat in the form of a 6-inch shell fired from Bulwana Mountain and filled with plum-pudding, with 'A merry Xmas' painted in white letters on the outside of the shell.

More messages of goodwill were received from the outside world on New Year's Day, and the enemy fired in a shell containing a piece of paper inside, on which they had written, 'A happy New Year to you; come out of your holes, you heroes,' the last word being crossed out and 'cowards' substituted.

From this time till the end of the siege, with the exception of the big attack on January 6, nothing took place in the brigade which might be described as a 'special event.' The daily desultory bombardment went on, and was responded to at longer and longer intervals from our gradually diminishing stock of ammunition; the daily lies were still just as freely circulated, till most of us were getting too weak to laugh at them. Rations went down or up according as bad or good news came from General Buller, till, at the lowest, they consisted of about one and a half ration biscuits and three-quarters of a pound of horse-flesh, *per diem*.

The failure of the operations round Spion Kop and Vaal Krantz caused hope of relief to be somewhat deferred and the heart to be a little sick in consequence, but all was forgotten on the glorious 28th of February, when at 1.30 p.m., as men off duty were lolling about the camp in various attitudes of repose, a single horseman was seen cantering down the road in the direction of the general's quarters. As he neared the naval camp he was recognised as General Hunter, and seeing some officers in camp, with his usual genial good nature he pulled up and the following conversation took place:

General Hunter: 'Heard the news?'

N.O.'s: 'No, sir; anything fresh?'

General Hunter: 'Helio just in from General Buller: "Gave the Boers a thorough beating yesterday, and am sending my cavalry on to ascertain in which direction they are going, as I believe them to be in full retreat."'

N.O.'s: 'Thank you, sir; that's good enough.'

And off galloped the general to impart the joyful tidings to Sir

George White.

This, then, was the meaning of the great Boer movement that had been anxiously watched through the long naval glass all day. Buller, with the tenacity of the British bulldog, had at last, after weeks of fighting over an almost impossible country, succeeded in forcing his way into the beleaguered town. At 6 p.m. an advance party of 180 of the Volunteer Cavalry under Lord Dundonald entered the town by way of Intombi camp, and the siege was at an end.

Bulwana Bill had fired his last shot during the forenoon, but it was not till about 3 p.m. that any signs of his removal became apparent. A little later a huge pair of 'shears' were seen to be erected over the gun, and then the naval guns 'weighed in,' 4.7's and 12-pounders vying with one another in their attempts to bring the shears down; no necessity for saving ammunition then, and the Boers got some idea of what was meant by a *quick-firing* gun. Down came the shears, disappearing in the cloud of dust raised by a lucky shell; our guns ceased firing, and awaited instructions. For the remainder of the day, and all through the night, occasional shells were sent into this gun position, but, in spite of them, the enemy managed to get their gun away by the morning.

A week later the brigade, or rather what was left of it, after being escorted to the railway station by the pipers of the Gordon Highlanders, left Ladysmith for Durban and thence for the *Powerful* at Simonstown. Here some of the officers and men, who had been landed with the Naval Brigade, which had fought under Lord Methuen and Lord Roberts, rejoined the ship from Bloemfontein, and, with her complement almost complete once more, H.M.S. *Powerful* started home.[1] Within six weeks of the relief, her crew was ashore in old England, was given a tremendous reception by the people of London, had the great distinction of being inspected by Her Majesty Queen Victoria at Windsor, and finally 'paid off' the ship which had been the home of officers and men for three years of so eventful a commission.

---

1. The marines still remained at Bloemfontein.

CHAPTER 1

Landing of the Brigade and Arrival at the Front

During the early part of November '99, shortly after the outbreak of war, the *Terrible*, *Powerful*, *Forte*, and *Thetis* lay at the outer anchorage off Durban, whilst the *Magicienne*, *Philomel*, *Racoon*, and *Tartar* were snugly moored in the inner harbour.

The *Powerful*, having sent her brigade to Ladysmith, steamed back to Simonstown, and to the remaining ships was entrusted the defence of the town itself.

With Ladysmith invested, and Boer commandoes sweeping south across the Tugela, there was not much time to be lost, so a large number of officers and men were landed from their ships, with 4.7's and 12-pounders, on Scott's mountings, and many machine guns. In all thirty guns were in position by November 8, forty-eight hours after the arrival of the *Terrible*, whose Captain, Percy Scott, became commandant of the town, and organised the defences.

During November a few small detachments of bluejackets[1] had been sent north—a few of the 'Tartars'—to work a 7-pounder in an armoured train; Lieutenant James and some more 'Tartars' with two 12-pounders for the defence of Maritzburg; Lieutenant Halsey with some 'Philomels' and two more 12-pounders for the same place, allowing James to move forward to Frere; and Lieutenant Steel eventually followed with some men of the *Forte* and the same armament, for the defence of the railway at Mooi River.

Everyone who had been eagerly looking forward to a trip up country, imagined sadly that this was all the navy would be called

1. *Victoria's Blue Jackets & Marines*: the Royal Navy during Queen Victoria's reign 1839-1901 by W. H. G. Kingston and G. A. Henty also published by Leonaur.

upon to do, and felt somewhat chagrined that no more active share in the fighting would fall to his lot.

However, we were not to be all disappointed, for about 2 o'clock on Sunday afternoon, November 26, a signal was made from the commandant to Captain E. P. Jones, of the *Forte*, ordering him to proceed at once to the front in command of a Naval Brigade to be attached to the Ladysmith relief column.

What a Sunday afternoon that was!

Two hours later amid much excitement we landed at the Point, finding a hundred men of the *Terrible* under Commander Limpus waiting for us with two 4.7's and four 12-pounders. These, their stores and ammunition having been stowed on railway-trucks, we steamed across to the town station, and, after a tedious delay of an hour, the two special trains containing the Naval Brigade started north, amidst a scene of great enthusiasm, continued at every little station we passed.

At Pine Town, where we halted after crawling nearly a thousand feet above sea level, the kind-hearted inhabitants offered the rather hungry and extremely thirsty bluejackets 'buns and flowers.' In exchange they wanted cap-ribbons and buttons, but, as we were 'flying light' and had not a surplus of these articles, the worthy souls had to be disappointed.

Three hours after leaving Durban, Inchanga, 2,500 feet up, was reached, and here a halt of an hour was made for supper, water-bottles were filled, and on we went again, very much on the alert, for the two trains were very valuable, the country north of this swarmed with Boer sympathisers, and the sharp railway curves, running along the precipitous sides of the hills, gave every opportunity to the most timorous train-wrecker.

Arriving at Maritzburg at midnight, orders were given that only the big guns were to go forward to Frere, and that the 12-pounders were to be left behind. Eventually they saw as much fighting as the bigger guns, but at the time the disappointment of their crews was intense.

This order necessitated the shifting of guns and ammunition from one train to another, and a busy hour and a half's work it was in the dark, sorting everything into the right trains.

After plenty of hard swearing it was accomplished and the lucky 4.7's were again on the road by 1.30 a.m.

At Mooi River, which was reached early next morning, things became more interesting, for only a day before marauding Boers had been seen in the neighbourhood.

Estcourt was reached by 9 a.m. Very hungry, we successfully raided the station restaurant, and returned to our train smiling and content, for this was probably the last good meal we should have for some time to come, and we had done justice to it. But when two hours had gone by, and the train was still 'as you were,' we began to think we were not getting much 'forwarder,' and chafed irritably at the delay, for away in the direction of Ladysmith heavy firing could be distinctly heard, and we felt sure something in the way of a fight was being missed.

Then along came a telegram, ordering us to remain at Estcourt—a horrible disappointment which, added to the discomfort of having baked and broiled in a siding in a hot railway carriage under a burning sun all the morning, seriously tried our angelic dispositions. There was nothing to do but pitch our tents, which was done, close to the railway, and, as it rained heavily that night, we were washed out, not having yet mastered the intricacies of trench digging round them.

Estcourt was crowded with troops, and the long khaki 4.7's on their trucks were the admiration of the Tommies, whose opinion was that 'they were the boys for the —— Bó-ers.'

While we remained here troop-trains rolled up from the south in incessant streams and rolled along northwards to the front. On the morning of November 29 orders came to move on, so camp was struck, the gear replaced on the trucks, an engine appeared from somewhere or other, and hauled the Naval Brigade to Frere sixteen miles away.

At last we breathed freely—we were now actually 'at the front.'

Chapter 2

Two Days' Bombardment of Colenso Trenches

Ox-teams for the guns, and ammunition and baggage ox-wagons were waiting for us, with their mob of native drivers, so the guns were taken off the trucks and the trains unloaded.

After much hard work we started our first trek—a short one of a mile—but it was over an awkward *drift* across the Blauwbank River, which gave us some idea of what we had in store later on. Once safely across our tents were pitched on sloping ground on the north bank, and close to the railway bridge, now lying in the river-bed wrecked by Boer dynamite.

One or two houses close by, which we visited, showed the wanton destruction caused by the enemy; the furniture broken to fragments, glasses smashed, mattresses picked to bits, books and music torn into little pieces and scattered all over the rooms. One thing was most noticeable—no picture relating to any sacred subject was ever touched. About a mile and a half towards Colenso was the remains of the wreck of the armoured train. In this train there had been some men of the *Tartar*, working a 7-pounder, and four of these had been captured and one killed. The upturned trucks lying on the *veldt* were silent witnesses of a gallant little action.

Two days after our arrival the *Terrible's* searchlight apparatus arrived, mounted on a railway truck and worked by its own engine and dynamo. It was invaluable, for though signals could be made fairly easily by 'helio' *from* Ladysmith, to the top of a hill near Weenen, and thence to Frere, it was very difficult to get a similar signal *into* the town.

The Boers hovered within three miles of the pickets, and one day a 12-pounder managed to wound two or three.

On December 4 we started off at 1 a.m. with one 4.7 and an escort, with the idea of proceeding to Chieveley, to shell Colenso. We travelled along, in pitchy darkness, over a country covered with huge boulders, and intersected with *dongas* and barbed wire fences.

There certainly was a guide, but, in the darkness, he was useless. Once or twice the gun nearly turned over into a *donga* or got embedded in mud. Just before sunrise we had gained a slight crest, from which the Boer position could be seen, but we were still four miles from Chieveley, it was raining hard, and it was impossible to reach the appointed position before day- light, so the expedition was abandoned, and camp formed two miles north of Frere, where we were presently joined by the second 4.7.

This trip reminded us somewhat of the 'brave old Duke of York,' and his time-honoured expedition.

December 6.—The four 12-pounders, left behind at Maritzburg, rejoined, and we were also reinforced by two officers and fifty men of the Natal Naval Volunteers, whose knowledge of the country, and of both native and Dutch languages, was very useful.

This same detachment was at Colenso when that place was hurriedly evacuated, after the investment of Ladysmith, and was told to leave its guns in Fort Wyllie, but the men would not hear of abandoning them, so rolled them down the *kopje* across the *veldt* to the train, and got them away safely. General Buller arrived at Frere on this date.

Two days later another detachment from the *Terrible* and *Philomel* arrived, with eight 12-pounders, under Lieutenant Ogilvy. This was a large addition to our brigade.

Next morning at sunrise the camp was struck, and the two 4.7's, all the 12-pounders, ammunition and baggage wagons, marched a couple of miles along the road to give the men practice and to test the transport arrangement. Everything being satisfactory, the Naval Brigade returned to camp.

With our fourteen guns and numerous wagons with their long ox-teams, the column made a brave show, stretching close upon a mile. The 4.7's were easily hauled along by sixteen oxen, though a spare team was always kept in readiness to assist up hills or through *drifts*.

The trails of the 12-pounders were at first made fast to the rear of wagons, but later on were supplied with their own oxen (twelve to fourteen).

December 12.—All were up at two o'clock, tents were struck, all gear stowed away in the wagons, and we left at 3.30 a.m., trekking some six miles to Chieveley with the 6th Brigade, and arriving at a *kopje*—Gun Hill— on which the guns were placed in position. This hill was about four hundred feet high, and from it the ground gradually sloped down to the Tugela at Colenso about four miles away. From the summit a good view of the Boer position was obtained, and behind it was pitched the naval camp.

It was a very stony spot, and it was with some difficulty one could pick out a place to sleep with any degree of comfort. Scorpions, snakes, and white ants were numerous; flies were unbearable, but mosquitoes were not very troublesome.

The heat in the morning had been terrific and in the afternoon there was a heavy thunderstorm, the difference in the morning and afternoon temperatures being very great.

December 13.—Orders were received to move forward another 2,000 yards, to a *kopje* nearer the Boer position, but a dense fog postponed this movement. Later on it cleared away, and at 7 a.m. the 4.7 guns opened fire, for the first time, on the Colenso trenches, and kept it going till 9.80, when the tremendous heat and mirage made satisfactory shooting at long ranges (7,000 to 11,000 yards) impossible. The guns and their mountings worked admirably and very good shooting was made, but there was no reply, and the Boers could be seen in the evening still busily digging.

General Buller came on from Frere with Ogilvy's six 12-pounders, so there were now two 4.7's and twelve 12-pounders with the Naval Brigade. Till the general's arrival most people were under the impression that only a feint was to be made at Colenso, and that there would be a big flanking movement in the direction of Potgieter's Drift.

At 7.30 next morning camp was shifted to the previously mentioned *kopje*, 2,000 yards nearer the Boer trenches. It afterwards was known as Shooter's Hill. The 4.7's opened fire at 9 a.m. and carried on intermittently daring the day. There was no reply and the enemy would not be tempted to unmask his guns, though we were well within range. Later on this day orders were received for the morrow. Two 12-pounders were to remain on Gun Hill, four to advance with the 4.7's to a more advantageous position, and six were to attach themselves to Colonel Long's batteries. (Two 12-pounders were still at Estcourt, two at Mooi River, and two at Frere.)

ONE OF THE 4.7's AND A 12-POUNDER IN ACTION AT THE BATTLE OF COLENSO

CHAPTER 3

The Battle of Colenso

December 15.—We were called at 2 a.m., made a hearty breakfast and, two hours later, moved down the slopes of Shooter's Hill with two 4.7's and four 12-pounders and marched towards Colenso. Day dawned, and the yells of the native drivers, and the rumbling and jolting of the gun and wagon wheels over the crisp *veldt*, alone broke the silence of that calm peaceful morning.

As the light became stronger we could make out, away across the river, the dim outlines of what we thought must be Boer gun positions, and being in the open and making a large target, we were naturally very anxious lest they should open fire on us, for had they done so, there is no doubt that our oxen and natives would have stampeded, and we should have been badly mauled.

However, they left us alone and the six naval guns were slowly drawn up a slight eminence, 800 yards to the left of the railway, facing Colenso and Fort Wyllie, and distant from the latter, the centre of the enemy's position, about 4,500 yards. Unmolested they unlimbered, and the first shot—the first shot of the day—was fired at 5.20 a.m. from a 4.7. Everyone expected this to have the effect of a stick in a wasps' nest, and bring a score of replies about our ears, but not a sign or a move did they make along their whole line.

We kept at it, steadily plugging rifle-pits and trenches for half an hour, whilst Hart and Dundonald slowly worked their way to the left and right respectively, and Long's batteries, with six naval 12-pounders in rear of them, marched slowly along the other side of the railway towards the centre to make their great artillery attack on Fort Wyllie and the neighbouring trenches and rifle-pits.

They appeared to have almost gained the river banks, and were just coming into action, when the pent-up storm burst, and a tremendous rifle-fire was opened on them from rifle-pits among the trees, from the river banks, and the triple row of trenches beyond it; Fort Wyllie also opened with pom-poms.

Firing now became general all along the line, nor could rifle-fire, more continuous and intense, be imagined. Pom-poms, cunningly concealed, added their horrid noise, and now, at last, the Boer big guns, very scattered and very well hidden, commenced to open fire, the smokeless powder they used making it most exceedingly difficult to locate them.

In half an hour. Long's guns were out of action in the centre, the naval guns with him could not keep down the fire and had to be withdrawn, Hildyard was barely maintaining himself in Colenso, and Hart was in difficulties on the left. The attack was a failure, and, to enable Hart to extricate himself, more batteries and Lyttelton's brigade were hurried forward in support. These batteries, coming into the open, were vigorously shelled by three long-range guns at 7,000 yards, to which they could not reply and were badly hammered, till we turned on the three and eventually silenced them.

Then a general retirement was ordered, and it was our job to cover it, and keep down the fire from the big guns. We discovered something like twenty of them, and our men sweated away in the terrible heat, silencing, temporarily, one after another, and making grand shooting; but our guns were all too few, and what with the mirage and the enemy using smokeless powder it was almost impossible to hit them.

It was now nearly midday—the heat terrible—and the weary troops, tortured with thirst and burning with anger, came slowly back, repulsed indeed, but no one who saw them turning sullenly, as occasional shells from big gun or pom-pom fell amongst them, could call them beaten.

Then came our turn to retire, and one gun after another was slowly withdrawn, but it was not till 2 p.m. that all were back again at Shooter's Hill.

Not a man had been touched with the 4.7's, though shells fell frequently all round the guns—fortunately they seldom exploded, but went bounding from rock to rock and finally burying themselves in the ground. Most amusing it was to see the bluejackets and the men of our escort chasing them.

Some of us jolted back to camp on an ammunition wagon and were made a target of, one shell dropping just behind it. We kept our seats, but concluded on the next similar occasion to avail ourselves of

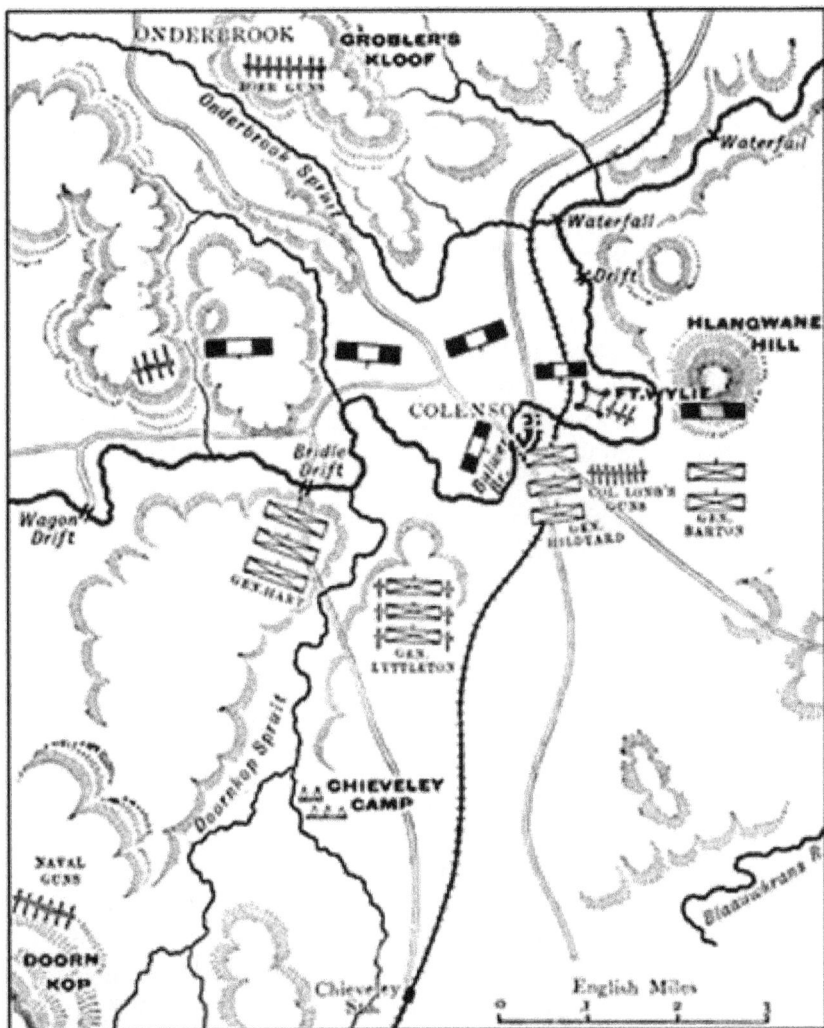

BATTLE OF COLENSO

a less conspicuous means of transport.

Close to Shooter's Hill the field hospitals had been established, and here the naval doctors lent a hand till a late hour, attending to the wounded, who were brought back the three miles and more from where they fell, by the volunteer stretcher-bearers—a very saddening sight.

Thus ended a memorable and ill-fated day.

The following account taken from Lieutenant Ogilvy's Report gives a very vivid idea of the work of his six 12-pounders attached to Colonel Long's batteries.

Acting under orders received from Captain Jones, R.N., I reported myself to Colonel Long, C.R.A., who directed me to attach myself to him until the guns had been placed in a suitable position. I therefore directed Lieutenant James of the 'Tartar 'to lead the battery behind the Royal Artillery field guns, and told him we were to form up on the left of these guns when they came into action. About 6 a.m., the guns being in column of route march with naval guns in the rear, I was riding in front beside Colonel Long about 450 yards from Colenso Station, when he directed Colonel Hunt to bring his guns into action just in front of a deep *donga* running across our front at right angles to the railway.

He then told me to come into action on the left, and proceeded to arrange our different zones of fire, while the Royal Artillery guns were getting into position. In front of us was a line of trees up to which our skirmishers had advanced, also a few artillery outposts. Just as I was about to direct my guns where to go, and as the Royal Artillery were unlimbering, the outposts turned sharply, and a murderous fire, both rifle and shell, was opened on the guns and ammunition column.

I immediately galloped back to my guns and found that the fire had caught them just as the two centre guns were going through a *drift* across another *donga* parallel to the first mentioned one but about four hundred yards in the rear. When I arrived I found that all the native drivers, with the exception of Lieutenant James's gun teams, had bolted. [*These men behaved with great gallantry and, turning up their coat-collars as if the pattering round them was only a rain shower, worked their teams with great coolness.—Original Ed.*] These guns had just crossed the *drift*, so I directed him to take up a position on the left and open fire on Fort Wyllie, from which the majority of the shell fire seemed to come. . . . The two rear guns under Lieut. Deas, of H.M.S. *Philomel*, not having crossed the *drift*, I directed him to take ground to the left and open fire also on Fort Wyllie.

The two centre guns under Mr. Wright, gunner, of H.M.S. *Terrible*, were unfortunately jammed with their ammunition wagons in the *drift*, the wheels of the wagons being locked and the oxen turned round in their yokes. I managed by the aid of some artillery-horses to extricate these guns from the *drift* and to bring them into action on each side of the *drift* to the rear of the *donga*, one of the horses being shot whilst doing this. I could not manage to move the ammunition wagons, as the rifle and shell fire was too severe at the time, a 1½-pounder Maxim-Nordenfeldt being particularly attentive, and sending three shells into the *drift* at every discharge.

Repeated messages for more men came back from the Royal Artillery batteries, and these were sent to the front by a Royal Artillery sergeant in charge of the ammunition column. After about half an hour's firing, as I should judge, the Royal Artillery guns were silenced, nearly all the men being apparently killed or wounded. Soon after this the fire from Fort Wyllie slackened considerably. The commander-in-chief now rode up and directed me to move our guns and ammunition as soon as I could. The guns were got away each by a team of artillery-horses who galloped them up the hill in the rear. The wagons were far more difficult, owing to their weight, the large circle they required to torn in, and to the fact that they had to be got out from the *drift* and turned round by the guns' crews before the horses could be put on.

About this time a most brilliant feat was performed by two teams of artillery, who galloped to the front, against a most murderous fire, limbered up and rescued two guns; a similar attempt by one other team, at least, resulted in the entire team, as far as I could see, being destroyed. . . . The conduct of our men without exception was particularly fine, the day being a very hot one and the work hard. The way Nos. 1 and 2 guns' crews of the *Terrible* got their wagons out of the *drift* under heavy fire from shell and rifle was quite up to the standard expected of all seamen. . . . Our loss was very small, three wounded, one of them very slightly, and I attribute this (1st) to the Fort Wyllie guns and rifle fire being directed principally on the R.A. guns, which were some three hundred yards nearer than we were; (2nd) to the enemy directing most of their fire on our ox-teams and wagons, they being so much more conspicuous than the guns; twenty-eight oxen were killed, wounded, or lost....

CHAPTER 4

Awaiting Reinforcements After Colenso

On December 17, two days after the big fight, the 4.7's and six 12-pounders—unobserved by the enemy—moved back early in the morning to Gun Hill at Chieveley, and at 7 a.m., from this position, the 4.7's opened fire on the Boer trenches.

Ogilvy's six 12-pounders had retired to Frere with the larger portion of the army, and for the next three weary weeks, waiting for reinforcements to arrive, had nothing whatever to do. We with the 4.7's worried the Boers nearly every day, chiefly at sunrise and just before sundown, for then there was no mirage; occasionally we loosed off a few rounds at night, and at other times were usefully employed covering reconnaissances—seldom were we altogether idle.

The Boers made many facetious signals, such as: 'How did you like your licking on Friday?' 'How is Mr. Buller?' 'What has Mr. Buller done that Roberts is coming out?' 'Let us know when you intend attacking again,' &c., &c.

In two months' time they had, however, forgotten to be funny!

On the 19th the 4.7's were ordered to destroy the footbridge at Colenso, and one gun plugged at it—it was 7,500 yards off— for half an hour, without any result, so the second gun was turned on, and William Bate, the captain of the gun, with his third or fourth shot, dropped a lyddite shell on top of it and completely wrecked one span; exceedingly good gunnery it was.

With this bridge destroyed, the Boers occupying Hlangwani Hill, to the south of the river, were isolated from the north bank and would find themselves cut off, if the river rose.

On the 22nd a spare 4.7 arrived from Durban to replace one

showing signs of wear. The railway brought it to the foot of Gun Hill whilst the guns were in action. The crew of the damaged gun ceased firing, dismounted it, rolled it down to the railway truck, hauled the spare one up, and had it mounted in less than an hour. No shears or tripods were used, and many soldiers took a lesson in impromptu naval repository drill.

A small party of bluejackets from the *Philomel* and *Forte* also arrived about this time to join the balloon section, and soon made themselves indispensable.

For three weeks the usual camp life was lived; very little to do, and a great deal of time to do it.

To fill up spare hours, the 4.7 crews, when not firing, worked 2,000 fathoms of 6-inch rope into mantlets for an armoured train, and kicked a football about in the cool of the evening.

Crowds of Tommies used to stand by for an opportunity of looking through the long ships' telescopes at the Boer trenches, and often came asking to be shown a Boer, for though many of them had been in the firing line at Colenso, they had never yet seen one.

'Long Tom' of Bulwana, twelve miles away, could be seen from here firing into Ladysmith, with the shells from the naval guns in the town occasionally bursting close to him. Through the telescopes we could even see men walking about near this gun position; so little wonder that, with the 4.7's sometimes firing and with our telescopic peep-show. Gun Hill became a very favourite resort.

It soon became christened Liars' Kopje, for among the officers and men who came to look on, most extraordinary yams, as to what the Boers and ourselves had done, or were going to do, were spun.

Thunderstorms and sandstorms were frequent, and the rapid changes of temperature, sometimes as much as 35°, were very trying; but the greatest trouble of all was the great scarcity of water, and what there was—an insipid khaki-coloured liquid—had to be brought daily from Frere.

Christmas Day was spent in peace; even the Boers left off their ceaseless digging.

Sports were organised in the afternoon, and two of our bluejackets, made up to represent John Bull and Mr. Kruger—Old Krugger the Tommies called him—caused much amusement. These two eventually had a tug-of-war, Kruger getting the better at first, but John Bull calling for reinforcements, and being backed up by Tommies and bluejackets, Oom Paul was rushed away with merry cheers.

GETTING THE SIGHTS ON

FIRE! 4.7 GUN IN ACTION ON GUN HILL

The Boers watching through their glasses must have thought we English took war very lightly.

January 6.—From the earliest hours of the morning till seven o'clock at night incessant and very heavy firing could be heard in the direction of Ladysmith.

This was the desperate attack on Caesar's Gamp and unfortunately little could be done to help the garrison; the force certainly did advance and threaten Colenso, and may possibly have kept a few Boers in the trenches there, but that is all. Knowing, as all did, that enteric and dysentery were raging in Ladysmith, and that the troops there were naturally enfeebled, it was very galling to be unable to assist them more; and, as the firing died fitfully away in the evening, anxiety as to the fate of the town was very great. The good news next morning was therefore very cheering and an intense relief.

CHAPTER 5

Commence the Second Attempt to Relieve Ladysmith

By January 9, Warren's reinforcements had commenced to arrive, and orders were received to march to Spearman's Hill, a great *kopje* overlooking Potgieter"'s Drift across the Tugela some miles to the west of Colenso.

We got the 4.7's to the foot of Gun Hill that night, all ready for the morrow, and the carpenter rigged up dummy guns in their place, but the Boers were not deceived for long by them, and heliographed next day: 'Do you take us to be such fools as not to know a dummy from a real gun?'

At 8.30 next morning, the two 4.7's got under way and marched west'ard, leaving four 12-pounders, and a newly arrived 4.7 mounted on a railway truck, at Chieveley, and meeting the main army with Ogilvy's 12-pounders, they marched along with them. There must have been 20,000 men in the column and it stretched, with its guns, ammunition, and baggage columns, a matter of twenty miles. Several *drifts* delayed the march, and at 7 p.m. we halted at the worst *drift* in the Colony—Pretorius Drift— and bivouacked under the wagons out of the rain. We had marched fourteen miles and had had nothing to eat all day, so were rather fatigued. The Naval Brigade was lucky to have wagons to crawl under, out of the rain, much more lucky than most units.

All night long Warren's division marched past us down to the *drift* and across the river, and so close was our bivouac to the road that the continuous tramping of feet, jingling of harness, and rattling of wheels prevented much sleep, and no one was sorry when day broke and our turn came to cross.

It was the worst *drift* we had had to tackle. The road down to it was all right, but that up the other side was only about twelve feet wide—a mere cutting in the river bank, with sides twelve feet or more high. It was very steep and sometimes as many as forty or fifty oxen were required, in addition to a couple of hundred soldiers hauling on ropes, to drag a wagon up this rise, and it took us two hours' hard work before the whole Naval Brigade was over, the wheels sinking to their axles and the oxen up to their houghs in the thick black mud.

We bivouacked on the other side, but received orders to march to Springfield, and arrived there at 9.30 p.m., crossing the little Tugela next morning by a substantial bridge—left intact by the Boers—and marching to Lindeque Spruit, which the previous day had been occupied by the enemy. Here we had a most refreshing bathe, and on the 11th marched to Spearman's Hill, the 4.7's being placed in position on Mount Alice, whilst the 12-pounders were placed across a loop of the very tortuous river.

The top of Mount Alice, from which direct communication was kept up with Ladysmith, was covered with long luxurious grass, and many cassia, mimosa, and cactus trees gave grateful shade and made the naval camp very pleasant. The air was bracing and the atmosphere was so exceedingly clear that we could see astonishing distances, and often fell into the error of underestimating ranges. At the foot of this hill was the *drift*, and being hauled slowly to and fro, across it, was the punt, so pluckily captured two days before by some South African Light Horse.

Through the *drift* ran the road to Ladysmith, winding its way upwards towards the centre of a great horseshoe of high hills, Vaal Krantz and Brakfontein on the right, Mount Tambanyama, ending in the prominent peak of Spion Kop, on the left.

Through our telescopes we could plainly see the enemy digging for dear life on the sides of these hills, extending their trenches and building *schanzes* and gun emplacements. Between them and the river, and not more than half a mile from the *drift*, were a few small *kopjes* which Lyttelton's brigade, a field battery and some 5-inch howitzers occupied on the 17th without much opposition, bluejackets being sent down to man the punt and doing good work. 'Worth their weight in gold,' was the general's verdict.

This brigade, with its guns backed up by the naval guns, was to 'contain' the Boers in their circle of hills, whilst Warren's division with Dundonald's mounted men still further to the left swept round the

SKETCH OF SPION KOP POSITION
JAN. 20-23.

Acton Homes

To Ladysmith

Mt Tabanyama

SPION KOP

Three Tree Hill

Tugela River

Trichard's Fm.

Trichard's

Potgieter's Drift

R.N.12

R.N.4

Mt Alice

Zwart Kop

Spearman's Hill

Spearman's Fm.

Tugela R.

Springfield

Little

Bridge

To Frere

N

Scale, 1 Inch = 3.94 Miles.

Miles 1 ½ 0 1 2 3 4 5 Miles.

Boer left, got behind them and crumpled up their whole line of defence.

From the 17th to the 23rd we bombarded Spion Kop and Brakfontein—the centre of the great horseshoe—helped by the 5-inch howitzers, but never drawing the fire of big guns and only occasionally, when the infantry made demonstrations, exposing one or two pom-poms. The big guns were all opposing Warren, whose force we could plainly observe pushing its way forward on our left in a northeasterly direction. Some of Lyttelton's howitzers were sent round to help him, but by the 23rd it was obvious that, with Tambanyama untaken, no further progress could be made, and, as Spion Kop appeared to dominate the rest of that range, Spion Kop had to be taken.

The 12-pounders, previously on the south of the river, now crossed the *drift* and took up position in the *kopjes* above it; Lyttelton's men were to demonstrate again against Brakfontein, immediately opposite Spion Kop, and all the naval guns were to back them up, whilst Woodgate's Lancashire Brigade, Thornycroft's Mounted Infantry, and the 17 Company R.E. climbed up the south-western slopes of Spion Kop under cover of darkness.

Morning dawned, hazy with a thick mist. Presently this cleared away and Spion Kop stood out boldly, and we could see our men streaming up it, others hastily entrenching themselves on the southern summit. We could also see Boers, gathering in clouds, dodging about among the great boulders behind the great *nek*, and preparing to drive them back. Directly the mist drove away, with every rifle and every gun they could get to bear, they opened fire on the summit, now crowded with our troops—most of them unable to get the least cover. Some guns began firing from the northern peak of Spion Kop, from a ridge, even higher than that to which our men were desperately clinging, others from Tambanyama itself, still others from hills behind it—all impossible to be reached by the naval guns on Mount Alice. Guns must be sent up, so James's two 12-pounders were ordered there and marched off; one of the 4.7's, too, was ordered to the west to get at the Boer guns on the other side of the hills.

Meanwhile affairs were becoming desperate up on the top of the ridge, with its feeble breastwork of stones behind which men and corpses were crowded together; and, to keep down the terrible fire, two of Lyttelton's battalions, away to the right, swung round and went straight up the steep side of the highest part of Spion Kop.

We pounded the rocks ahead and above them as hard as our men could work, and they carried the summit in the most gallant manner. More men were sent up to reinforce Woodgate's men as night fell; the Boer fire had slackened considerably, and the possession of the hill seemed to be assured, and our infantry holding its own. James's 12-pounders and a mountain battery started to haul their guns up the narrow precipitous path, choked with bearers bringing down the wounded, and men carrying up water. Progress was terribly difficult in the darkness and terribly slow. Worse than all, when half-way up, they met the worn-out troops streaming down from the top, learnt that Spion Kop had been evacuated, and had to return, sore at heart.

It was not till next morning that we, on Mount Alice, heard the bad news, and our disappointment after witnessing the gallant fight of the previous evening, and now learning that a general retirement to the south of the river had been ordered, was very great.

The Boers were as surprised as we were, for, when morning broke, they began pounding the fatal ridge again, till they discovered that it was evacuated.

By the 29th practically all the troops had recrossed the river. The second attempt had failed, just as success had seemed within grasp, but there was no mistaking the men— they meant to get through somehow or somewhere.

From this date to February 4 not a shot was fired, and all wondered when the next move was going to take place.

Six of the 12-pounders were hauled to the top of Zwaart Kop, a steep *kopje* on the right of Mount Alice—a very tough job but much relished by the bluejackets—and one of the 4.7's was shifted to the eastern end of Mount Alice, supported by two old naval 5-inch guns manned by garrison artillery.

Pontoon bridges were thrown across the river, and on February 5 the army recrossed once more.

Spion Kop having been found too difficult a nut to crack, Vaal Krantz, the opposite side of the horseshoe, was now to be attacked. Six batteries of R.F.A. were to cover the advance, supported by every gun that would bear. Moving eastwards towards Vaal Krantz they came under a plunging fire from three guns on Spion Kop. These guns were very difficult to locate, but we turned our 4.7's on to them, and managed to smash up one, and chip the muzzle of a second, so that his shooting became erratic. The third we could not reach. It was a fine sight to see these six batteries in action and under a fire to which they could not possibly reply. Plump would fall a big shell right among them, a whole gun and its crew would disappear in the smoke and dust, yet frequently that gun would fire before the smoke cleared away. The only possible way to describe the attitude of the Royal Artillery under fire is this—they absolutely and literally disregard it. Next morning, more Boer guns had been brought up and commenced harassing our people from the eastward; a 6-inch was especially annoying to the infantry on the lower slopes of Vaal Krantz.

One of our 4.7's started to hunt him out of it, and with a lucky shot blew up his ammunition and kept him quiet for some time. We never managed to hit that gun, but whilst we were engaging him his shells only came at long intervals, showing that our own were falling uncomfortably close. The range was very great, 11,500 yards.

Some of these guns were mounted on rails and often retired from view after firing, and this fact alone made the difficulty of hitting them exceedingly great.

Nothing much happened next day—the balloon was busy, but very little fighting occurred, and the infantry did not advance.

Indeed, the reports from the balloon were so bad—the whole road to Ladysmith bristling with guns, covered with gun-emplacements and trenches, in fact every hill the whole way a fortress— that the attempt in this direction was given up, the infantry fell back across the river daring the night, and by the 9th everybody was again on the south bank and marching back to Chieveley.

More than two thousand men had been lost in the fortnight's fighting.

The 4.7's came down from Mount Alice in the evening, and the whole Naval Brigade, with the exception of two 12-pounders left behind with the flanking guard, marched back to their old position at Gun Hill without incident, arriving there on the morning of the 11th, travelling along well, for most of the *spruits* and *drifts* had been filled in with earth and stones.

VAAL KRANTZ.

CHAPTER 6

The Fourth Attempt

If Ladysmith was not to fall by starvation there was no time to waste, so on the 14th—the third day after our arrival—the fourth scheme for penetrating the Boer positions was commenced.

This time Hlangwani, the isolated *kopje* on the south side of the river, was to be captured; and once in our hands it would command the *drift* at Colenso and all the Boer positions there, in fact crush in their left and centre.

Early in the morning a small force, supported by Ogilvy's 12-pounders, seized Hussar Hill, a *kopje* to be used in developing the attack on Monte Cristo and Cingolo, two eminences which dominated Hlangwani and were not strongly held by the enemy.

Hussar Hill was only held by Boer pickets, the advance seemed to have taken them by surprise, and the reinforcements hurried out arrived too late. On this hill sandbag emplacements were hastily made for the naval guns, and these were next day reinforced by two 6-inch R.G.A. All day the naval guns on Gun Hill in the rear were occupied covering the advance of the troops.

Daring the next two days—excessively hot they were— an artillery duel took place, without mach result, whilst reconnaissances were being made. On the evening of the 6th a 6-inch naval gun, mounted on a travelling carriage and just sent up from Durban, was put in position on Gun Hill, and early the following morning opened fire, quickly finding a worthy antagonist, for a Boer 6.2-inch opened on Hussar Hill from a *kopje* opposite Colenso.

In a few rounds the 6-inch silenced it, making splendid shooting at the great range of 16,000 yards.

By the evening the infantry had pushed up the slopes and occupied Cingolo, the Boers apparently not being in great force. But next morning they were hurrying reinforcements over to it in great numbers and had brought up more guns—wonderful was the way they shifted their heavy pieces—and began going for Cingolo for all they were worth, one gun at Bloy's farm, close in under Monte Cristo, especially giving much trouble. The 6-inch at Gun Hill, always on the lookout for such customers, went for him and drove him away with the third shot, a lucky shot, for the range was 18,500 yards (10½ miles).

Gun Hill was very busy all that day, and at 1 p.m. a Boer 6.2 opening on Hussar Hill, the naval 6-inch and three 4.7's (one on a railway truck) concentrated their fire on him, and drove him out of it again at the sixth round. Later in the evening they also extinguished a Boer searchlight.

Our infantry now showed up along the sky-line of Monte Cristo and gradually swept the Boers off it. By the evening the enemy were falling back on their centre, were all across on the north of the river, and had left several *laagers* in our hands. Every one's spirits rose exceedingly.

Gun Hill was now too much in the rear, so at 5.30 a.m., February 19, we advanced with two 4.7's, trekking past Hussar Hill, over awful roads— bridle paths really—the guns bumping and crashing over enormous boulders, fallen trees, through *dongas*, and eventually through an almost dry *spruit*, fetching up at last under Monte Cristo, for the oxen had had just about enough of it, and struck work. The great heat troubled them, poor brutes, even perhaps more than us.

The 5-inch were merrily in action ahead of us, so, after a rest, we borrowed a hundred men from a regiment and hauled the guns up alongside them by hand, and opened fire. Many shells dropped round them but without doing any damage.

We were close to a *laager* evacuated, the day previously, in a great hurry, horses, tents, flour and ammunition having been left behind.

The position was not commanding enough, however, so before daylight we shifted to a spur of Monte Cristo, and were there soon snugly ensconced behind *schanzes*, and, though hidden among trees, could get a grand view of the country north of the river. The R.E. helped us with our *schanzes* and gave us sandbags.

General Buller arrived at 9.30, and we came into action, continuing firing most of the day. Just before dusk we either destroyed or at any rate completely silenced a Boer gun. From the top of Monte Cristo we had our first view of Ladysmith, ten miles away as the crow

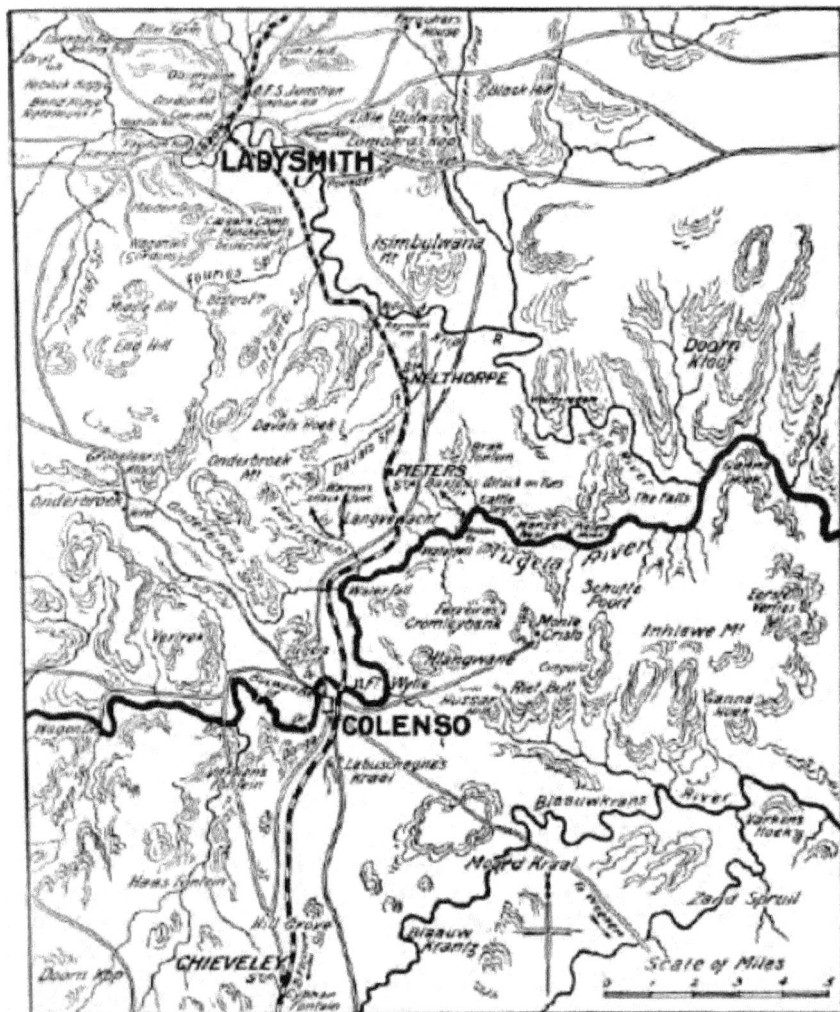

DISTRICT BETWEEN COLENSO AND LADYSMITH

flies, and with Boer *laagers* lying in between.

Ogilvy, meanwhile, had got two of his 12-pounders up to the top of Monte Cristo. Next day Hart's brigade got into Colenso, and took the Colenso *kopjes* and Fort Wyllie, James's 12-pounders going with him and taking up a position a mile to the north of the river.

The Boer centre was falling back on Pieter's and Railway Hills, and our army, to get at them and drive them back still further, had to incline to the west to cross at Colenso.

At dusk the 4.7's were brought down to the river and bivouacked near the pontoon. On the way we had to pass Bloy's Farm, and there saw very marked evidences of the 6-inch lyddite shells which had silenced a gun there three days before. We travelled over one of the worst pieces of ground it is possible to imagine, bad enough in the daytime, but a thousand times worse at night. This was a good test of the strength of the gun carriages, and they stood it right well.

We expected to cross at once, but were ordered to remain on the south bank till morning. Morning broke, and, as we were preparing to cross, orders were received to come into action at once, which we did, only a hundred yards from the bridge, and soon were engaged with a number of Boer guns over a wide front. Shells dropped round us all day, but were apparently chiefly intended for the pontoons, which, luckily, they failed to hit. Two more 12-pounders went across and were soon briskly engaged beyond Colenso.

The Boers, seeing our army inclining towards their centre, had evidently taken heart and were coming back. They showed plenty of fight during the next two days.

In the evening, firing having slackened, we moved down to the bridge, and directly the first gun and its carriage (five tons and three-quarters) got on the pontoon this began to crack, so it was drawn back as quickly as possible.

One of the oxen dropped overboard and had to be cut away, being washed over the falls a little way lower down, and though dropping thirty feet was rescued undamaged.

The break-down of the bridge was a great nuisance, and so unexpected was it that the steep *donga* leading to it was choked with wagons waiting to cross. The oxen and mules had first to be removed and the wagons dragged out backwards—a very slow process.

It seemed fated that the 4.7's should never cross.

It was too late to begin again, so the guns were taken off their carriages and placed on wagons all ready for the morning.

At 5.30, February 23, they crossed in this manner without a hitch and, safely landed on the north bank, were quickly remounted.

Four 5-inch R.G.A. guns came across as well, and all were posted close to the 12-pounders among the Colenso *kopjes*.

Meanwhile Ogilvy had got six 12-pounders to the top of Hlangwani, and a 4.7 on a platform mounting had come to the assistance of the big 6-inch on Gun Hill.

Right ahead was Terrace Hill, supported a little to the right and rear by Pieter's and Railway Hills, all strongly held by the enemy, who could be seen hurrying up reinforcements of men and guns. They had at least three 45-pounders, a dozen 12-15-pounders and several smaller long-range guns, besides pom-poms and some of our own artillery lost at Colenso.

We were soon very hotly engaged.

Captain Jones's despatch well describes this day's fighting:—

At 9 a.m. all the guns opened fire, which was replied to by a brisk fire from the enemy. During the day our infantry advanced and took the southern slopes of a commanding, strongly-fortified, and entrenched position at the summit of a range of hills close to the route to Ladysmith [Terrace Hill].

Towards evening General Hart, with the Irish Brigade, assaulted the summit, but did not succeed in taking it, and at dusk entrenched himself just below the last ridge leading up to it. He left, however, many killed and wounded on the glacis.

During the whole day the enemy shelled very vigorously, and it is beyond my comprehension how so small an amount of damage was done, as they were shooting with great accuracy. A dozen shells, mostly 40-pounders, fell within a radius of twenty yards round the 4.7 guns, and a great many passed over, while others fell a very little short.

I took the big glass up to the 12-pounders which were engaging on Grobler's side (the left) to try to discover guns, and there, I think, it was even warmer, for we had a pom-pom on us as well as two or three big guns. It was here that my coxswain, Thomas Tunbridge, who was sitting down on a stone, was struck by a shell which tore away half his thigh. Fortunately the shell did not burst, as there was a little knot round the glass where an officer was pointing out the position of a gun to me. Only four men were wounded all day by shell, and one shot by a rifle bullet in the evening. So soon as it was dark the enemy began to snipe our hills pretty freely; in fact, about 9 o'clock it amounted to a considerable fire. We got the men under cover, and no damage was done. The firing continued till daylight.

By next morning we were secure against sniping, having, during the night, built sandbag emplacements round the guns.

All day Saturday the duel continued in a drizzling rain, but the enemy paid more attention to the 6-inch than to us. Hart's infantry could do nothing against Terrace Hill—in fact, were only holding their own, their left even being menaced—so it was decided, without giving up the ground we had gained, to extend to the right, cross the river, and swing round from right to left, taking Pieter's and Railway Hills, which supported Terrace Hill, in detail; so at dusk the 4.7's were taken down to the pontoon, making heavy weather through the muddy roads, bivouacked there, crossed early Sunday morning to the south bank and took up a position on a spur of Hlangwani—close to the four 12-pounders sent across previously—and all in a position to enfilade Terrace Hill.

CHAPTER 7

A Heavy Day's Fighting

After the 4.7's and 12-pounders had been placed in position on Hlangwani, two platform-mounted 4.7's were brought up from Gun Hill, and all Sunday night (February 25) the bluejackets were busy mounting one of these on a *kopje* a thousand yards in front and below the wheeled 4.7's, less than a thousand yards from the Boer snipers, and only 2,500 yards from the big trench on Terrace Hill. A regular fusillade of sniping broke out at 9 p.m., and all night long our working party was incessantly annoyed by snipers. It was very heavy and tiresome work in the dark, and the glimmer of a lantern always immediately drew fire.

Monday, February 26.—Desultory firing took place but no move of importance. The long-range naval telescopes were much used during the day by headquarters staff.

At night the second platform gun was successfully mounted, and, being in such an exposed position, the R.E. rigged a sandbag defence for both.

The *schanzes* on the little Colenso *kopje* we had evacuated on Saturday were literally blown away by the Boers today. They must have been under the impression that the naval guns were still there. Lucky for us that they were not.

At 7 a.m. the big guns opened fire, nor were the enemy slow to reply, and, as the field guns joined in, the noise of the great bombardment gradually swelled. Whilst the naval guns were busy engaging their opponents' guns, the howitzers and field guns threw lyddite or shrapnel into the endless tiers of trenches on Pieter's, Railway, and Terrace Hills.

All the forenoon the infantry were getting into position to assault these hills, and at noon Barton's men were launched at Pieter's and up they went, every gun that would bear clearing the ground in front of them. Pieter's was in our hands in a couple of hours, and just about this time came the news of Cronje's surrender, the cheering of our troops as the good news flew along probably disconcerting the enemy somewhat.

Then came Kitchener's turn to take Railway Hill, and presently we could see his men working up the eastern and western slopes; but those on the western slope were enfiladed from Terrace Hill, made but slow progress, and their advance was checked.

Captain Limpus, of H.M.S. *Terrible*, in his diary thus describes the events immediately following:—

.... for nearly half an hour they did not gain 100 yards. Then the guns redoubled their efforts. The shell bursts seemed almost continuous, lyddite and shrapnel throwing up earth and stones at each trench. One could now see the Boers as they rose up to fire, and the way in which they managed to keep their fire going won our admiration, but we felt that they must be crushed down by shell fire and that our men must be helped all we knew. The bombardment was now terrible, especially at a little mischievous entrenched *kopje* near the top of the *nek*; several times the Boers had to be brought back by a determined man who seemed to be in charge, until at last he himself disappeared in a great lyddite shell that burst—and that trench was silenced. We then moved our shell on to another.

A few of Kitchener's men then rose and charged for- ward splendidly. In a moment the whole lot rushed forward; the oth- er guns ceased, but the two naval 4.7's and four 12-pounders went on as hard as they could. It was felt that there must be no mistake about it this time—those rifles must be cowed and unsteadied until our men were right up to them—so we went on in spite of rapid questions from watching staff officers. To them it looked dangerous: we, with our great telescopes, could be certain how long we might safely continue. At last our men were up, our shell fire swept round up to Terrace Hill, and on Railway Hill the bayonets got to work, and this hill and its ad- joining *nek* were ours.

This was at about 5 p.m.

Norcott's men were now ascending Terrace Hill, and our guns

were shelling the top where the Boers were splendidly standing their ground. The Lancashires, feeling the rifle fire from Terrace and having secured Railway, swung round and charged up Terrace Hill too. This was too much. The Boers wavered, looked behind them, and began making off, hunted by bursting shell, which stopped only to let the Lancashires in again with the bayonet Norcott's men came up and soon the whole hill was in our hands, and the men began making cover against the pom-poms and sniping which now assailed them. But the day was ours. We felt, we saw that the Boers were really beaten, thoroughly beaten and running away; and the relief was tremendous. . . .

Darkness fell amid preparations for going on, and we felt that the battle which decided Ladysmith's fate had now been fought—and won—and that too on Majuba Day.

Captain Jones's despatch also graphically describes the peculiar work of the naval guns:—

I remained with these two guns [platform 4.7's] during the fighting on that great day, the 27th, and not only saw every detail of the fight from relatively quite close to, but also the finest shooting from one of them that I have ever seen in my life.

Once mounted, and at the ranges at which they are required to fire, the platform has a great advantage over the wheeled mounting. Having once got the range, of course you can put as many shots in as you like and as quick as you like. A man from the *Philomel*, Patrick Casham, was the captain of the gun, and a born shot. . . . At least ten different guns always claim to have put some particular gun out of action, so I will only observe that through the big glass I saw this gun put three lyddite shells in one minute into the embrasure of a gun on Grobler; the gun never fired again, nor were the wheels visible afterwards, though I had previously seen them distinctly [range =9,000 yards]. At about 7 or 7.30 a.m. the fusilier brigade advanced to cross the pontoon, and Col. Reeves, of the Irish fusiliers, pointed out to me as he passed the positions up the hill to which they and the Scotch were to go.

This enabled me, I think, to help the Irish considerably. The Scotch, however, went further to the right than I was aware of, and did not get much assistance, as when they swung round to

THE TWO 4.7'S CLEARING THE WAY FOR THE ATTACK ON PIETER'S
AND TERRACE HILLS (HLANGWANI HILL IN THE BACKGROUND)
The haze in front of the gun that has just fired is due to the dust of
the *veldt* being disturbed by the explosion.

THE 6-INCH GUN IN ACTION ON GUN HILL

the left, after surmounting Pieter's Ridge, about 1 o'clock to take the other hills in flank, I could not see how far they had got and would not fire in front of them.

I believe, however, this was admirably done by the 12-pounders and the other two 4.7 inch guns on Hlangwani.

The Scotch started with their bagpipes, and the Irish whistling and joking, and the battle was half won before they started.

. . . Just about this time the news came of Cronje's surrender, and the cheering of the various units as the news reached them did them no harm either.

Wednesday, 28th.—At daybreak the Boer positions were found evacuated and by the evening our mounted troops had entered Lady-smith, thus ending the siege of 112 days.

About noon we crossed the river to the north bank for the second time, and bivouacked in the dip between Terrace and Railway Hills, close to an enormous trench, into which a large number of Boers had bolted the previous evening, and in which a great number had been buried. Many women and children were found in the trenches; prob-ably they had come out to see the English badly 'slated' again. Some of the prisoners stated that they had not been out of their trenches for weeks, some in fact, had been there on the day of Colenso and had, naturally, taken no part in that fight.

At 8 a.m. on March 1 we marched towards Ladysmith, crossing the railway at Pieter's Station, and on to Nelthorpe, along the Colenso-Ladysmith road, bivouacking close to the station.

We had expected the Boer guns round Ladysmith—especially those on Bulwana—to oppose our advance, but the Boers had no more fight left in them and were dragging them away north to the Biggarsberg.

During the afternoon a few of us rode into Ladysmith—about ten miles—and before leaving crammed our holsters with whisky, tobac-co, and cigarettes for the Powerfuls, but our route lying through the neutral camp and hospital of Itombi, we were pretty well plundered before we ever saw them.

We all thought the garrison looked more robust than we had ex-pected. On returning to Nelthorpe after a very cordial meeting with the 'Powerfuls', we examined the dam in the Klip River which the Boers fondly imagined would flood Ladysmith. Not less than half a million sandbags had been already used in its construction, and all round were traces of the hurried flight of the enemy—hundreds of spades, pick-axes, and bales of new bags scattered over the ground.

On March 8 the 4.7's were taken to Ladysmith by train, and the Naval Brigade with its 12-pounders and wagons trekked there, marching through the town and pitching tents two miles to the north-east.

On the 7th the Powerfuls returned to their ship homeward bound, and four days later the Terribles were detached from the Naval Brigade and were sent down to rejoin their ship at Durban, *en route* for China, where they eventually arrived just in time to form part of the Pekin Belief Force. Before they left a telegram was received from Her Majesty, the Queen, thanking the officers and men of the Naval Brigade for their services, and congratulating them on their success.

During the relief operations the 4.7's had fired 4,000 rounds, the 12-pounders 12,000, so small wonder that some of the guns were showing signs of wear.

The strength of the brigade was as follows:

39 officers and 403 men of the Royal Navy.
2 officers and 50 men of the Natal Naval Volunteers.

The guns were:

1 6-inch.
2 4.7's on travelling carriages.
2 4.7's on platform mountings.
1 4.7 on a railway truck.
18 12-pounders, 12 cwt., on travelling carriages.
1 7-pounder, 'Tartar's' armoured train [captured].

CHAPTER 8

Rudely Disturbed by Shells

When Ladysmith had been relieved and both the 'Terribles' and 'Powerfuls' had been sent back to rejoin their ships, the Naval Brigade, although reinforced by the crews of the 12-pounders which had remained on the lines of communication, numbered ten officers and ninety men, only just sufficient to man two 4.7's and four 12-pounders. The remaining guns were handed over to the army.

From March 3 to 19, the diminished brigade was encamped to the north of Ladysmith, and early on the morning of this latter date marched six miles along the Newcastle road, and bivouacked close to the site of one of the big Boer *laagers*, used by them when besieging the town.

Trekking to Elandslaagte (ten miles) the following day, camp was pitched two miles beyond the railway station and a mile south of Sunday's River. General Clery commanded the forces here.

We were left in absolute quiet till April 10, when at 8 a.m. the enemy, quite unexpectedly, opened fire on the camp from four different gun positions, the shells coming fast and pitching right in among the wagons.

This was the first time we had known them begin the game—the trouble had always been, heretofore, to make them reply to our guns.

The six naval guns came into action with great rapidity, and quickly knocked out at least one of their opponents, and shortly managed to subdue the fire of the others.

In the meantime the *Kaffir* drivers and Cape boys had gone after the oxen, which were peaceably grazing some distance away, driven them in, and inspanned. This they did with the most commendable alacrity and coolness, though all the time shells were falling pretty freely among the ammunition wagons. One shell alone smashed a wheel and unfortunately killed two men of the *Philomel*, wounding two others. These were the first men killed in this brigade. The body of one was completely pierced by the case of the shrapnel shell.

Directly the gun teams were brought in, they were hooked on to the guns and dragged them into little emplacements which had been previously made in readiness for just such an occasion, and from these they quickly got the mastery of the Boer guns.

There were several very lucky escapes that morning. Perhaps the most lucky was that of an officer who was superintending the wagons, and heard several men shouting to him to jump aside. This he did, and a big piece of shell went whizzing by, grazing his leg as it passed. These men had seen the shell burst, had seen the fragment flying in his direction, and if he had not jumped aside when they called, it would have caught him clean in the body. A gun limber was smashed up by another shell, and a box of 12-pounder ammunition was completely perforated, the cordite cartridges being cut in two.

The Naval Brigade had, in fact, been more roughly handled than in all its severe fighting south of Ladysmith.

At dusk the force retired on Elandslaagte, and the 4.7's took up a position on the very *kopje* so gallantly captured by our men at the commencement of the war.

The Naval Brigade earned General Clery's especial commendation that day, for the men showed great steadiness under a fire at times very severe, though most of them had previously formed the crews of the guns on the lines of communication, and had never been in action before.

The camp was then left in peace till the 21st, when Boers were seen swarming to the south of the river, where they had occupied a small *kopje*, and on both flanks. The 4.7's opened fire and two Boer guns, one on each flank, promptly replied, but one was quickly smashed up and the other soon ceased firing (range, 4,500 to 4,800 yards).

Then we went to sleep again for nearly three weeks, j whilst everything was being prepared for Buller's great advance.

CHAPTER 1

Very Hard Trekking

On Wednesday, May 9, after our long spell of inactivity, the Natal Field Force commenced a general advance, and from that time until June 24, when I returned with most of my men to H.M.S. *Forte*, we had no cause to complain of inactivity.

The Boers, after raising the siege of Ladysmith, had fallen back to a position of immense natural strength in the Biggarsberg, a range of bold hills stretching across the apex of Natal.

From this they had to be driven, and, to do it, General Buller commenced a wide turning movement to the eastward, sweeping across Sunday's River and through Helpmaakar to Dundee. At the same time the division under General Hildyard crossed Sunday's River near Elandslaagte, and protected Buller's left flank during his advance, working round to the west and clearing the country through Wessers Nek and Waschbank and, forcing his way through the beautiful pass of Glencoe, to Glencoe itself.

As Hildyard advanced and secured positions, the naval 12-pounders followed him and occupied advantageous ground to cover his flank. Thus two crossed Sunday's River on May 13 and the remaining two followed next morning.

The two 4.7 guns which were in position on Battle Hill(the scene of the first battle of Elandslaagte) formed the last unit to leave, which they did on the 17th, with their escort of Natal Volunteers. We were very glad to be on the move again, as the long idle camp-life had told very much on the health of the men, oxen, and horses. This at once commenced to improve, despite the extremely hard work that followed for the next five or six weeks. All tents and heavy baggage were left behind and never pitched again till we got to Volksrust, in the Transvaal, on June 13.

Our first point was Wessel's Nek, where, on our arrival at 2 p.m., we received orders to go on to Waschbank.

It was fair trekking, but one or two very bad *dongas* had to be crossed, and we didn't arrive in camp till 10.30 p.m., when we were most hospitably received and fed by Major Manifold, R.A., whose bivouac adjoined the ground we occupied.

A pretty place this, and most grateful we and our oxen found the river, which flowed alongside and enabled us to give the oxen a good drink next morning, before our start at 7 a.m. for another very long and hard trek, but a very beautiful and extremely interesting one, up through the Pass of Glencoe. We passed enemy's camps still warm, so to speak, and gun positions that, if held, might have kept an army at bay indefinitely, but every Boer had cleared out. General Buller's arrival at Helpmaakar had started them, and by the time he got to Dundee they were off to the Drakensberg, as fast as they could get.

It was 'collar work' for most of the way, and the brigade was halted at a stream for two hours in the middle of the day to graze and water the oxen. A halt of less than this is useless, as oxen must be outspanned—they cannot either eat or drink while inspanned—and as they had had nothing to eat for twenty-four hours, and then only a brief 'snack,' they had plenty of leeway to make up.

We had a very stiff afternoon's trek, across a *drift*, and then up the long steep hill that terminates on the heights of Glencoe. We arrived at the top about 6 p.m., and the animals certainly could not have done it but for their midday halt. Even here they were not to have much of a rest; just time for a drink of muddy water and a mouthful of excellent grass, and then on again at 8 p.m. to a place called Hatting Spruit, only seven miles or so, but the oxen were pretty well 'played out,' and we didn't get to the top of the long hill, where we were to bivouac, till midnight.

We started on again next morning for Danhauser, but when about half-way were stopped by a most optimistic messenger from General Buller, who informed us that we held Laing's Nek and the tunnel, so we were turned back and marched to Glencoe again that night, everybody declaring the war was over. However, it turned out, like so much more of our information, to be merely a stretch of the imagination. They had *seen*, not *held* Laing's Nek, and had ample opportunity of gazing their fill at it for the next month.

We were really turned back, I think, because General Buller was apprehensive about supplies for so large a force, and we therefore halted at Glencoe for two or three days, all the Naval Brigade wagons being requisitioned to bring up supplies.

It was a very welcome halt in some ways, for several of our wagons were sadly in need of going into 'dock,' and we were now able to fit new wheels, and have repairs done in Dundee, which abounds in wheelwrights' shops, as, indeed, does every village in this country.

Here Steele got thrown off his fiery steed one day and was laid up with 'concussion,' Burne had just recovered sufficiently from his fall at Elandslaagte to take charge of his own guns again, and Lilly turned up from sick-leave, having walked all night from Waschbank, with Massey Dawson, to catch us up.

We left Glencoe again on the 23rd, and marched to Danhauser, getting there at midnight, a long wearisome day with the usual amount of *dongas* and *spruits* to cross.

On the 26th, the wagons of the various units having returned, we went on to Ingagane and the following day to Newcastle, which place, in common with all the others we had passed, had been wrecked wantonly by the Boers. There were still, however, a few houses not much damaged. It is a pretty little town with picturesque surronndings and the grand Drakensberg mountains overlooking it.

We crossed the river and camped in some fields on the other side, with plenty of water close at hand and splendid grazing, and hoped we should have a chance of recuperating the oxen. But no! we had scarcely settled down when orders were received to advance next morning across the Buffalo River, with another brigade, to march to Utrecht and capture it.

We crossed at a place called Wool's Drift, where a handsome stone bridge had been erected between the Transvaal and Natal, this having been the dividing line, and were now in that part of Zululand which had been annexed to the Transvaal.

We camped for the night just on the other side, and our 12-pounders were posted on various hills around to protect the camp.

This is a fine river, and the easy access to good water was a great boon to us, as we generally had to make shift with little and bad, and frequently had to drive the oxen many miles to get even that. We were also lucky in getting a good many eggs here, and a few vegetables, these latter being perhaps the greatest luxury, for the compressed vegetables served out by the commissariat did not seem to satisfy the craving for fresh ones.

From this camp we could see a 'Long Tom' mounted on a hill close to Laing's Nek, and occasionally throwing shell into General Clery's camp close to Mount Prospect.

Next morning we moved on to a bivouac about five miles out of Utrecht, near a fine Dutch farm. We did not arrive till after dark, and had to send the oxen a long way back for water. The farm had a cordon of sentries round it, and was as jealously guarded and taken care of as the crown jewels. Even our horses and oxen were not allowed to be watered on the farm, although two rifles and a little ammunition had been found there, after the old man had declared that he had none.

I strolled over early next day, and the old *vrau* graciously sold me four fowls for about double the price she had ever got before, and also gave me some coffee. They all talked English, and the girls told me they had been taught it in the schools at Utrecht, where they were educated.

Nearly all the books—hymn books, *Ancient and Modern*, &c.—that I picked up in this house were in English.

The parson of Utrecht was there, and I had an amusing discussion with him about the war. He seemed to think, or pretended to think, that it was very unfair that sailors should come upcountry against them.

I was obliged to take a wagon at this place, giving a receipt, as usual, for the value, and when my A.D.C. went with the conductor and a team to bring it away, the old rascal grumbled very much and wanted more money. The midshipman said to him, 'Look here! what do you think your countrymen would do if they came to an English farm and wanted a wagon?' He laughed and said, 'Oh, yes, I know; but then they are very bad men.'

This farmer made a 'good thing' out of us, quite 100 *per cent*, on everything he chose to sell.

The following day we all advanced to the capture of Utrecht, but had no fighting, for the *landdrost* came out and surrendered the town. We posted notices on the church and returned to our bivouac near the farm, and next day trekked back to Wool's Drift and thence to De Wet's Farm, north of Newcastle, where we arrived two days later.

From Wool's Drift we started off Steele, into Newcastle, with a couple of oxen in a gun limber, to fetch some gun-wheels we were expecting, mails, and anything he could pick up. It was very amusing to see the start.

The oxen, not accustomed to work in couples, were 'all over the shop,' and the last I saw of them was going full tilt over a hill in the opposite direction. However, he turned up at De Wet's Farm all right a couple of days afterwards, laden with mails, wheels, and other valuables.

Chapter 2

Cross the Pass and Bivouac in the Orange River Colony

On June 6, being in bivouac at De Wet's Farm in Natal, I received orders to ride with Major-General Coke to make a reconnaissance of a hill called Van Wyk, some six or seven miles away, immediately opposite Botha's Pass and about seven thousand yards distant from it, with a view to finding a position for the naval guns. This was the first hint I had had that the real attack to force the passage of the Drakensberg would be made in this direction. We had been 'backing and filling 'for so long in the region of Laing's Nek that I couldn't guess where the ultimate attack would be made.

Well! General Coke took with him half his brigade, the S.A.L.H., and a battery of R.A., which latter was halted about three miles from Van Wyk, and also the infantry. General Hildyard and some of his staff rode up here and the two generals and myself, with Col. Byng and some of his S.A.L.H. in advance, rode on, and very soon the Light Horse were engaged, small parties of Boers keeping up a desultory fire at long range from the adjoining hills, till we arrived at a *nek* close to Van Wyk, when, after a lively interchange of rifle fire, they cleared off and we went on.

Having selected positions for my guns I was ordered to go back to camp, picking out on the way a route by which they could be brought up after dark.

The Boers had discovered our game and it was quite apparent that the hill must be held there and then. This the S.A.L.H. (dismounted) had to do until the rest of the brigade could be brought up, and a pretty stiff time they had of it. Before I left the enemy had opened fire with three or four guns across the valley, and during the afternoon collected all their available men and attacked in force, but the foremost regiment arrived on the scene in time to repulse them. I have not seen much credit given to the S.A.L.H. for their performance on this occasion, which was most creditable and important, and not the least of their brilliant achievements.

I got back with my A.D.C. and found Halsey with his two 12-pounders going to a point near Yellowboom Farm, also facing the Drakensberg, and at 7.30 started with the two 4.7's and Burne's two 12-pounders.

The route was exposed to the enemy's guns for two-thirds of the way—that was why we had to wait till after dark. Now it is one thing to ride in daylight to a distant hill clearly in sight, even though across a strange and difficult country, but quite another to drag 4.7 guns, drawn by bullocks, in the dark to the same place. Especially, as in this case, when the enemy has set the grass on fire in the interval and obliterated all one's most cherished landmarks. What was not a blackened waste was a roaring sea of flame. However, we did not go so much out of our way, but what with some very bad *drifts* to cross, and the oxen, maddened by the flames, breaking away from their *rheimes*, progress was very slow, so about midnight I pushed on the 12-pounders, guided by Ledyard, my A.D.C., to try and get them up by daylight. The 4.7's were not intcoided to go beyond the *drift* at the foot of Van Wyk in the dark.

However, one of the 12-pounders capsized in a *drift* and we caught them up, got it to 'rights' and pushed on to the foot of the hill.

The blazing country made it as light as day and helped us a good deal; indeed, I think on the whole we scored by the fire.

Another 12-pounder capsized in the *drift* at the foot of Van Wyk, but was righted and the two crossed and pushed up the steep slopes of the hill. One of them broke an axle and was left halfway up, but a shot from the summit, just after daylight, announced that the other had arrived all right.

The 4.7's halted near the *drift* at the bottom of the hill till daylight. There was very great difficulty in getting them through this *drift*. The guns were dismounted and carried across on wagons, and during the morning we commenced the ascent. It is a very steep and long pull up over rotten ground, and sixty oxen were used for each gun and wagon of ammunition, pulling them up bit by bit. We had them in position by 2 p.m. I really think the Boers never dreamt that we should get heavy guns up there, or they never would have let us get possession of the hill. This was the hardest job we had through the whole campaign.

Despite the opinions at home about the wonders the Boers achieved in getting their guns into inaccessible positions, I venture to say that they never got guns, large or small, into such difficult places as we did, during the whole of the Natal operations. I visited nearly all their gun positions after we had driven them out, and with very few exceptions there was an easy ascent on the reverse side. In many places, looking up at them from our point of view, perched on top of a frowning precipitous hill, it looked impossible for guns; but then the Boers didn't get them up that way.

During the afternoon the trail of the 12-pounder was broken whilst firing at some wandering Boers, but by dint of working all night with our armourers, carpenters, and two wheelwrights lent by the R.A., both that gun and the one with the broken axle were repaired and in position ready for action on the day of the fight (9th). The wheels and axle of a limber were fitted to one 12-pounder, and the trail of the other was cut and scarfed.

The infantry advanced to the attack at 11 a.m. and, an hour or so before, our four guns on Van Wyk, the military 4.7's, and Halsey's two 12-pounders, away to the right, searched every *donga* and the approaches to the line of works, to the left and right of Botha's Pass.

The enemy had several guns along the ridge, but immediately our guns were in position they took them back out of sight, thus leaving our troops unmolested by artillery fire whilst making the actual ascent, an enormous advantage, secured entirely by the presence of the guns.

The infantry swarmed up the hills and over the crest with little opposition, and then the real fight began. The enemy opened on them with guns, pom-poms, and rifles. They had got their guns away to the left of our advance, and enfiladed it from behind a dense cloud of smoke which prevented us seeing them. But the infantry went steadily on all day, driving the enemy from their works to lines further back, till the whole of the works were taken, and by sunset the Boers were in full flight and the place was in our possession.

During all this time our guns were firing over the heads of the infantry, and helped materially to clear the ground in front of them, driving the enemy out of several of their trenches and *schanzes* before our men got up to them. We ceased fire at dusk, when the battle was practically over. It was bitterly cold and a heavy dense fog came on, and by 7.30 all our people had settled to sleep under their wagons with all the blankets they could muster over them. Half an hour later I was roused out and ordered to take my guns down the hill during the night, and a regiment was ordered to meet us at the top of the gully, by which we had to descend, to help get the guns down. Every one buckled to with a will, guns were got down from their positions, dismounted and put on the wagons, oxen inspanned, wagons packed, and we were at the *nek*, the appointed place, by ten, the appointed time, but no regiment turned up.

The oxen had to be outspanned before making the descent, and we waited and sent in all directions to look for the troops, but the fog was so thick we could not see twenty yards. I went twice to the general to try to obtain troops, but he was powerless to get any, and we never saw them till next morning about 7, when they stumbled on us at the bottom through the fog, having been wandering about, lost, all night.

We waited for them till past 11 p.m., and then, being determined to get down if possible, we started easing the wagons and guns down the gully, one by one, with drag-ropes and trek-chains, putting every man of the force on to each. We had to get them down like this nearly three-quarters of a mile before the oxen could be inspanned; and after each 'package' was lowered the men had to climb the hill again with their ropes and repeat the operation—eleven times in all—most fatiguing work, and the men working splendidly, aided by two companies of infantry forming our escort. However, we got them all to the bottom by 4 a.m., when men, officers, and oxen dropped where they stood, and got what rest they could, in the long grass, till six o'clock, when the work of getting the guns across the ravine commenced.

The 12-pounders smashed one of the wagons during the descent and injured two oxen so severely that they had to be killed. It is an ill wind, &c., &c., and the 800 Tommies, hungry after their night's wandering, soon left nothing of them.

At 8 a.m. we were ordered to a position a little in advance of Yellowboom Farm, and had just outspanned to graze and water the oxen, which were sorely in need thereof, when I received orders to proceed at noon with General Coke's brigade through Botha's Pass, a long tedious pull up, the road blocked by strings of store and provision wagons. We arrived at our bivouac, just over the pass and in the Orange River Colony, soon after dark. At last we were over the Drakensberg, and had outflanked the Boers at Laing's Nek; but there was much still to be done before they shifted from that historic ground.

Next morning we moved on with the division in the direction of Grandsvlei—very good going, and the trekking quite a pleasure, after some of our former experiences. The field artillery and our 12-pounders were frequently brought into action on this march to clear the enemy from hills along the advance, and at a place called Piet Uys Farm we had quite a little brush; but they continued to retire. Here we came up with the enemy's ambulances, which of course were unmolested, and the farm round which they were gathered, itself adorned with many white flags, was tenderly guarded by sentries to prevent anyone entering.

This was somewhat exasperating, for the place was evidently a depot of the enemy, and there were enormous stacks of sweet-smelling hay garnered there, the scent of which caused many of our half-starved animals to break away. But we were not allowed to take any or to destroy it, though it was palpably stored for the enemy. There were also large stocks of poultry and sheep.

We halted here for an hour or so, and a few officers managed to buy some fowls at enormous prices. General Coke and I tried to buy a sheep, but they were not disposed to sell, and we had to go without, and passed on, leaving the place with all its stores to be used by the enemy, should they think fit.

I considered our position somewhat critical for the next few days, for we had only about three days' provisions, and could get no more till we got it through Laing's Nek, out of which the Boers had first to be driven.

General Clery's division was in front of Laing's Nek, and Lyttelton's further to the east, towards Utrecht, and our business was to work round in rear of them. We got up to Grandsvlei about 5 p.m. and found firing going on and the S.A.L.H. engaged storming a hill in advance. They lost somewhat heavily.

Next morning, June 12, before daybreak, all naval guns and the artillery advanced to positions about two miles ahead and proceeded to clear the ground for the infantry advance, and when they had gone on we followed (11 a.m.) a few miles further, and found them and a mountain battery hotly engaged, the enemy holding a strong position on both sides of Allman's Nek, through which our road lay. We took up a position, under fire, along a hill about five thousand yards from the *nek*, with some army 4.7's on our left, and the howitzer battery at the foot of the hill in our rear. There was a nasty cross-fire from guns and pom-poms for some little time, but as soon as we discovered them we quickly stopped their game, and about 1 p.m. the infantry advanced to the attack.

Hamilton's brigade assaulted the hills to our left of the *nek*, Coke's men those to the right—very precipitous and rocky hills they were. The army 4.7's covered the left attack, our naval ones the right, aided by the howitzers, which did excellent work. On this side there was a tremendous fight, one of the best in the campaign. The troops plodded on in the face of a tremendous fire and heavy loss, till at last they gained a sugar-loaf hill overlooking the pass, and were on the enemy's flank. Thence they worked along the ridges to the right. The Boers on the other side did not wait long for Hamilton and were soon on the move, but the others resisted stubbornly, though just as the sun went down, a gorgeous splendour behind the hills, the whole range was in our possession and the Boers in full flight, leaving the country in a blaze behind them, as usual.

We continued to throw shell over the hills in the direction of their retreat, and although we could no longer see them, some at least took effect, as we discovered next morning. We also discovered some ghastly sights of Boers 'hoist with their own petard,' fire, in the form of several corpses burnt to cinders. They were probably wounded men unable to keep ahead of the flames.

The water cart was our only casualty in this fight.

It was a very thorough beating and a very important one, the last of any consequence before we got to Volksrust, and was the signal for the Boers to abandon Laing's Nek, Majuba, &c.

Next morning we moved on, and about noon the 4.7's came into action and shelled Sandspruit Station, and parties of Boers as they disappeared over the hills in fall retreat.

That night we bivouacked five miles outside Volksrust and heard of the evacuation of Laing's Nek. Next day we marched into the town, Charlestown being occupied at the same time.

On the following day (15th) I rode over to Laing's Nek and Majuba Hill. The position was quite impregnable, I should say, and nothing but a very wide flanking movement could have turned them out. For miles each side of the *nek* the place was entrenched and fortified— deep narrow trenches that nothing could touch from below. Majuba also, which flanks the *nek*, was thoroughly entrenched, as were the hills to the westward of it, which in turn flanked Majuba.

It was a stiff climb to the top of Majuba, and it seemed to me almost incomprehensible how such a disaster as we met with there could have occurred. The graves are not in a very good state. A wooden cross records the fact that Braizier (no rank) and twenty men of the Naval Brigade lie buried there. There is a similar one to the soldiers who fell, and a stone cross to an army officer.

Poor Romilly, General Colley, and other officers are buried at Mount Prospect, a small hill four miles away.

On my return to Volksrust, after examining these trenches and gun positions, I found orders waiting to march at daybreak next morning with the 11th Brigade on Wakkerstroom. Lyttelton had met with opposition to the eastward and we were despatched to see it through.

We arrived on the morning of the 17th without opposition and bivouacked near the town. We stayed there over the next day, and then, 'as per routine,' cleared out and left it to its own devices, much to the disgust of the inhabitants, who had given up their arms, taken the oath of allegiance, and were now left to the tender mercy of their brethren in arms. As a matter of fact the *landdrost's* son was shot within twenty-four hours afterwards by the Boers.

After a weary trek we reached Sandspruit on the 20th, and here I received orders to return to my ship with all the men of the *Forte*, leaving behind only the men of the *Tartar* and the *Philomel* under Lieutenants Halsey and Burne.

Proceedings Subsequent to June 24

After the departure of Captain Jones and the 'Fortes,' Lieut. Halsey remained at Volksrust until June 28, with two 12-pounders, manned by men of the *Philomel.* This detachment accompanied a flying column from Sandspruit, which advanced towards Amerspoort, found the enemy in considerable force, and fell back according to orders. The long-range fire of these naval guns was instrumental in forcing the enemy to disclose their strength and guns, and afterwards covered the retirement on Sandspruit. Here the 'Philomels' remained till July 10, when they proceeded by train to Standerton. At this place the two guns were horsed from a field battery—a very successful experiment which considerably increased their mobility.

Although on one or two occasions during slight skirmishes they went into action 'at the trot,' the carriages were not injured by this extra strain. On July 24 they marched to Greylingstad, having been employed during this time covering the repair of the railway towards Heidelberg, remained there a month, and then returned to Standerton, one 12-pounder taking up a position near this town and the second being eventually sent to garrison Heidelberg.

Lieut. Burne's detachment of 'Tartars' with the remaining two 12-pounders took part in the series of operations to the east of the railway resulting in the capture of Wakkerstroom and the position of Gras Kop, a lofty hill which dominates the whole surrounding country. On this hill one gun was placed permanently in position, the second being shifted first to Opperman's Kraal and latterly to Paarde Kop.

Of Gras Kop, Lieut. Burne says in his report of proceedings, dated October 17:—

The whole of the intelligence from Gras Kop as to the movements of the enemy since July 24 up to this date has been furnished by my lookouts with their long telescope, and this,

I need scarcely say, has been a considerable and arduous duty for the men, under the conditions of violent winds, rains, mists, and storms which prevailed up here (a height of 6,500 feet) since we occupied the hill. These windstorms have destroyed our tents once, sometimes continuing for days, and have caused much discomfort to ourselves and the troops, and I have lost a good many oxen by exposure and lung sickness.'

Both detachments were withdrawn to their ships in the latter part of October 1900.   Original Editor.

Appendices

1

OFFICERS OF NAVAL BRIGADES.

BRIGADE LANDED TO DEFEND STORMBERG.

H.M.S. 'Powerful.'

Com. A. P. Ethelston. [Killed Graspan.]
Lieut. F. J. Saunders, R.M.L.I.
Surgeon C. M. Beadnell.
Mid. T. C. Armstrong.
Mid. G. E. Lewin.

H.M.S. 'Doris.'

Major J. H. Plumbe, R.M.L.I. [Killed Graspan.]
Capt. A. E. Marchant, R.M.L.I.
Lieut. W. T. C. Jones, R.M.L.I. [Wounded Graspan.]

Lieut. G. W. McO. Campbell, R.N.
Fleet Surgeon J. Porter.
Sub.-Lieut. R. F. White.
Ass. Paymaster B. C. Allen.
Mid. C. A. E. Huddart. [Killed Graspan.]
Mid. T. F. J. L. Wardle.

H.M.S. 'Monarch.'

Lieut. F. W. Dean.
Lieut. Guy Senior, R.M.A. [Killed Graspan.]

FIRST BRIGADE REINFORCED AND PLACED UNDER ORDERS OF LORD METHUEN.

H.M.S. 'Doris.'

Capt. R. C. Prothero, R.N. (in command). [Wounded Graspan].

Lieut. the Hon. E. S. H. Boyle.
Gunner E. E. Lowe.
Mid. Egerton.
Mid. W. W. Sillem.
Mid. J. F. Houstoun.

232

REINFORCEMENTS AFTER GRASPAN.

H.M.S. 'Philomel.'

Capt. J. E. Bearcroft (commanded Brigade till it was recalled).

H.M.S. 'Doris.'

Sub-Lieut. M. G. Newton.
Surgeon E. P. Mourilyan.
Gunner H. Ball.

Mid. Robertson. [Died Modder River, enteric.]
Mid. J. W. Rainier.
Mid. F. P. Saunders.

H.M.S. 'Monarch.'

Com. S. V. Y. de Horsey. [Wounded Pretoria].
Capt. R. H. Morgan, R.M.L.I.
Lieut. L. O. Wilson, R.M.L.I. [Wounded Belfast.]

JOINED AT MODDER RIVER.

Lieut.-Com. W. J. Colquhoun, Royal Victorian Navy.

H.M.S. 'Monarch.'

Lieut. E. J. K. Newman.

Lieut. W. S. Poë, R.M.A.
Lieut. G. I. Raikes, R.M.A.

H.M.S. 'Powerful.'

Major A. G. B. Urmston.

GRANT'S GUNS.

H.M.S. 'Doris.'

Com. W. L. Grant.
Mid. G. H. Lang.
Mid. J. Menzies. [Died enteric.]

H.M.S. 'Barrosa.'

Lieut. J. A. Fergusson.

H.M.S. 'Monarch.'

Surgeon T. T. Jeans.
Gunner J. Cannon.

JOINED AT PAARDEBERG AND POPLAR GROVE.

H.M.S. 'Doris.'

Major S. D. Peile, R.M.L.I.
Lieut. A. H. French, R.M.L.I.

Mid. J. E. G. Cunningham.
Mid. Lloyd. [Died enteric.]

JOINED AT BLOEMFONTEIN.

H.M.S. ' Monarch.'	H.M.S. ' Philomel.'
Lieut. E. P. C. Back, R.N.	Paymaster W. B. Penny.

JOINED AT PRETORIA.

H.M.S. ' Doris.'

Mid. B. M. Denison.

Total number of officers	46
Killed	4
Wounded	4
Invalided	19
Died	8

OFFICERS OF NATAL BRIGADE.

H.M.S. ' Forte.'

Captain E. P. Jones (in command).
Lieut. F. W. Melvill.
Lieut. G. P. E. Hunt.
Staff Surgeon F. J. Lilly.
Act. Lieut. J. M. Steel.
Gunner E. Holland.

H.M.S. ' Terrible.'

Com. A. H. Limpus.
Lieut. F. C. A. Ogilvy.
Lieut. S. R. S. Richards.
Lieut. J. S. Wilde.
Lieut. G. P. England.
Sub-Lieut. S. Newcome.
Surgeon E. C. Lomas.

Surgeon C. C. Macmillan.
Engineer J. F. Arthur.
Engineer A. E. J. Murray.
Ass. Eng. F. J. Roskruge.
Gunner J. Wright.
Gunner E. J. Cole.
Gunner E. Williams.
Mid. P. F. Willoughby.
Mid R. T. Down.
Mid. R. B. C. Hutchinson.
Mid. A. C. Ackland.
Mid. A. E. Sherrin.
Mid. H. E. W. C. Whyte.
Mid. G. M. Skinner.
Mid. G. L. Hodson.
Mid. W. W. Hallwright.
Mid. H. S. W. Boldero.
Mid. J. A. G. Troup.

H.M.S. 'Tartar.'

Lieut. J. E. Drummond.
Lieut. H. W. James.
Staff Surgeon J. Hughes.

H.M.S. 'Philomel.'

Lieut. A. Halsey.
Lieut. C. R. N. Burne.

Lieut. A. Deas.
Lieut. F. A. Clutterbuck.
Mid. W. R. Ledgard.
Clerk W. T. Hollins.

Natal Naval Volunteers.

Lieut. Anderson (in command).
Lieut. Chiazzari.
Lieut. Barrett.

The Ladysmith Brigade consisted of 17 officers and 267 men, the names and ranks of the officers being as follows :

Captain the Hon. Hedworth Lambton (in command).
Lieut. F. G. Egerton. [Killed.]
Lieut. A. W. Heneage.
Lieut. L. Halsey.
Lieut. M. H. Hodges.
Fleet-Paymaster W. H. F. Kay. [Died, enteric.]
Surgeon J. G. Fowler.
Engineer E. H. Ellis.
Engineer C. C. Sheen.
Gunner W. Sims.
Midshipman J. R. Middleton.
Midshipman H. T. Hayes.
Midshipman R. C. Hamilton.
Midshipman the Hon. I. L. A. Carnegie.
Midshipman Alick Stokes.
Midshipman E. G. Chichester. ⎫ from H.M.S. 'Terrible.'
Midshipman C. R. Sharp. ⎭
Lieut. E. C. Tyndale-Biscoe (late R.N.) and Lieut. E. Stabb, R.N.R. [died, enteric], joined the Brigade after arrival at Ladysmith.

The 267 men included the guns' crews, small-arm companies, 2 engine-room artificers, and 6 stokers as a gun-mounting party, 42 stokers as stretcher-bearers and ammunition carriers, 3 armourers, 2 cooks, 3 marine servants, and a ship's steward's boy, besides a ship's corporal and a sick-berth attendant, blacksmith, and carpenters.

The casualties among the officers and men of the Ladysmith Brigade were:

	Officers.	Men.
Killed or died of wounds	1	5
Died of disease	2	25
Wounded	1	4

2

List of Distinctions Awarded for Service With Naval Brigades in the South African War.

COMPANIONS OF THE ORDER OF THE BATH.

Captain the Hon. Hedworth Lambton, R.N.
Captain E. P. Jones, R.N.
Captain R. C. Prothero, R.N.

Captain J. E. Bearcroft, R.N.
Major S. P. Peile, R.M.L.I.
Major A. E. Marchant, R.M.L.I.

COMPANIONS OF THE DISTINGUISHED SERVICE ORDER.

Lieutenant G. P. E. Hunt, R.N.
Captain W. T. C. Jones, R.M.L.I.
Surgeon E. C. Macmillan, R.N.
Staff-Surgeon E.C.Lomas, R.N.
Lieutenant W. J. Colquhoun, Victorian Navy.

Lieutenant N. W. Chinzzari, Natal Naval Volunteers.
Captain Leslie O. Wilson, R.M.L.I.
Captain F. J. Saunders, R.M.L.I.

CONSPICUOUS SERVICE CROSS.

Ernest E. Lowe, Gunner, R.N.
Joseph Wright, Gunner, R.N.
T. C. Armstrong, Midshipman, R.N.

T. F. J. L. Wardle, Midshipman, R.N.
R. B. C. Hutchinson, Midshipman, R.N.
C. A. E. Huddart, Midshipman, R.N. [Killed Graspan.]

PROMOTIONS.

COMMANDERS TO BE CAPTAINS.

Commander A. H. Limpus, R.N.

Commander W. L. Grant, R.N.

Commander S. V. V. de Horsey, R.N.

LIEUTENANTS TO BE COMMANDERS.

Lieutenant F. G. Egerton (promoted after being mortally wounded).

Lieutenant F. C. A. Ogilvy.

Lieutenant F. W. Dean.

„ Arthur Halsey.

„ H. W. James.

„ J. A. Fergusson.

Major A. G. B. Urmston, R.M.L.I., to be Brevet-Lieut. Col.

Captain A. E. Marchant, C.B., R.M.L.I., to be Major.

Lieutenant W. T. C. Jones, D.S.O., R.M.L.I., to be Captain.

Fleet-Surgeon J. Porter, R.N., to be Deputy Inspector-General of Hospitals and Fleets.

Staff-Surgeon F. J. Lilly, R.N., to be Fleet-Surgeon.

Surgeon C. M. Beadnell, R.N. } to be Staff-Surgeons.
„ E. C. Lomas, R.N.

Assistant-Paymaster B. C. Allen, R.N., to be Paymaster.

Engineer E. H. Ellis, R.N. } to be Chief Engineers.
„ C. C. Sheen, R.N.

Gunner W. Sims, R.N., to be Lieutenant, R.N.

NOTED FOR EARLY PROMOTION.

Lieutenant E. P. C. Back.

„ J. E. Drummond.

Lieutenant C. R. N. Burne.

Surgeon J. G. Fowler.

The majority of the midshipmen were recommended for early promotion, on qualifying for the rank of Lieutenant.

A List of Petty Officers, Non-commissioned Officers and Men of the Royal Navy and Marines Specially Mentioned in Despatches.

LADYSMITH BRIGADE.

Captains of Guns.

H. W. C. Lee, P.O.I., Captain of 4·7 on Junction Hill.
P. T. Sisk, P.O.I.,   „   „   at Cove Redoubt.
A. O. Pratt, L.S.   „ 12-pounder at Leicester Post.
A. G. Withers, P.O.I. „   „   at Gordon Post.
S. E. Hemmings, L.S. „   „   at Manchester Camp.

THE NATAL NAVAL BRIGADE.

Geo. Crowe, M.A.A.

Chief Petty Officers.—Thos. Baldwin, Wm. Bate, Ben. Stephens, Alex. A. Munro.

Petty Officers, 1st Class.—Pat. Cashman, T. Mitchell, J. Mulliss, J. Weatherhead, J. Venness, N. Symons, H. Harrison, J. Funnett.

Petty Officers, 2nd Class.—G. H. Epsley, E. A. Harvey, C. Challoner, T. Sargent. Leading Seaman W. H. Franklin.

Able Seamen.—P. Treherne, D. Shepherd, H. House, W. Jones, E. Cheeseman, D. Smith, J. Macdonald, G. Baldwin, J. Sawyer, H. Wright, T. Payne, F. Ryall, W. Wiltshire.

Ordinary Seamen.—A. E. Reading, H. Harwood, F. Tuck.

www.ingramcontent.com/pod-product-compliance
Lightning Source LLC
Chambersburg PA
CBHW032048080426
42733CB00006B/197